D0204275

THE POLITICAL DEVELOPMENT
OF TANGANYIKA

DT444
T3

THE
POLITICAL
DEVELOPMENT
OF
TANGANYIKA

J. Clagett Taylor

STANFORD UNIVERSITY PRESS
STANFORD, CALIFORNIA
LONDON: OXFORD UNIVERSITY PRESS
1963

81547

Stanford University Press
Stanford, California

London: Oxford University Press

© 1963 by the Board of Trustees of the
Leland Stanford Junior University

All rights reserved

Library of Congress Catalog Card Number: 63–12043

Printed in the United States of America

937.82
T 215

PREFACE

The inspiration for this study came from a speech given by Tanganyika's first Prime Minister, Julius Nyerere. In February 1960, I heard Mr. Nyerere address a gathering at All Souls' Unitarian Church in Washington, D.C., on "Tanganyika's March to Independence." At that time Tanganyika had not attained independence or even reached the stage of responsible government, but it was already clear that something out of the ordinary was happening there. Accompanying Mr. Nyerere on this trip to the United States were two other members of Tanganyika's Legislative Council, one a European resident of the country and the other an Asian. These three leaders were a symbol of the racial cooperation existing in Tanganyikan politics.

It was this outward appearance of racial good feeling that I chose to examine. Since there seemed to be so much racial antagonism in other parts of Africa, I was curious whether the racial cooperation spoken of in Tanganyika was only so much window dressing. After beginning my research, I soon realized that I would not be able to limit my study to the period following World War II, but would have to trace Tanganyika's history back to 1920, when the period of British administration began, and even to 1880, when Germany first seized control of the territory. This study therefore presents the history of Tanganyika's political development from 1880 to December 1961, when Tanganyika achieved independence. The part played by racial cooperation is emphasized throughout.

For patient advice and assistance I am greatly indebted to Professors Emmett Mittlebeeler and Mary Bradshaw, my research advisers at The American University, Washington, D.C. I am grateful also to Miss Helen Conover of the Africana Division of the Library of Congress for helping me track down reports and documents, and to Mrs. Barbara Graham for typing the manuscript. My colleague Roy Harrell gave freely of his time and advice, especially after I had left the United States.

Most of all, my thanks are due my wife, Patricia, without whose continuous support this task might never have been completed. For the interpretation of facts, the conclusions drawn from them, and the various shortcomings of the work, I remain wholly responsible.

J.C.T.

Mrewa Mission
Southern Rhodesia

CONTENTS

CONTENTS

THE POLITICAL DEVELOPMENT
OF TANGANYIKA

We would like to light a candle, and put it on top of Mount Kilimanjaro, which will shine beyond our borders, giving hope where there was despair, love where there was hate, and dignity where there was humiliation.

JULIUS NYERERE
October 1959

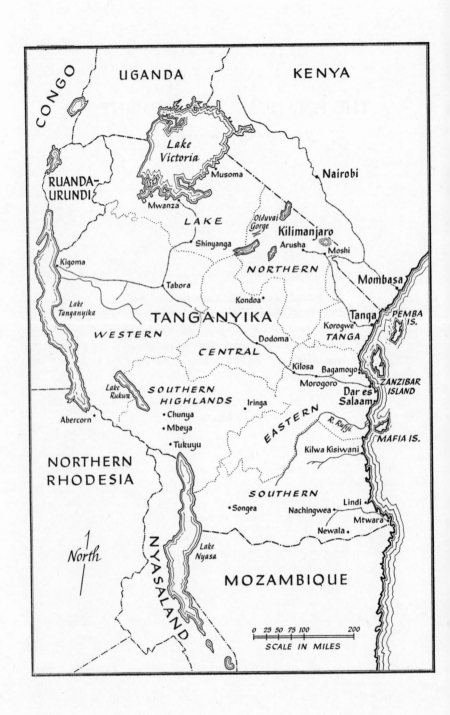

1

THE HISTORY OF TANGANYIKA
PRIOR TO THE MANDATE

Tanganyika is the largest country in East Africa. It lies between the great lakes of Central Africa—Lake Victoria, Lake Tanganyika, and Lake Nyasa—and the Indian Ocean. It is bounded on the north by Kenya and Uganda, on the west by the Republic of Congo, on the southwest by Northern Rhodesia and Nyasaland, and on the south by Portuguese East Africa. It contains the two topographical extremes of the whole continent—snow-capped Mount Kilimanjaro (19,340 feet), and the deep, trough-like depression filled by Lake Tanganyika, the second deepest lake in the world, with recorded depths of over 4,700 feet.

Tanganyika's area is 362,688 square miles, which includes 19,982 square miles of inland water. It is therefore larger than France and Germany combined, or more than six times the size of England. On the map, Tanganyika extends from 1° S. to 11° S. and from 29° E. to 40° E., and is some 740 miles long and 760 miles wide. It has a coast-line of about 550 miles. More than nine million people live within its borders, the overwhelming majority of whom are Africans. Only slightly over one per cent of the population is non-African. This non-African segment consists of about 100,000 Asians, mostly Indians, and about 20,000 Europeans.

The formation of the country has been likened to that of a giant bowl—mountains to the north, east, and south, with a great plateau in the middle. In the northeast, near the coast, lie the Usambara and

Pare mountains, and to the northwest lie Mount Kilimanjaro and Mount Meru. In the east is the Ruhebo mountain system, and in the south, between Lake Nyasa and Lake Tanganyika, lie the Njombe highlands, the Livingstone mountains, the Kipengere range, the Porotos, and the Mbeya range. In the middle and to the west lies the vast Central Plateau, ranging from 3,000 to 4,000 feet in altitude; to the east are the coastal plains. Most of the land is the usual African bush country of flat, open grassland with a thin cover of trees. Unfortunately, much of it is tsetse-infested. Because of this and the lack of water, nearly two-thirds of the country is entirely uninhabited. Although Tanganyika lies very near the equator, its altitude prevents it from having the extreme heat one expects to find in the tropics.

Tanganyika contains one of the remarkable geographical phenomena of the world—the Great Rift Valley. From near the mouth of the Zambezi in Portuguese East Africa, it runs northward through Tanganyika, Kenya, Ethiopia, and the Red Sea to the Dead Sea in Jordan. Owing to the effects of tectonic action, whole blocks of country have been elevated above the surrounding terrain. The Rift Valley is responsible for the formation of Lakes Tanganyika, Nyasa, Rukwa, Kivu, Manyara, and Natron. It lies in a huge shallow depression, 3,717 feet above sea level. There are few permanent rivers of any size, the Pangani, the Wami, the Ruvu, the Rufiji, and the Ruvuma being the most important. All these flow into the Indian Ocean. Kilimanjaro and other mountains indicate that Tanganyika was once a land of intense volcanic activity. The Ngorongoro Crater to the east of the Serengeti Plain is probably the most spectacular wild animal preserve in all Africa. Not far away is the Olduvai Gorge, the site of important archaeological discoveries.

Tanganyika has few large towns. The population of its capital, Dar es Salaam, was approximately 129,000 in 1957. Next in size was Tanga with 38,000. All the other towns—Mwanza, Tabora, Morogoro, Moshi, Dodoma, Mtwara, Lindi, and Arusha—had populations of under 20,000. Dar es Salaam, Tanga, Lindi, and Mtwara are the principal ports on the Indian Ocean, while Mwanza is the only port of any size on Lake Victoria. The country is divided into nine provinces or regions. Reading from north to south, they are Lake, Northern,

Tanga, Western, Central, Southern Highlands, Eastern, Dar es Salaam, and Southern Provinces. Most of the principal centers are now interconnected by roads of fair standard. Railway lines are fewer. In the north the Usambara line connects Arusha and Moshi with Tanga on the coast. Further south, the Central Line spans the breadth of the country from Dar es Salaam to Kigoma on Lake Tanganyika; from Tabora there is an important branch line leading to Mwanza on Lake Victoria. Near the Ruvuma River in the south is the Southern Province Line, which was built as part of the Groundnut Scheme in the late 1940's; it runs between Nachingwea and the new port of Mtwara.

Tanganyika is not a rich country. There are no large mineral deposits, nor is there much industrial development. The average per capita income, including an allowance for the value of subsistence agriculture, is only about $56 a year, which is on a par with India and Pakistan. A revenue of about $60,000,000 a year is all that the whole country has at its disposal for economic development. Yet, politically, Tanganyika has the potential of being one of the richest countries in Africa.

EARLY HISTORY TO 1500

Dr. L. S. B. Leakey's discovery in 1959 of the 1,750,000-year-old skull of *Zinjanthropus,* the so-called "Nutcracker Man," in the Olduvai Gorge presents the possibility that the whole history of mankind started in Tanganyika. Since 1959, Leakey has uncovered the remains of another hominid thought to be even older; but so far *Zinjanthropus* remains the oldest member of the family of man who is known to have made "tools to a set and regular pattern," the characteristic distinguishing man from "near-man."[1]

The ethnographic history of East Africa is still something of a mystery, but most authorities agree that the present residents, the Bantu, were late arrivals on the scene. Before them were the Bushmen and the Hamites. Among the early inhabitants were a group called by the anthropologists "Boskopoids"; their only lineal descendants extant today are thought to be the Bushmen of the Kalahari

Desert and the Pygmies of the Congo. Leakey thinks that the Hamites were developing in East Africa from about 5000 B.C. onward. These Hamitic people appear to have been of the same basic stock as the Caucasians who populated Europe, although they were not "white" in the sense we know today. Whether these people developed first in Asia and migrated to Africa and Europe or developed first in Africa is still under question.[2]

Around 5000 B.C. a new group known as Negroes appeared in Africa. Although their origin is unknown, they made their first appearance in northeast Africa. These people were an important element in the civilization of ancient Egypt, as is witnessed by the numerous Negro skulls that have been found. Scholars have also found rock paintings in which Negroes feature prominently; these paintings date back to around 4000 B.C. and come from the Sahara area.[3] It is generally assumed that as the Sahara gradually became the desert we know today, its inhabitants migrated from the area. Sometime after 1000 B.C. these Negro people arrived in East Africa and began to intermarry with the Hamitic people they found there. This mixture has resulted in the Bantu inhabitants of today.[4]

It is still unknown when the first contacts between East Africa and the outside world began to be made. There is some evidence that the Egyptians and Phoenicians were the first outside people to visit the area. According to Herodotus, a voyage was made in about 600 B.C. by a group of Phoenicians, who sailed down the Red Sea into the Erythraean Sea, the ancient Greek name for the Indian Ocean, and along the East African coast. The account suggests that these sailors may have circumnavigated the whole continent before returning to Egypt.[5]

Over much of the last two thousand years there appears to have been contact between the east coast of Africa and the neighboring coasts of Asia. Before the beginning of the Christian era, trade connections existed with Arabia and India. There was a continuous migration of Himyarites from southern Arabia and neighboring lands to this part of Africa. Traders readily took advantage of the pattern of winds in the Indian Ocean that made an annual voyage from Asia to Africa one of comparative ease. The northeast monsoon, which blows steadily from November to February, carried their dhows across the Indian Ocean to East Africa; the southwest monsoon, which blows from April to September, carried them home again. This pattern of trade was certainly established by the first century A.D., when an anonymous Greek trader wrote the *Periplus of the Erythraean Sea,* an account of commerce in the Indian Ocean at the time when Egypt was a province of the Roman Empire. Reference is made to the island of Menouthias and to a town called Rhapta. The former may have been either the islands of Zanzibar or Pemba, and the latter either present-day Pangani in Tanganyika or a town in the delta of the Rufiji River.[6] The Greek geographer Ptolemy (about A.D. 150) also gives some account of East Africa as then known.

As the East African trade prospered, permanent trading posts were established on the numerous islands along the coast. These settlements grew in size, and substantial buildings were erected. As a result of the spread of Islam, Arab penetration and colonization from Oman began in the eighth century A.D. Persians were also present on the east coast of Africa about this time, but it is uncertain whether they preceded or followed the Arabs. The oldest known town in Tanganyika is Kilwa-Kisiwani ("Kilwa on the Island"), although ruins on other nearby islands also show signs of early settlement. The oldest ruins of all may be those on Sanje ya Kati, a small island to the south of Kilwa-Kisiwani.[7]

There is an Arabic chronicle that records the history of Kilwa-Kisiwani from the tenth century A.D. down to the time of the arrival of the Portuguese in the sixteenth century. According to this account, settlers from Shiraz in Persia reached Kilwa in about A.D. 945. The early period of Kilwa's history was one of wars with adjacent Songo and Xanga, a struggle from which Kilwa eventually emerged triumphant. The island of Mafia, which had also been settled by people from Shiraz, was likewise subjugated during this period. The foundations were thus laid for the powerful Zenj Empire, which had Kilwa as its center. During the twelfth century, Kilwa secured a foothold at Sofala (near Beira in what is now Portuguese East Africa) and gained control of the lucrative gold trade there. The gold came down to the coast at Sofala from the gold mines of Monomotapa in what is now Southern Rhodesia.

The connection between Kilwa and Sofala lasted until the end of the fifteenth century and gave Kilwa commercial and political supremacy along the whole of the East African coast during this period. Numerous trading towns grew up at the points at which the various trade routes reached the Indian Ocean. In addition to the large coastal trade, fleets of trading vessels came from India, the Persian Gulf, and southern Arabia, bringing with them cloth and other commodities and taking back gold, ivory, tortoise shell, ambergris, and slaves. Recent archaeological discoveries indicate that these trading towns reached the height of their prosperity around the year 1500.[8] Chinese fleets paid several visits to the east coast of Africa during this period, the last of such expeditions being in 1430.[9] Chinese porcelain has been discovered at Kilwa and at many other sites along the coast of Tanganyika.

Although these medieval towns were Muslim trading centers, there was practically no spread of Islam into the interior. The Arab settlers intermarried with the coastal Bantu people, and the result of these intermarriages was the creation of the Swahili people. At the same time the Swahili language developed from a mixture of Arabic and Persian with the local Bantu languages. The present-day Swahili civilization of the coast thus had its beginnings during this period.[10]

Of the interior, less is known with any certainty; but the discoveries of archaeologists and anthropologists give us an interesting view of an old civilization that existed there. This early civilization has been called the "Azanian" civilization, deriving its name from the old Greek term for East Africa. Archaeologists have found evidence of a people unusually skilled in using dry stone for building, some of the settlements showing as many as a hundred houses clustered together. One of the most spectacular ruins is a city situated 300 miles from the coast in the hills of the Kenya-Tanganyika border. Although this city, Engaruka, is probably no more than 300 years old, it seems to be part of a highly developed civilization.

Another characteristic of the Azanian civilization was the elaborate terracing of cultivated land. Examples of terracing are found all the way from Ethiopia to the Transvaal, an indication of how far these people migrated. They also dug irrigation canals, raised cattle, mined iron and other minerals, and worked them both for their own needs and for export. Just how extensive their contact with the coast was is still uncertain. Trading did take place, but it appears to have been on a small scale.

G. W. B. Huntingford has suggested a date of about A.D. 700, or perhaps earlier, for this stone-building, metal-using civilization of the interior. The people responsible for it may have retreated southward into East Africa from the north as a result of the spread of Islam. This civilization, Huntingford believes, probably came to an end around the fourteenth or fifteenth century. His theory about its origin is borne out by tribal legend in East Africa, which frequently refers to northern beginnings.

There are indications that this relatively well-developed civilization of the "Azanians" was overwhelmed and slowly destroyed by pastoral nomads from the Horn of Africa—the Galla, the Somali, the Masai, and others—who, though technically more primitive than the Azanians, were militarily superior to them. Before the coming of the first Europeans, then, this purely African civilization flourished in the hinterland of East Africa.[11]

PORTUGUESE AND ARAB RULE

Vasco da Gama sailed along the east coast of Africa on his way to India in 1498, the voyage that opened up the Indian Ocean to the Western world. He stopped at Sofala and had intended to stop at Kilwa, but was prevented by ocean currents. Further up the coast he called at Mombasa and Malindi before proceeding to India. The first Portuguese to call at Kilwa was Pedro Alvares Cabral, the discoverer of Brazil, who sailed into the harbor with six ships on July 16, 1500. The following year a second fleet under the command of John da Nova also put in at Kilwa. Both men were coldly received by the inhabitants, who viewed their visitors with the greatest suspicion. These early voyages showed the Portuguese that the East African ports were useful stopping places for water and fresh provisions on the way to India; and since their intention was to monopolize trade with India by controlling the whole of the Indian Ocean, they decided to seize control of the East African coast from the Arabs.

On July 12, 1502, Vasco da Gama arrived at Kilwa with a large fleet. By threatening to destroy the town, da Gama extracted a pledge of loyalty from the local Amir as well as a promise to pay a considerable annual tribute to Portugal. When the first year's tribute had been paid, da Gama sailed away. In 1505, Francis d'Almeida arrived at Kilwa with another large fleet. Kilwa had subbornly refused to pay the tribute for a few years. D'Almeida captured the town and established a garrison to control it. Seven years later the garrison had to be withdrawn because of losses from disease and continuing friction with the local populace. Kilwa, however, never regained its former importance.

Throughout the sixteenth century the Portuguese exercised control over the whole East African coast, but their rule was never firmly established. This was partly because they depended upon the assistance of tributary Arab sultans, many of whom were not loyal. Mombasa was particularly recalcitrant, and continued to resist Portuguese control until the end of the century, when Fort Jesus was erected there. Portuguese rule could in any case survive only as long as Portugal held control of the sea routes, and this was lost early in the seventeenth century.

The rising state of Oman, situated in the southeast portion of the Arabian peninsula, was the next conqueror of the East African coast. After they had managed to drive the Portuguese off the island of Ormuz near Oman, the Omani Arabs raided Zanzibar and Pate in 1652, and destroyed the Portuguese settlements there. From that time on, Omani squadrons raided up and down the coast, the Portuguese not having sufficient strength to repulse them. In March 1696 a fleet from Oman arrived at Mombasa and laid siege to Fort Jesus. After 33 months, resistance crumbled and the fort was taken. Although Fort Jesus was recaptured in 1728 and held for nearly two years by the Portuguese, its fall in 1698 marks the effective end of Portuguese rule north of the Ruvuma River. Only Mozambique was left to them. Except for a few fortifications in the coastal towns, there are few traces of this Portuguese period in Tanganyika.

After the fall of Mombasa, all the towns and islands along the coast recognized the authority of the Sultan of Oman. The loyalty of Kilwa remained under suspicion, and the Omanis captured the town in 1698, in the course of which it was partially destroyed by fire. The Arab system was to appoint a governor in each town along the coast. However, some towns—notably, Mombasa, Zanzibar, and Kilwa—showed signs of independence, a situation that the Sultan was unable to remedy, since dissensions in his own state often left him too weak to interfere in East Africa. When the Busaidi overthrew the Yorubi as the ruling family in Oman in 1741, the Mazrui governor of Mombasa seized the opportunity to renounce the overlordship of Oman. The ensuing struggle between the Busaidi and Mazrui houses was to continue for the next century and lead to the rise of Zanzibar to power. The rulers of Oman were repeatedly unsuccessful in their attempts to dislodge the Mazrui at Mombasa.

Kilwa followed Mombasa's example and in 1741 revolted against Omani rule. This state of affairs continued until 1776, when the Sultan of Kilwa closed a treaty with a French merchant, agreeing to supply him with 1,000 slaves annually for the French plantations on the Ile de France (Mauritius) and Bourbon (Réunion). The French were then permitted to occupy the fortresses at Kilwa. During the next few years a number of French vessels called at Kilwa to load cargoes of slaves. The growing importance of the slave trade at Kilwa induced the Sultan of Oman to send a fleet—probably in 1784 —to reassert his sovereignty along the East African coast. Zanzibar, Mafia, and Kilwa all fell into line, and an Omani Governor was appointed at Kilwa. Under the new regime the slave trade prospered and expanded. Muslim, Swahili-speaking towns, trading in ivory and slaves, sprang up all along the coast. During this period the Arabs did little to introduce Mohammedanism in the area or to subjugate the countries of the interior.

Although Oman managed to retain its hold on Kilwa and Mafia, the Mazrui further to the north continued to resist. In 1798 an important treaty was signed between the Sultan of Oman and Great Britain: in return for the Sultan's pledge not to allow any part of his realm to be conceded to the French or the Dutch, Britain agreed to help the Sultan against his enemies in Oman and East Africa. This support was extremely valuable for the Sultan and began a long period of friendship between Britain and the Sultans of Oman.

In 1805 an energetic young ruler, Said bin Sultan, the fifth of the

Busaidi line, acceded to the throne in Oman. For the next fifteen years the new Sultan was occupied in maintaining his position in Oman and was unable to pay great attention to Africa. However, in 1822 an expedition from Zanzibar wrested control of Pemba from the Mazrui. Two years later the Mazrui persuaded the captain of a British warship to place Mombasa under British protection. The British flag flew above Fort Jesus for the next two years, but in the end the British government honored its treaty with the Sultan of Oman and withdrew the British flag. In 1828 Said bin Sultan personally led an expedition against Mombasa; the expedition had some measure of success, but it was not until 1837 that the power of the Mazrui was finally broken.

After the attack on Mombasa, Said bin Sultan proceeded to Zanzibar and was so taken with the place that in 1840 he transferred his capital there. This move from Oman to Zanzibar inaugurated a new period in the history of East Africa, since it brought with it a great development of trade. More and more Arabs began to go into the interior in search of ivory and slaves, with the result that the interior and the coast became more closely joined. For the first time events on the coast began to affect the tribes of the interior. And once again the coast itself was under a single ruler.

Said had considerable difficulty in administering the two parts of his realm. In fact, the stronger he became in East Africa, the weaker became his rule in Oman. His long absences from Oman led to trouble, and he was constantly being summoned home to save his throne from external attack or to put down internal intrigue; on more than one occasion the British government in India helped him to overcome his domestic crises. These circumstances led to his making the wise arrangement that at his death his unwieldy kingdom should be divided between two of his sons.

Said exercised only minimal political control over the Arab and Swahili trading centers along the coast. He appointed governors to act as his personal representatives at the more important of them; but they did little more than collect the customs duties levied at each port, and the townsmen were as a rule allowed to manage their own affairs. Political control was only of secondary interest to Said; his primary interest was in trade. Impressed by the high fertility of Zanzibar Island and Pemba Island, he encouraged the planting of cloves. He concluded commercial treaties with the United States, Great Britain, France, and the Hanseatic States. Not content with the haphazard methods by which the coastal people carried on trade with the Bantu in the interior, he organized the regular dispatch of caravans; by 1839, caravans were being sent into the interior once a year. The principal trade route was that leading from Bagamoyo on the coast to Tabora, virtually the same route that the railway from Dar es Salaam follows today. (Tabora owed its importance to the fact that it was the junction of the trade routes from Ujiji on Lake Tanganyika to the west and from the regions bordering Lake Victoria to the north.) The caravans were usually led by Arab or Swahili traders from the coast. No attempt was made to annex territories in the interior, and relations with the tribes along the trade routes went no further than buying ivory or slaves, or purchasing safe passage.

The results of Said's economic policies were impressive. By 1856, the year of his death, he had multiplied his African revenue ten times. Zanzibar, once an insignificant settlement, had become the principal port in East Africa. It had become the source of almost all the world's supply of cloves, the biggest slave market in the East, and a major market of ivory and gum copal. As the importance of Zanzibar increased, the importance of the small trading centers along the coast declined. Much of Said's economic success was due to the rapid and far-reaching penetration of the African mainland that took place during his reign.

Said was succeeded in the rulership of his African realm by Majid, his third surviving son. The throne of Oman was left to Thwain, Majid's elder brother. As it turned out, Thwain was dissatisfied with his portion and put to sea in 1859 to attack Zanzibar. Only the intervention of the British staved off hostilities, and Thwain was forced to return to Oman. Majid carried on the policies of his father during his fourteen-year reign. On the mainland the trade routes were pushed further westward. The situation in the interior remained much the same as in Said's time. Although many Bantu chieftains recognized Majid's overlordship, there was no question of his exercising any control over them. The commercial life of Zanzibar continued to flourish. In 1866, Majid began building a town on the mainland opposite Zanzibar to which he gave the name Dar es Salaam ("Haven of Peace"). When he died in 1870, he was succeeded to the throne by his brother Seyyid Barghash.

Seyyid Barghash's reign (1870–88) was an eventful one. Explorers had been busy in the interior, following up the discoveries of Livingstone; there was a great increase in missionary work; the British intensified their efforts to abolish the slave trade; and the international "scramble for Africa" began in this period.

One of the chief reasons Britain was interested in East Africa during the nineteenth century was that she hoped to abolish the slave trade there. Attempting first to restrict slave traffic, the British government signed a treaty with Said bin Sultan in 1845 that applied certain limits to the trade. The opening up of the interior, however, increased the traffic in slaves, and before long whole areas had been depopulated. Realizing that half measures would no longer serve, the British government instructed its consul at Zanzibar, John Kirk, to try to negotiate a treaty abolishing the slave trade altogether. Seyyid Barghash was at first reluctant to put a stop to such a lucrative business, but he was finally persuaded by Kirk to sign the treaty on June 5, 1873. Although slavery itself would be slow to die out, this treaty at least put an end to the slave trade in East Africa.

Besides suffering constant slave raids by the Arabs on the coast, the people of the interior were also affected by the movement across East Africa of Bantu tribes from the north and south, a migration that had been going on for the past four or five hundred years. Repeatedly, warlike tribes invaded the interior, killing and pillaging as they went. During the nineteenth century the slave trade encouraged many of the larger tribes to attack their weaker neighbors in order to sell them to the next passing caravan. This had the effect of consolidating tribal power.

For these reasons—the tightness of the tribal unit, the lack of external contact, and the ravages of the slave trade—most of the African peoples of the large area later to be known at Tanganyika continued to exist in a backward and often semiprimitive state right up to the time of the coming of the Europeans.

GERMAN EAST AFRICA

Sir Reginald Coupland has pointed out that the familiar phrase "the scramble for Africa" has usually been used "to denote the process by which the unoccupied territories of Tropical Africa were hastily appropriated in one form or another by rival European Powers between 1884 and 1891." Coupland continues:

But in East Africa—and it was much the same in West Africa—a kind of unofficial scramble had begun some years before 1884. From the time of the Egyptian invasion of 1875–76 onwards a multitude of Europeans— explorers, scientists, traders, financiers, missionaries—were scrambling everywhere, at the Sultan's palace in Zanzibar or far inland by the Great Lakes, scrambling for new knowledge, for a reputation, for markets, for concessions, for pagan souls.[12]

When the partition of Africa by the Great Powers began, several European nations eyed Sultan Barghash's East African possessions with interest. An earlier attempt by Egypt to get a foothold in East Africa had been thwarted through the intervention of Great Britain. Between 1877 and 1884 the Belgians, the French, and the Germans all made expeditions into East Africa, but without success.

Great Britain was the country with the best claims to the territories in question. Not only were British explorers and missionaries the first Europeans to penetrate and settle in the interior, but—even more important—Britain's role in the abolition of the slave trade had been of immeasurable benefit to the people of East Africa. Britain, however, showed little interest in establishing a protectorate over the Sultan's mainland possessions. When, in 1882, Barghash asked the British government to be responsible for seeing that his son succeeded him, Gladstone politely refused, thereby rejecting any sort of commitment in East Africa. Britain's last opportunity to stake out a claim came in 1884, when Sir Harry Johnston concluded an agreement with Mandara, the most powerful Chagga chief, for a settlement on the slopes of Kilimanjaro; but the British cabinet refused to acknowledge the agreement. Despite the quickening pace of the scramble, Britain's East African policy remained the same as it had been at the beginning of the century: to support the Sultan and encourage the extension of his authority on the mainland, which meant a parallel extension of British influence as well.[13]

Germany had also had an opportunity to establish an East African protectorate: in 1870 the Sultan had made overtures to the German government, but Bismarck had turned the offer down. The German Empire had only just come into being, and Bismarck was more concerned with Germany's new position in Europe than with colonial expansion. A number of Germans, however, felt that their country should not fall behind other nations in building up an overseas empire, and in 1880 the German African Society of Berlin was formed; this society immediately dispatched an exploratory expedition to Lake Tanganyika. In 1884 Dr. Karl Peters founder of the Society for German Colonization, led a small party into the East African interior. In the space of six weeks he concluded twelve treaties with African chiefs in Usagara, Uzeguha, and Ukami, whereby large tracts of land were handed over "for all time" in exchange for a few trinkets.

When Peters returned to Germany in 1885, Bismarck's attitude toward colonization had changed. This was no doubt due to pressure from certain north German firms that had interests in East Africa.[14] On February 27, 1885, the Kaiser issued a charter extending his protection to all the territory acquired by Peters and granting the management of this land to the Society. Peters subsequently formed the German East Africa Company and transferred to it all the rights he had secured in his treaties of 1884.

When he learned of the German claims, Barghash sent a strong protest to the Kaiser, but to no avail. Five German warships anchored in the harbor at Zanzibar in August 1885, and Barghash was forced to give in to the German demands. He was further persuaded by the British consul, John Kirk, who had been instructed by his government to encourage Barghash to agree to the German protectorate. In view of the French threat to Egypt and the recent triumph of the Mahdi in Sudan, Gladstone was in no position to quarrel with Bismarck.

Prior to this, Britain, France, and Germany had been discussing the possibility of appointing a joint commission to investigate the

Sultan of Zanzibar's claims to certain territories in East Africa, and to determine the precise limits of his territory.[15] This proposal was eventually agreed to, and the so-called Delimitation Commission was set up, consisting of one representative from Great Britain, Germany, and France, respectively.

The Commission began its work in January 1886, and during the next few months it visited every major port between Cape Delgado in the south and Mogadishu in the north. Countless interviews were held. Colonel Kitchener, the British representative, writing to Lord Roseberry at the Foreign Office, reported that "the Sultan's government was found everywhere firmly established, and the Commission was unable to find any contrary tendency."[16] On this point the three members of the Commission were agreed in their findings; but when it came to determining how far the Sultan's power extended into the interior, the German representative insisted on opposing the opinion of his British and French colleagues that in places the Sultan's control stretched as far as 40 miles inland. However, since it had been decided that only the unanimous findings of the three commissioners would be presented, the final report of the Commission recommended that the Sultan should have the ports and a ten-mile strip of land along the coast—without mentioning that two of the Commission's three members considered that he should have an additional 20 to 30 miles of territory inland as well.

After the Commission's report had been received, a partition agreement was concluded on November 1, 1886, between the British and German governments, by which (1) Britain and Germany recognized the Sultan's authority over the coast to a depth of ten miles from the River Ruvuma in the south to Kipini (in what is now Kenya Protectorate) in the north, and over the islands of Zanzibar, Pemba, and Mafia; and (2) German and British spheres of influences over the territory between the rivers Ruvuma and Tana were divided by the line that is now the boundary between Kenya and Tanganyika.[17] At no time during the investigations of the Delimitation Commission or the negotiating of the partition agreement was Barghash asked for his views. He was left with no choice but assent.

The treaty, however, did not satisfy the ambitions of the Germans, who were bent upon obtaining actual control of the coastal area through which they had to pass to reach the sea. Following the death of Barghash in 1888, his brother and successor, Seyyid Khalifa bin Said, concluded a new agreement with the German East Africa Company, whereby he handed over to it the right to administer that part of the ten-mile coastal belt which lay adjacent to the German protectorate. By this time the rapidity of German expansion in East Africa was causing anxiety in government circles in Britain. It was feared that since the 1885 Anglo-German agreement had left un-defined the western boundaries of the German and British protectorates, the Germans might have designs on the region northwest of Lake Victoria later to be known as Uganda. This rich agricultural area had recently become a center of increasing commercial interest to Britain. As it turned out, British suspicions were justified, for in 1890 Peters led a party into Uganda and concluded a treaty with Mwanga, the ruler of Buganda.

Peters' efforts, however, were defeated by the Anglo-German agreement of 1890, which adjusted the disputes of the two countries as regards their spheres of interest in many parts of East, West, and Southwest Africa. This agreement, like that of 1886, was determined by the politics of Europe; but this time the terms favored Britain, for Germany, facing the danger of war with France and Russia, needed British friendship. Under the agreement signed on July 1, 1890, Germany (1) recognized the British protectorate over Zanzibar, (2) abandoned all her claims on the coast or inland north of the River Tana, and (3) accepted the extension of the frontier dividing the two "spheres of influence" westward to Lake Victoria and across it to the boundary of the Congo Free State. For her part, Britain ceded Heligoland to Germany and undertook to use her influence with the Sultan to "cede absolutely" to Germany the ten-mile coastal strip already leased to the German East Africa Company in return for an "equitable indemnity." It was later agreed that this sum should be four million marks (£200,000).[18] On September 25, 1890, Seyyid Ali bin Said, who had succeeded his brother Khalifa as Sultan of Zanzibar, reluctantly gave his consent to the agreement. The British Protectorate of Zanzibar was proclaimed on November 4, 1890.

The whole area between Mozambique and the British "sphere of influence" to the north became German East Africa. This huge area, as demarcated by the agreements of 1886 and 1890, was substantially the same as that of Tanganyika today, except that German East Africa included the Ruanda and Urundi areas on the border of the Congo Free State.

For some time after the acquisition of their new territory, the Germans were engaged in putting down revolts. They did this with an iron hand. Indeed, Karl Peters, the man who set the pattern of early colonization, was generally known by the Africans as *Mkono-wa-damu,* "the man with the blood-stained hands."[19] Because of his cruelty, Peters was removed from his position as Imperial High Commissioner for the Kilimanjaro District and recalled to Germany in 1893. Some Germans, however—Emin Pasha, Franz Stuhlmann, Wilhelm Langheld, Baron von Eltz, and others—proved to be able colonial administrators who showed understanding of the African people and inspired their trust. (They also played a large part in stamping out an illicit slave trade.) Others, notably Hermann von Wissmann, the explorer, took a genuine interest in the people, but were forced to follow a policy dictated by Berlin. And so long as Berlin was bent upon achieving complete control of the interior with the utmost speed, punitive expeditions were inevitable. This gave militaristic junior officers and noncommissioned officers an opportunity to pursue the policy of *Schrecklichkeit* ("frightfulness") advocated by Peters.[20]

In the year that the German East Africa Company assumed the administration of the coastal belt, a widespread revolt among the coastal Arabs broke out. Under the leadership of an Arab named Bushiri bin Salim el Harthi, the revolt spread not only up and down the coast, but as far inland as the Southern Highlands. Even though the German government sent a force under Hermann von Wissmann to assist the Company, the revolt was not completely put down until the end of 1889, when Bushiri was captured. The intensity of the rebellion proved that the Company was incapable of administering its East African territory without the aid of the government. Therefore, on January 1, 1891, a protectorate was proclaimed, and the German Imperial government assumed the administration of the territory.

Even after the Company had handed over its administrative

powers to the German government, the situation did not improve. The effect of the coastal rebellion in 1888–89 was to create widespread anti-European feeling. In 1888, General Lloyd Mathews, the head of the Sultan's forces, wrote to John Kirk, who had recently retired, to inform him that "the feeling is against all Europeans. The whole coast and interior is in a ferment."[21] The coastal rebellion had scarcely been put down, when a revolt broke out with the Hehe of the Southern Highlands, a warlike people who resented German intrusion into the area. Their paramount chief, Mkwawa, had previously allied himself with Bushiri at the time of Bushiri's rebellion, hoping that his ally would be able to expel the Germans from the coast. Mkwawa was in the habit of raiding caravans passing through his territory, and in 1891 Lieutenant von Zelewsky, von Wissmann's successor, decided to put a stop to this practice. Mkwawa, however, received warning of the expedition and laid an ambush for von Zelewsky, virtually annihilating his entire force. A second expedition against the Hehe in 1894 put down the main body of the revolt, but Mkwawa continued to wage constant guerrilla warfare until 1898, the year of his death.

In 1892, after several successful forays against the Germans around Tabora, the Nyamwezi, under their paramount chief Siki, succeeded in completely closing the caravan routes to and from Tabora. This uprising was put down the following year, when a strong German column attacked and destroyed Siki's fortress. During these early days the Gogo were constantly causing trouble on the caravan route between Tabora and the coast, and several punitive expeditions were sent out to deal with them. The hinterland behind Kilwa, Lindi, and Mikindani also remained in ferment and from time to time occupied the attention of the Germans.

None of these revolts, however, constituted a real danger to German rule. It was not until the Maji-Maji rebellion of 1905 that the German position was seriously threatened. The rebellion broke out among the tribes south of the Rufiji River, and it extended from Lake Nyasa in the interior to Kilwa on the coast. According to Moffett, its main causes were "the misdeeds and acts of oppression of certain German officials and of many more of their Arab, Sudanese and Swahili subordinates."[22] One account of the rebellion points out that it "was chiefly remarkable for the combined effort of a number of tribes, for while it was never doubted that any one tribe might at any time give trouble, concerted action by many tribes was generally considered to be out of the question."[23] The bond uniting the tribes was the widespread belief that magic water obtained at a place named Ngarambi had the power to turn the Europeans' bullets into water.

Maji-Maji was the most widespread revolt East Africa has ever seen. The initial local successes of the original insurgents encouraged malcontents in other parts of the country to take up arms against the Germans. The revolt began with the murder of a number of isolated Arab, Sudanese, and Swahili traders in the area of Samanga and Madaba. Soon, however, ill-armed and ill-disciplined bands of Africans were roving over a wide area, attacking government outposts and mission stations as they went. Their hatred of German rule continued to unite them even after heavy casualties dulled the original fanaticism derived from their belief in the power of the Ngarambi waters. Unable to suppress the rebellion so long as the people continued to give passive support to the rebels, the Germans ruthlessly destroyed villages and crops over the entire area. By 1907, when the death of one of the bravest and most intelligent of the original insurgents, Abdulla Mpanda, brought an end to the revolt, devastation was almost complete in the south of German East Africa. The inhabitants had been robbed, killed, and enslaved by the German askaris; crops and villages had been destroyed and cattle carried off. Casualties from warfare and famine numbered about 120,000 people. According to Lord Twining, a recent British Governor of Tanganyika, the country has still not fully recovered from the severity of the German reprisal.[24]

The Maji-Maji rebellion marked the end of the first phase of German colonization. Reports of German brutality in putting down the rebellion, an uprising in the Cameroons in 1904–5, and the Herero War in German Southwest Africa all combined to effect a reform in German colonial policy. If Germany's colonies were to provide a place for her surplus population to emigrate and settle, as did the colonies of Britain, France, and the Netherlands, something clearly had to be done to bring about peace, order, and good government.

Up to this time, colonial affairs had been the concern of a sub-

department of the Chancellor's office. A separate Colonial Office
was now established, and Dr. Bernhard Dernburg was appointed
as the first Secretary for the Colonies. A so-called "scientific colonization" policy was adopted.[25] Dernburg and his successor, Wilhelm
Solf, were largely responsible for a changed official attitude toward
the African population in German East Africa. Seeing the colony
as a source of raw material for German industry, Dernburg viewed
the African inhabitants as the colony's most valuable asset rather
than as so much labor for German plantations. He advocated a land
policy in favor of African ownership and production. The sale of
land to settlers was greatly restricted, and forced labor was made
illegal except for public works. (These measures were unpopular
with the German settlers and proved to be largely ineffective.) Dernburg was also instrumental in bringing about the construction of the
Central Railway Line in order to open up the interior. Work was
begun in 1907, and by 1914 the line stretched from Dar es Salaam on
the coast to Kigoma on Lake Tanganyika.

Although the Germans were primarily interested in the economic
development of the territory, Dernburg also initiated a number of
administrative changes. He encouraged the appointment of a civilian
to the post of Governor—previously the governorship had usually
gone to a military man—and placed the territory's military forces
under a separate commander. (The Governor, however, remained
the supreme civil and military authority.) He instituted an advisory
council composed of three officials and from five to twelve unofficial
members to assist the Governor. The unofficial members, who were
appointed by the Governor, had to be natives of Germany. All financial estimates and proposed legislation had to be submitted to the
council, which was required to meet at least three times a year.

With regard to African administration, Dernburg boldly advocated the adoption of British methods in the face of strong opposition
from militarists and others. Dernburg, and Solf after him, gradually
saw their ideas prevail. It was found that the pre-German tribal organization had broken down in many parts of the territory, largely
because of the numerous punitive expeditions carried out prior to
1907. Where tribal organization remained intact, namely, in Ruanda,

Urundi, and Bukoba, residencies were created, and the inhabitants continued to be ruled by their traditional rulers under the supervision and direction of a German Resident. The remainder of the country was divided into 21 districts under direct German rule, since in these parts the Germans considered tribal authority too weak to be useful. Two of the districts were left in military charge, but the rest were placed under a civilian officer, who was called a district commissioner. Each district commissioner was responsible to the Governor for the maintenance of law and order in his district as well as for the collection of taxes.

District administration was similar in many ways to the earlier Arab system. A district was broken down into groups of villages, consisting of some 20,000 to 30,000 people, administered by an official known as an *Akida*. Each *Akida* was vested with certain magisterial powers and was held responsible for law and order in his group of villages. Each village was then placed in charge of a village headman bearing the title of *Jumbe*. These headmen were likewise given magisterial powers and held responsible for law and order within their respective jurisdictions.

The system never really had a chance to prove itself owing to the outbreak of World War I. Its chief weakness was the lack of German supervision. Each district was too large for the European administrative staff (who in 1914 numbered only 79 for the whole country) to exercise effective control over their subordinates. Therefore the actual functioning of the administration depended largely upon the *Akidas,* who were usually Arab or Swahili and prone to ride roughshod over native customs. Many of the *Akidas* were competent officers, but many others were guilty of corruption and abuse of authority. An official German report later pointed out that "the Akidas were in the habit of resorting to oppression and fraud, which made the administration detested by the people."[26] The quality of German administration therefore depended a great deal upon the individual administrative officer, whose power for good or evil was extensive. If we are to conclude that the German system of administration in Africa was a failure, it should be remembered that the Germans entered the field of colonial enterprise very late in the day. They had no experience either in colonial administration or in dealing with African races, and this was a considerable drawback in their attempt to administer the varied population of German East Africa.

Although the administrative efforts of the Germans were not particularly successful, their achievements in other fields were considerable. As has already been pointed out, their main concern throughout their rule was with the economic development of the land, rather than with administration. Except for attempts to encourage African cotton cultivation, the Germans concentrated on developing European plantations. The three most important plantation regions were Usambara in the north, the area along the line of the Central Railway, and the hinterland behind the port of Lindi. Other more isolated areas were the district of Iringa, the shores of Lake Victoria, and the lower slopes of Kilimanjaro. Although only about 3,115 square miles of land were alienated to Europeans for the purpose of planting economic crops—i.e., less than 1 per cent of the total area of German East Africa—this land was situated in some of the most fertile regions. This was especially true in the vicinity of Kilimanjaro.[27] The two most important economic crops were sisal, which was introduced from Florida in 1892, and rubber. Other plantation crops were coffee, cotton, coconuts (for copra), and kapok. The plantations developed by the Germans still form the backbone of the country's economy. The most thorough early agricultural research in East Africa was done by the Germans at Amani, where a biological and agricultural institute was established in 1902.

Another product of the period of German administration was the Usambara Railway, which was started from Tanga in 1896 and finally reached Moshi in 1912. The main reason for constructing this line (and the Central Railway, also built by the Germans) was to assist plantation development. These two lines established Tanganyika's basic communications system, and, except for the addition of certain branch lines, this system remains unchanged today.

Credit must also be given the Germans for the measures they took to improve African education during their short period in East Africa, measures that contrast quite favorably with those taken in the adjacent British protectorates. A report of the German Colonial Institute states that in 1911 there were over 1,000 schools and 66,647 pupils in the colony. Most of these schools were in the hands of missionary societies, only 83 schools being supported by the government. The vast majority were lower-level, elementary schools. In addition to three government and 14 missionary industrial schools, there were 17 "schools for practical work," whose aims were "to turn out artisans for the Europeans, and women for domestic work, to develop old Arab handicrafts, and introduce new culture."[28]

In the social field, steps were taken to bring about the gradual extinction of domestic slavery. A 1907 decree declared that all children born after 1906 of slave parents were *ipso facto* free; slaves born before that date had the right to purchase their freedom. Considering the place of slavery in the Arab-Swahili society of the coast, such measures were nothing short of a social revolution.

German rule came to an end with the defeat of Germany in World War I, during the course of which German East Africa suffered heavily from hostilities within its borders. Soon after the outbreak of war, clashes occurred between British and German troops along the northern frontier of the German colony. An attempted invasion of German East Africa by British and Indian troops in 1914 was repulsed by the German forces under the command of General Paul von Lettow-Vorbeck. No large-scale attack was made until February 1916, when a large body of British, South African, Rhodesian, and Indian troops, led by General Jan Christian Smuts, crossed the border, defeated the Germans near Kilimanjaro, and occupied the town of Moshi in March. The advance continued southward, Dar es Salaam falling into the hands of the invading forces on September 4, 1916. By the end of the year, all of German East Africa north of the Central Railway was occupied by British or Belgian forces, the latter having entered the colony from the Belgian Congo. On January 1, 1917, General Smuts set up a provisional civil administration over the occupied area and placed Horace Byatt at the head of it.

The Allied advance was resumed in mid-1917 and was now led by General Jacob van Deventer. General von Lettow-Vorbeck continued to resist with a small German force, but was finally driven across the Ruvuma River into Portuguese territory in November 1917.

He continued to hold out here until September 1918, when he re-crossed the Ruvuma into German territory. At the end of October he was forced to retreat into Northern Rhodesia, where he remained until the signing of the armistice. On November 25 he formally sur-rendered his battle-weary force to the British at Abercorn. Later von Lettow-Vorbeck summed up the German achievement: "In cold truth our small band, which at the most comprised some 300 Euro-peans and about 11,000 Askari, had occupied a very superior enemy force for the whole war. According to what English officers told me, 137 Generals had been in the field, and in all about 300,000 men had been employed against us."[29]

German East Africa suffered more from the war than any other part of East Africa, since most of the fighting took place there. Much of the country was turned into a wasteland. Africans serving with the army died by the thousands from malaria and dysentery in the waterless and tsetse-infested scrub country. Disease and famine fol-lowed the army across the territory, reducing the population and bringing much of the economy to a standstill. Sir Donald Cameron, a later Governor, estimated that 30,000 Africans died of famine alone.[30] Thousands of others died of the influenza epidemic of 1918–19.

By Article 119 of the Treaty of Versailles Germany renounced in favor of the Principal Allied and Associated Powers all her rights over her overseas possessions, including her East African colony. All former German colonies were placed under mandates, which were administered by the League of Nations through its Permanent Man-dates Commission, the mandatories being responsible for sending the Commission regular reports upon the administration of their terri-tories. Originally, the Big Four had intended to hand over the whole of German East Africa to Great Britain; owing to Belgian opposition, however, it was decided that Belgium should receive the Mandate for the areas of Ruanda and Urundi in return for her part in the East African campaign. Britain received the Mandate for the part of Ger-man East Africa referred to as Tanganyika Territory, a name that was officially given to the British area in January 1920.

This system of international trusteeship was instituted as a com-promise between those who held that imperial control should pass into the hands of the League and the imperial powers themselves, who were anxious to divide up Germany's overseas possessions. The Treaty of Versailles came into force by the exchange of ratifications on January 10, 1920. The Council of the League of Nations confirmed the Mandate for Tanganyika on July 20, 1922.

In undertaking the Tanganyika Mandate, Great Britain assumed certain international responsibilities outlined in Article 22 of the Covenant of the League of Nations and the Mandate Agreement for Tanganyika. Leopold Amery, the British Secretary of State for the Colonies, writing in 1926, likened these responsibilities to those "undertaken at home in the whole conception of trusteeship and administration of British dependencies." In point of fact, the obligations undertaken by Great Britain in Tanganyika were much more precise than those undertaken by her in any other part of Africa.[31]

The terms of the Mandate for Tanganyika placed the following requirements upon Great Britain: "to promote to the utmost the material and moral well-being and the social progress of . . . Tanganyika's inhabitants" (Article 7); to suppress the slave trade and work for "the eventual emancipation of all slaves" (Article 5); to "protect the natives from abuse and measures of fraud and force by the careful supervision of labour contracts and the recruiting of labour" (Article 5); to "respect the rights and safeguard the interests of the native population . . . in the framing of laws relating to the holding or transfer of land" (Article 6); to "ensure in the territory complete freedom of conscience and the free exercise of all forms of worship which are consonant with public order and morality" (Article 8); and to refrain from using the territory for military purposes (Article 4). As far as aliens were concerned, Britain agreed "to secure to all nationals of states [that were] Members of the League of Nations the same rights as are enjoyed in the territory by [British] nationals in respect of entry into and residence in the territory" (Article 7).

2

THE PEOPLE

German East Africa had an area of 370,000 square miles and a population of about 7,600,000. Nearly half of this population was densely settled in the two native kingdoms of Ruanda and Urundi, which were sliced off from the former German colony and granted to Belgium as a mandated territory following World War I. The British Mandate, Tanganyika Territory, although the largest of the mandated territories (it contained an area of 362,688 square miles, which included about 20,000 square miles of water), was more sparsely populated owing to sleeping sickness, tribal wars, and harsh treatment by the German administration.

The first attempt at a census by the British administration was that of 1921, which placed the total African population at 4,107,000. In 1913 the Germans had estimated the population of the same area to be about 4,063,000—in other words, there had been only a slight increase over a period of eight years.[1] This was due to the fact that although the population in the interior had continued to increase (except in three districts where great numbers died as a result of the war and the famine of 1919), the population in the coastal districts had decreased owing to a steady decline in the birth rate.

The accuracy of the early censuses is questionable. The vastness of the territory and the tendency of the African population to scatter across it made an accurate census difficult to obtain. Two more enumerations, in 1928 and 1931, were undertaken by the British during the period of the Mandate. Both showed considerable increases in population; this, however, must be attributed largely to the greater accuracy of the enumeration procedures. Table 1 sets out the African population as recorded in these four enumerations, with estimates of the increase and the mean annual increase.

According to German figures shortly before the war, there were about 15,000 non-Africans resident in German East Africa. Of these, 5,336 were Europeans and the remainder was made up of various Asian groups. At the time the British assumed the mandate, the composition of the non-African population had changed somewhat: the census of 1921 showed that the number of Europeans had decreased to 2,447 (owing to the deportation of German subjects), but that the number of Asians had increased to 14,991, a figure that was made up of 9,411 Indians, 4,041 Arabs, 798 Goans, and 741 unclassified peoples.[2]

The two Asian groups showing the greatest increases during the early years of the Mandate were the Indians and the Arabs, with the Indians easily in the lead. As nationals of a member state of the League of Nations, Indians were free to enter the territory and to acquire land under Article 7 of the Mandate, and they accordingly immigrated in large numbers. The immigration of Indians into Tanganyika was considerably greater than that of Europeans, the 1931 census recording the Indian population as 23,422 and the European as 8,228. Although immigration slackened off after 1931 as a result of the depression, the influx continued, and in 1938 the Asian population was estimated at 33,784, of which more than 25,000 were Indians, as compared with a European population of 9,345.[3] The

TABLE I.—AFRICAN POPULATION, 1913–1931

Year	Total African population	Years between censuses	Increase since preceding census (per cent)	Mean annual increase (per cent)
1913	4,063,000	—	—	—
1921	4,107,000	8	1.7	0.1
1928	4,741,000	7	15.4	2.1
1931	5,023,000	3	5.9	1.9

SOURCE: Hill and Moffett, p. 34.

large increase in the Indian community during these years is one of the most striking features of the period.[4]

The European community in Tanganyika was marked by its heterogeneity. As the report of the Commission on Closer Union of the Dependencies in Eastern and Central Africa pointed out in 1929, "if officials and their families are left out of account the proportion of non-British to British is considerably more than two to one."[5] Of the total European population in 1938, the British element numbered 4,054, the German 3,205, and the Greek 893. There were also Dutch, Italian, American, French, Swedish, and Danish settlers, but in much smaller numbers.[6] Germans in Tanganyika in 1938 were actually more numerous than in the former German colony.[7]

The territory's population has steadily increased since the end of World War II. According to the 1948 census, the population consisted of 7.4 million Africans, 57,512 Asians, and 10,643 Europeans. In other words, approximately 99 per cent of the total population was African, 0.9 per cent Asian, and 0.1 per cent European. An intermediate census of the non-African community in 1952 showed that the number of Europeans and Asians had increased to 17,885 and 77,609, respectively.[8] The most recent census was taken in 1957. It showed the population to consist of 20,598 Europeans, 102,532 Asians, and 8,665,336 Africans, making a total of 8,788,466 (see Table 2).

TABLE 2.—Non-African Censuses 1948, 1952, and 1957
Comparison by Race

Race	1948	1952	1957
European	10,648	17,885	20,598
Indian	44,248	56,499	65,461
Pakistani	—	—	6,299
Goan	2,006	3,240	4,776
Arab	11,074	13,025	19,100
Somali	—	2,060	3,114
Colored	1,335	1,576	2,257
Other	849	1,209	1,525

source: Hill and Moffett, p. 37; East African Statistical Department, *Tanganyika Population Census 1957* ([Nairobi?], 1958), Table 1. The non-African census in 1948 excluded Somalis. Before the census of 1957, Pakistanis were included with the Indians.

The rate of increase in the three sections of the population is explained in various ways. The rapid increase in the Asian community (about 3 per cent per annum[9]) is due partly to the fact that the Asian population has now reached a size that results in a considerable natural increase and partly to immigration. The rate of natural increase for the African population has been rising as a result of improved health conditions. The European population is so small that its increase in size is largely due to immigration.

The great majority of Africans still live in the traditional tribal type of society. Although official sources do not always agree, the number of tribes found in the territory is usually given as 120. The administration has always found it difficult to establish the exact limits of a tribe; thus the number of tribes may vary from census to census. Tanganyika contains a great many tribes in relation to its area, and no one tribe represents a large percentage of the total population. In 1948 tribes ranged from very small groups to groups numbering as many as 800,000 people. Many had fewer than 10,000 members, and only six had more than 250,000 members. The Sukuma, who inhabit the area around Lake Victoria, are the most numerous, representing in 1948 some 12 per cent of the total African population.[10] Table 3 shows the size of the seven largest tribes in 1948.

Tribalism is still of enormous importance in the life of the Tanganyika African. The great majority of members of any one tribe are still to be found living together within their own tribal boundaries, and within a given area at least 90 per cent of the inhabitants usually

TABLE 3.—POPULATION OF THE LARGEST TRIBES

Tribe	Total	Percentage of grand total
Sukuma	888,000	12.0
Nyamwezi	362,829	4.9
Ha	286,112	3.9
Makonde	281,320	3.8
Gogo	278,755	3.8
Haya	269,142	3.6
Chagga	237,343	3.2

SOURCE: Hill and Moffett, p. 32.

belong to the local tribe.[11] Although tribal loyalties are beginning to give place to nationalist loyalties, no wholesale change should as yet be expected. Nationalism has its strongest grip on the "de-tribalized" Africans living in the towns or other commercial centers. Its effect, therefore, on the ordinary "man in the bush" is not great. Even though the Tanganyika African National Union now has a membership of over 1,000,000, this is still only about one member for every nine Africans.

The majority of the African population are descended from the Negroid, Hamitic, and Nilo-Hamitic peoples who have from time to time settled in East Africa. These movements began long before the time of Christ and continued right up to the coming of the Europeans. There has been considerable admixture of blood, and this has resulted in the present very diversified African population. There are five identifiable ethnic groups—the Bushman group, the Nilotic group, the Hamites, the Nilo-Hamites, and the Bantu—and some unidentifiable elements. These groups are mainly distinguished by their physical characteristics, but there are also differences of language, social organization, and mode of living.

The Bushman group are descended from the early inhabitants of southern Africa; the best known of these short-statured folk are the Bushmen of South Africa. In Tanganyika there are two tribes of Bushman origin, the Kindiga and the Sandawe. The former still live the life of the nomadic hunter and food-gatherer, whereas the latter have settled down to cattle-raising and agriculture. Both tribes speak a click language peculiar to the Bushman people.

The only tribe of Nilotic origin is the Luo, who live on the east shore of Lake Victoria. They are the only relatively pure example of Negroid stock in Tanganyika.

The Hamitic group are tall, light-skinned, fine-featured people similar to the predynastic Egyptians and to the Abyssinians of today. They are not descended from the early Hamites who inhabited East Africa prior to the coming of the Negroes, but from a later group that moved into East Africa probably in the sixteenth century. They imposed themselves as rulers over large numbers of the Bantu, particularly in Ruanda, Urundi, and Buganda. Although for the most part these Hamitic people have blended with the tribes they rule, they still retain a position of power, and it has been estimated that almost two million of the present population are under their political influence.[12] However, other members of the group, generally referred to as the Tusi, have no political interest and have settled as cattle herders.

The Nilo-Hamitic group are a blend of the Nilotic and Hamitic groups. This mixture occurred long before these people entered East Africa. The largest and best-known segment of the group is the Masai. There are also the Barabaig, Kismajeng, and Taturu tribes, all of whom fall under the Tatog classification. The Nilo-Hamites have none of the political talents of the Hamites; their interests are solely in their cattle and the maintenance of their grazing lands. Although they occasionally raided their Bantu neighbors, there was no attempt at political subjugation. The Masai, in particular, have long held the respect of colonial administrators for their proud aloofness and absolute indifference to European ways. Although they numbered only about 60,000 in 1948, the Masai occupy a large area west of Mount Kilimanjaro and Mount Meru known as the Masai Steppe.

The fifth ethnic group, the Bantu, are by far the largest group. In 1948 they numbered about 7,000,000, or about 94 per cent of the total African population. The four groups already described made up the remaining 6 per cent.[13] They are believed to be a mixture of various Hamitic and Negro stocks, and the many Bantu tribes that exist vary greatly according to the different degrees of admixture that have occurred. For the most part the Bantu are agricultural people engaged in subsistence production; many are at the same time cattle-owners. Cattle are a prized form of wealth and are sometimes associated with religious and magical beliefs and practices.

Every well-known Bantu tribe of today is a blend of recent origin. For instance, the Gogo, the Hehe, and the Chagga, each about a quarter of a million strong, are all recent conglomerations of many elements. The Sukuma, the Ha, the Haya, the Zinza, the Hangaza, and the Subi are Hamitic-dominated agricultural tribes living in the northwestern part of the country. East of the Masai Steppe live some of the most advanced tribes, notably the Chagga and the Meru. Owing to the favorable climate, these tribes have become relatively prosperous agriculturists. They have had particular success with the cultivation of coffee and have established highly effective co-operative unions to handle this product.

Conditions on the Central Plateau, on the other hand, are harsh and have retarded the economic progress of the tribes living there. These tribes, typified by the Gogo to the east and the Nyamwezi to the west, are agriculturists and cattle-owners. The tribes in the region of Lake Nyasa and Lake Tanganyika, the largest of which are the Nyakyusa and the Fipa, are among the least economically advanced. This is due both to their isolation and to the havoc caused by the slave trade, which was particularly active here.

The tribes living along the coast and in the Southern Province are the weakest in traditional political organization, the institution of the chief being almost entirely lacking. An unhealthy climate, the effects of especially severe slave-raiding, and, in the Southern Province, the fighting that took place during the Maji-Maji rebellion and World War I have inhibited population growth and economic advance. The mode of living is particularly influenced by Islam, which is more widely accepted here than in any other part of the country. The language of the coastal people is Swahili, which is understood in most parts of the country and is a useful *lingua franca*. Bantu in origin, it is enriched by many words of Arabic, English, Persian, Hindustani, and Portuguese derivation.

The bulk of the African population are peasant farmers engaged in feeding and housing themselves and their families. When these basic needs have been met, the individual farmer may become a migrant laborer or a small producer of a few cash crops such as cotton and coffee. The Bantu, in particular, are different from peasant farmers in other parts of the world in that they do not have to leave their homes in order to go to the fields every day: they live in family groups, sometimes small, farming the land around their huts. Often it may be some distance to their nearest neighbor.

There are three types of population movement of economic and social importance: the long-established, semi-nomadic migrations of pastoral tribes, movements resulting from population pressure, and changes of habitat brought about by a search for work. Except for certain health controls, particularly in the case of sleeping sickness, such movements are theoretically free of any restrictions. In practice, however, although a man is free to leave his own tribal area at any time, his right to settle in another tribe's area depends upon acceptance by the people of this second area and their willingness to make land available to him.

The distribution of the population is determined largely by the lack of water and the prevalence of the tsetse fly. In order to avoid these two evils, the population has scattered itself across the territory. The most densely populated are the elevated areas, particularly in the Usambara Mountains, around Mount Kilimanjaro and Mount Meru, on the shores of Lake Victoria, and in the Southern Highlands. It is also in the areas of greatest density that the rate of population increase is greatest. Density figures for the provinces range from approximately 12 people per square mile in Western Province to approximately 47 people per square mile in Lake Province. Even within the provinces the density figure for one district may vary greatly from that of a neighboring district.[14]

Although Christian missionaries have been active in the country for more than a hundred years, and although Islam has spread rather widely, the majority of Tanganyika Africans are animistic. This is not to say that they have no religion, but simply that such external signs as temples, priests, and sacrifices are lacking. Since religious practices vary from tribe to tribe, it is dangerous to generalize, but certain beliefs do appear to be held in common. Among these is a belief in the unity of the dead and the living. The soul is believed to originate in an unseen world composed of the spirits of the dead and other spirits. The basis of religious ideas and observance is therefore ancestor worship; and although this survives only in a fragmentary form, it is nevertheless definitely present.

A belief in magic and the practice of witchcraft are common to many of the Bantu tribes and in some areas still play an important part in tribal life. The chief, or some other person believed to have special powers, may perform certain rites on behalf of the people to secure the protection of the tribe from misfortune, to ensure the fertility of the soil, or to bring rain. In some of the more remote and backward areas there is still a tendency to place the blame for every misfortune on some evil influence.[15]

The two most important nonindigenous religions are Islam and Christianity. During the last 150 years, Islam, long present on the coast, has become well established in a number of inland districts, especially those on the routes of the Arab caravans of last century. The prevalence of Arab names among Africans throughout the country testifies to the gradual spread of Mohammedanism. The spread of Christianity has been more recent, occurring during the last fifty years, and Christianity is now the predominant religion in several districts. Lutheran, Anglican, and Roman Catholic missionary societies have been particularly active in Tanganyika.

In its traditional form, tribal authority was generally exercised by a chief, assisted by subchiefs, village headmen, and elders. However, some Bantu and Nilo-Hamitic tribes have no tradition of centralized organization. Among the politically centralized tribes, subchiefs either were members of the recognized ruling clan, or were appointed by the chief for their personal qualifications or as a reward for services rendered. During recent years there has been an attempt to modify the tribal structure and bring it more into line with modern ideas of local government. The traditional forms of tribal constitution have been modified, the basis of administration has been broadened, and the principle of popular representation has been quite widely accepted and established.

More than three-quarters of the non-African population are Asians, consisting mainly of the Indian and Arab communities. The Asian group also include small numbers of Goans, Sinhalese, Somalis, Seychellois, Syrians, Comorians, Baluchis, and a very few Chinese.[16] Yet despite the heterogeneity of the Asian group, many of whose members have retained their own creeds, traditions, and customs, the Asians have increasingly adopted a local outlook.

Indian traders have been present on the East Coast for centuries. They were welcomed by the Germans, during whose administration they spread throughout the interior. Today Indian petty traders have penetrated to every corner of the country. They have introduced a money economy and the advantages of such commodities as cloth, knives, lamps, matches, shoes, and tea to the local inhabitants.

The Indians' place in the economic life of Tanganyika has been considerable. During the 1920's, for instance, all the commercial property of Dar es Salaam, except for two European retail firms, was in Indian hands.[17] In 1952 just over half of the gainfully employed Indians were engaged in wholesale and retail trade, 14.1 per cent in the manufacturing industries, 13 per cent in the public services, and only 5 per cent in agriculture, forestry, and fishing. Their interest in trade and commerce, office work, and craftsmanship has naturally made them a more urban group than other sections of the population. In 1952, excluding Goans, Indian urbanization was 82.7 per cent as against 51.1 per cent for the Europeans and only 38.9 per cent for the Arabs.[18]

Trade has also been the principal means of livelihood of the Arabs, although they have less influence in this field than the Indians. The Arab inhabitants have to a considerable extent intermarried with indigenous elements of the population, and nearly two-thirds of their number now live in rural areas. In 1952, 78.1 per cent of the gainfully employed Arabs were engaged in wholesale and retail trade. The rest were employed in agriculture and fishing, and to a lesser degree in the public services. As an ethnic group the Arabs are more backward in education than either the Indians or the Europeans.[19]

Europeans make up Tanganyika's smallest racial group. During the early period of British administration, Europeans were engaged primarily in agriculture and the public services. The European population of Dar es Salaam came to only a handful at this time: in 1928, out of the city's total population of 25,000, there were only 800 Europeans as against 4,500 Asians and 19,700 Africans.[20] In 1957 the country's European population consisted of representatives of thirty different nationalities. Quite naturally the largest number were British; Greeks took second place. As in the period before World War II, they were primarily engaged in farming, the civil service, missionary work, industry, and commerce. In spite of its small size, the European community has had a pronounced influence on the political development of Tanganyika, an influence that derives its strength from a concentration of economic power coupled with educational advantages and social cohesion.[21] However, their diverse background, combined with a lack of contact resulting from poor communications, has prevented the Europeans from forming as strong a settler group as is found in Kenya.

A. K. Datta has analyzed the composition of the various income groups in Tanganyika. He found that the higher income group consists mainly of Europeans and a few Asians. In the middle income groups the Asians predominate, with the lower fringe of the European population and the upper fringe of the African population also falling within this group. In the lower income group the indigenous people are the overwhelming majority, and the rest are Asians. "Thus in the pyramidal class-structure of the Territory the top is white and the base is black, while the middle which joins the two and merges black and white is overwhelmingly brown."[22]

The population of the main towns of Tanganyika has grown right along with the increase in total population. However, a study made in 1957 found that urbanization itself was "only slowly increasing." It noted that in 1931 the ten largest towns contained 1.2 per cent of the total African population; by 1951 this figure had risen to a mere 1.9 per cent. In 1952 only 205,869 Africans lived in the ten listed townships out of the total African population of 7,407,517. This amounts to only 2.75 per cent of the entire African population.[23] Dar es Salaam, the largest city in Tanganyika, also has the largest non-African population of any town in the territory. In 1957 the city's population

TABLE 4.—POPULATION OF THE MAIN TOWNS

Town	Population	Town	Population
Dar es Salaam	128,742	Moshi	13,726
Tanga	38,053	Dodoma	13,445
Mwanza	19,877	Mtwara	10,459
Tabora	15,361	Lindi	10,315
Morogoro	14,507	Arusha	10,038

SOURCE: East African Statistical Department, *Tanganyika Population Census 1957* ([Nairobi?], 1958), Table 3.

consisted of 4,479 Europeans, 30,900 Asians, and 93,363 Africans. The other large towns have considerable non-African populations, too; but these are made up mainly of Asians, the European population in each case being quite small. The population of the ten largest towns in 1957 is shown in Table 4.

3

TANGANYIKA
UNDER BRITISH MANDATE

The British Mandate for Tanganyika came into force on January 10, 1920, when the exchange of ratifications of the Treaty of Versailles took place. By an Order in Council known as the Tanganyika Order in Council, 1920, issued on July 22 of that year, provision was made by Great Britain for the civil administration of the mandated territory. The office of Governor and Commander in Chief was vested with the chief executive authority. The Governor, the representative of the Crown in the territorial government of Tanganyika, was appointed by the Crown and, according to the Tanganyika Order in Council, 1920, was "authorised, empowered and commanded to do and execute all the things that belong to his said office, according to the tenor of any Orders in Council relating to the Territory, and of such Commission and Instructions as may be issued to him" under the Royal Sign Manual and Signet, by Order in Council, or by the Crown through one of the principal Secretaries of State. Thus Great Britain established complete control over the administration of Tanganyika, in setting forth policy as well as in its actual execution. Although Tanganyika was a mandated territory of the League of Nations, its links with the British Crown were as close and active as in the case of any colony.[1]

The Governor was responsible for peace, order, and good government in the territory, and extensive executive, legislative, and judicial powers were accordingly conferred on him. His powers, however, did not go so far as to allow him to formulate basic policies. For this he was required to obtain instructions from the Colonial Office, after which it was his responsibility to see that they were carried out. The Governor therefore acted as a link between the territorial government and the metropolitan government.

The Governor was originally assisted in his executive work by an Executive Council, which was established by the Royal Instruction under the Royal Sign Manual and Signet passed on August 31, 1920. The function of the Executive Council was to advise the Governor on such questions as the law prescribed should be dealt with by the Governor in Council and on such other matters as he saw fit to submit to it. The decision in all such questions, however, remained with the Governor, who could act in opposition to the advice given to him. In this event he was bound to report the case to the Secretary of State, giving the reasons for his action.

Article XIII of the Instruction establishing the Executive Council stipulated that in the execution of his duties the Governor was legally bound to consult the Council in all cases. The only three exceptions to this provision were: (1) when it was in the public interest not to hold such consultation; (2) when the issues to be discussed were too unimportant to be so discussed; and (3) when the matters were too urgent to admit of the Council's advice being sought. In the third case, the Governor was required to communicate his decision to the Council at the earliest opportunity.

The Executive Council was at first composed of only ex officio members, but later unofficial members nominated by the Governor were added. The ex officio members held their seats by virtue of being the heads of certain important departments of the territorial government.

When first established in 1920, the Executive Council consisted of only four ex officio members. These were the Chief Secretary, the Attorney General, the Treasurer, and the Director of Medical and Sanitary Services. Subsequently, the Director of Education and the Secretary for Native Affairs became members of the Council by the Tanganyika Order in Council of 1926.[2]

During the period of the Mandate, the Chief Secretary's importance far exceeded that of the other members of the Council. Administrative authority was concentrated in his office. As the principal executive officer of the Governor, he was appointed to act as Governor during the latter's absence or incapacity. Normally he was the administrative head of the Civil Service and was responsible not only for the main executive decisions, but for provincial and district administration as well. He also acted as a link between the Governor and the Provincial Commissioners, the heads of various departments, and the general public. This concentration of power in one office was broken up during World War II, however, because of an increase in the amount of work.

The unofficial members of the Executive Council, who were appointed by the Governor, could also be suspended by him, upon sufficient grounds, under Article 10 of the Tanganyika Order in Council, 1920. Thus the question arises whether the unofficial members were free from government control. Unlike the ex officio members, they were not committed to support all measures proposed by the government side in the Council, and theoretically they were in a position to voice nongovernmental interests in a moderate manner. Provision for an unofficial group, even though nominated, on the Executive Council acted as a safety valve for discontent among the more mature section of the population. It was hoped, therefore, that the unofficial members would offer responsible and constructive criticism of government policy.[3] However, the Council had no unofficial members until 1939; in that year, four unofficial members were appointed, three Europeans and one Asian.

When Sir Donald Cameron, the second Governor of Tanganyika, arrived in the territory in 1925, one of the first things he did was to recommend to the Secretary of State for the Colonies that a Legislative Council "with a liberal representation of the unofficial community" be set up. He proposed "the constitution of such a Council whereby means would be afforded . . . of sharing responsibility for legislation and for the Annual Budget with public men appointed for the purpose from the unofficial side of the community." He explained: "I was literally unhappy at the idea of having to enact legislation and prepare the Annual Budget of expenditure without proper ventilation and discussion of each measure."[4]

Subsequently, the Tanganyika (Legislative Council) Order in Council of March 19, 1926, was proclaimed. It provided for a Legislative Council consisting of thirteen official members, committed to support the government, and a maximum of ten unofficial members; in other words, there was to be a permanent official majority. Although the previous lack of a Legislative Council had been a source of complaint to the European population,[5] Cameron records that he was "blamed at the time in certain quarters for instituting a Legislative Council at such an early date in the political history of the Territory." He declared that his difference with such objectors was "fundamental," since he believed strongly that the territory could not be administered properly "from an office in comparative seclusion, with but little contact with the outer world and that little only of one's own seeking." He stated that he believed in administration "in the field of action where one is in constant day to day contact with unofficials and officials."[6]

Up to 1943, the Governor's authority in the Legislative Council, as in the Executive Council, was supreme. He served as President of the Council and had other powers similar to those of a Prime Minister. He could initiate legislation, and then as President he conducted the discussion on such matters. Finally, as the representative of the Crown he made the final decision on any bill passed by the Legislative Council. A further alternative was for him to reserve decision for the Crown itself. Clause XIV of the Tanganyika Order in Council, 1926, pointed out the relationship between the Governor and the Legislative Council: "It shall be lawful for the Governor with the advice and consent of the Council to make laws for the administration of justice, and the raising of revenue and generally for the peace, order and good government of the Territory."[7]

The first session of the Legislative Council was held at Dar es Salaam in December 1926. The thirteen official members consisted of the six ex officio members of the Executive Council plus seven other high government officials. Lord Milner once stated in the House of Lords that "the only justification for keeping an official majority in any colony is that we are convinced that we are better judges, for the time being, of the interests of the native population than they are themselves."[8] Although certain allowances were made for conscientious scruples, it was generally understood that if an official member found that his conscience did not permit him to support the policy of the government, it was his duty to resign his office.

The unofficial members of the Legislative Council were nominated and appointed by the Governor, subject to disallowance or confirmation by the Crown, and they held office for a term of five years. They were nominated without regard to representation of particular races, interests, or public bodies, being chosen purely on suitability for the job. Although it was not mentioned specifically in the Order in Council establishing the Tanganyika Legislative Council, the authorities intended eventually to give some of the unofficial seats to Africans who had learned enough English to allow them to participate in the proceedings of the Council.[9]

As a consequence of the stipulation that members of the Legislative Council take an oath of allegiance to the King, only British subjects were eligible to become members. This caused some dissatisfaction later on, when the Germans and other European communities together outnumbered the British in the territory. But even though representation of these communities may have been desirable, especially since the territory was held under Mandate, no way was seen around the oath.[10] Appointment of Indians to the Council was possible, however, since they were British subjects. In 1938 three Indians were among the unofficial members of the Council.[11]

Although the British had recently introduced a system for the election of unofficial members of the Legislative Council in Kenya, Sir Donald Cameron wrote in his memoirs that "it was generally accepted . . . that the Territory was still politically too young to consider the adoption of a system of direct representation." He predicted, with accuracy, that the question of an electoral system "will present special difficulties in the Mandated Territory when the time may arrive for its more serious examination."[12]

Both the Executive and the Legislative Councils were created primarily as subsidiary advisory organs. But in practice, because the Governor was physically incapable of dealing with every detail of administration, their opinions carried considerable weight. This applied chiefly to advice given by the official members of the councils, but also to the opinion of the unofficial members. Since the colonial officials were often less familiar with the history, geography, and social and economic life of Tanganyika, the unofficial members, as representatives of the permanent element in the territory, were depended upon for such information. The Governor, therefore, despite official majorities in both councils, would probably reconsider any measure that had the unanimous opposition of the unofficial members.[13]

THE INTRODUCTION OF INDIRECT ADMINISTRATION

Sir Horace Byatt, who formerly had been the administrator of the British-occupied portion of German East Africa, was appointed the first Governor of Tanganyika in 1920. He served in that capacity until 1924. He faced the formidable task of restoring order to a country that had been ravaged first by war and then by famine. Trade and revenue in 1920 stood at less than half of what they had been before the war.[14]

The administrative staff was not only small, but inexperienced. Some officials had been lent by other governments in East Africa and the Union of South Africa; others until recently had been military officers serving with the forces in East Africa. During this transitional period, few changes were made in the German methods of administration, since the British had quite enough to do coping with the problems left by the war without embarking on large-scale reorganization. German ordinances and regulations remained in force unless they actually conflicted with British law; political officers in the coastal region continued to work through *Liwalis, Akidas,* and *Jumbes* who had not shown anti-British feelings; and the district organization that the Germans had installed was maintained.

During this period, the British administration was largely occupied with the disposal of German lands and assets. Auctions of former German plantations began in 1921, and by 1924 the majority had been disposed of. Most of them were bought by British, Indian, and Greek settlers. When the Germans returned to Tanganyika, some of these estates were resold to their original German owners.

The period of postwar reconstruction came to an end in 1925. By that time, revenue had begun to match expenditure. The former

German plantations were again producing, and native agriculture was back on its feet.[15] By 1925, Tanganyika was exporting twice as much as it had done before the war. Considering the difficulties that had faced him, Sir Horace Byatt had achieved a great deal in the field of economic recovery.[16]

Although the German system of native administration had been continued at first, it was not long before the system of indirect administration found in other British territories was put into effect in Tanganyika. This system consisted of ruling a territory through its native chiefs and was in theory almost diametrically opposed to the German practice of ruling through alien officials, a practice which, according to one Tanganyikan official, "actively promoted the disintegration of such tribal organization as had previously existed."[17]

The British system was introduced in 1923, when an ordinance known as the Native Authority Ordinance conferred upon administrative officers, native chiefs, and headmen the power to issue orders and regulations for matters concerning the maintenance of order and the prevention of crime. The Ordinance came into operation only gradually, the German system being abolished first in parts of the Mwanza district and in Kondoa Irangi. The government could not abolish it elsewhere right away because of the difficulty of finding out who the real rulers in each tribe were. However, owing to the gradual removal or disappearance of the intermediaries through whom contact had formerly existed between the government and the Africans, district officers were at least in closer touch with native affairs. Indeed, in many cases they issued the orders and regulations themselves, a practice that hardly fulfilled the intentions of the recent ordinance establishing native authority.[18] This was the situation when Sir Donald Cameron arrived in Tanganyika in April 1925.

Cameron, who had served as Chief Secretary in the Nigerian government before his appointment as the second Governor of Tanganyika, took over the government from John Scott (later knighted), who had been serving as Acting Governor since the departure of Sir Horace Byatt the year before. Cameron found that native administration was a problem needing his immediate attention. He has since

written: "So far as I could judge on arrival the Provincial Administration had little or no guidance, and in the Districts—there were
as yet no Provinces—work was being done at a scramble—or left un-
done—owing to shortage of administrative staff and lack of any sort
of settled policy." He placed no blame on Scott, however, for not
attempting any major reforms in the short time at his disposal, since
such reforms would have had to be "of a very comprehensive and
radical character."[19]

The urgency of reforming the system of native administration was
further heightened by the government's recent assumption of an obligation to pay a number of tribal chiefs an annual stipend in place of
the tribute and service they had been accustomed to receiving from
their subjects. The rendering of tribute and service was usually accomplished by a tribesman's giving so many days' free labor during
the year to work on the chief's gardens and plantations. Each person's total obligations, expressed in terms of cash, were not fixed, with
the result that the individual African often suffered from capricious
and burdensome exactions demanded at the pleasure of his chief. The
rendering of such tribute and service was also considered objection-
able on the grounds that Africans already paid one direct tax in the
form of the hut and poll tax and therefore should be free from any
other direct taxation.

Shortly before Cameron arrived in the territory, the government
had arranged for the chiefs to give up this custom in exchange for
annual stipends from the territorial treasury, approximately the cash
value of the tribute formerly received. An increase in the hut and poll
tax had provided the extra revenue necessary to carry out the plan.
Since no payments had as yet been made to the chiefs, Cameron decided that they should at least contribute something toward the £96,-
000 that the government had committed itself to pay out annually,
and he suggested that this contribution should take "the form of
responsible service on behalf of their people."

Drawing on his own experience in Nigeria and that of three of
the territory's senior administrative officers, Cameron devised the
system of indirect administration that was instituted in Tanganyika

during his governorship. When the cash value of the tribute and service formerly received by each chief had been determined, this amount was to be paid into the treasuries of the tribal authorities involved, which were to be constituted at the same time. Then, in return for serving as head of the local administration, each chief who had been receiving tribute and service was to be paid a fixed salary from the native treasuries according to the extent of his duties and responsibilities.

Since this system of administration depended upon locating the local authority recognized by the members of a particular tribe or subtribe, Cameron felt that "if a people continued to render tribute and service to a particular man it was fairly safe to assume for the time being that they recognised him as their Chief in accordance with native custom." In ambiguous cases, inquiries were made in order to discover what local authorities were still recognized by the people.

Cameron wished it to be understood that he had not gone to Tanganyika "itching to introduce the Nigerian system of 'Indirect Rule' "; he had simply adopted the system that best suited the circumstances. He said that in Nigeria he had not belonged to the group "which blindly worshipped 'Indirect Rule' " and that the modification of it adopted in Tanganyika was "more liberal . . . from the point of view of the people and not the Chiefs."[20]

Apart from administrative expediency, Cameron later gave two other reasons for introducing indirect native administration in Tanganyika. "I believed that the people would in addition derive material as well as moral advantage from it . . . I hoped to afford a means acceptable to the African that would build up his sense of responsibility and in the long run make him proud of being a member of his own society."[21] In formulating these two aims, Cameron was aware of Britain's commitment in Article 3 of the Mandate "to promote to the utmost the material and moral well-being and the social progress" of Tanganyika's inhabitants. This is not to suggest that he felt constrained to refer to the terms of the Mandate at all times; he wrote later that he never had any difficulty in keeping to his commitments under the Mandate because they embodied "the ordinary and recognised principles of British Colonial Administration."[22]

An elaboration of Cameron's purpose as set out above can be seen in his address to the administrative officers of the territory in July 1925, which reads in part:

Everyone, whatever his opinion may be in regard to direct or indirect rule, will agree, I think, that it is our duty to do everything in our power to develop the native on lines which will not Westernize him and turn him into a bad imitation of a European. . . . We want to make him a good African and we shall not achieve this if we destroy all the institutions, all the traditions, all the habits of the people, superimposing upon them what we consider to be better administrative methods, better principles; destroying everything that made our administration really in touch with the customs and thoughts of the people. We must not, in fact, destroy the African atmosphere, the African mind, the whole foundations of his race, and we shall certainly do this if we sweep away all his tribal organisations, and in doing so tear up all the roots that bind him to the people from whom he has sprung.

Cameron went on to decry the idea that the chiefs should be used "as our mouthpieces through whom the orders of the Government are issued to the people" because this would undermine traditional authority. He warned that if nothing were done to build up native institutions, tribal organization would break down altogether, the process of disintegration having already begun under the Germans, when the country was ruled entirely through alien officials.

With the decay of the tribal organisation we shall get a numerous body of broken and disgruntled chiefs, disaffected, quite naturally, and hostile to the Administration. The natives will have ceased to be tribesmen and, no longer attached to their tribal institutions, will have become mere flotsam on the political sea of Tanganyika. . . .

On the other hand we could employ the other method of trying, while we endeavored to purge the native system of its abuses, to graft our higher civilisation upon the soundly rooted native stock, stock that had its foundations in the hearts and minds and thoughts of the people, and therefore on which we could build more easily, moulding it and establishing it into lines consonant with modern ideas and higher standards, and yet all the time enlisting the real force of the spirit of the people, instead of killing all that out and trying to begin afresh.[23]

On another occasion Cameron wrote that in attempting to organize native society in the territory he hoped "to find for it—and leave for it—a full place in the political structure when the time might arrive for such a consummation." An additional purpose of indirect administration, therefore, was to teach "the chiefs and people habits of responsibility in public affairs, probity in the handling of men and money and obedience to constituted authority."[24]

Cameron felt that this was an obligation the British government could not escape in light of the responsibilities assumed under the Covenant of the League of Nations. He noted that the reason for creating the mandate system was that the territories to be placed under it were, according to Article 22 of the Covenant, "inhabited by peoples not yet able to stand by themselves." Therefore, he pointed out, the Mandate assumed by Great Britain for Tanganyika

is not a permanent and absolute one and is to be exercised only until the people "can stand by themselves." That being so, it is clearly, I submit, the duty of the Mandatory Power to train the people so that they may stand by themselves, at least as part of the whole community of the Territory, however long that training may take, and to make its dispositions in such a manner that, when the time arrives, a full place in the political structure shall be found for the native population.[25]

The Europeans in the territory did not agree with Cameron on this subject, being of the opinion that it was best to let sleeping dogs lie. In substance they said, "Do not interfere with the political side so far as it affects the native, in any event do nothing that will give him the idea that a place in the community belongs to him." Cameron's reply to them was that the policy they advocated was a policy of negation; "a policy which clearly would allow our obligations under the Covenant to go by default; a policy which no British Government would care to declare to the world." He added:

You, in the meantime, press insistently for the development of the political side so far as it affects not the natives, but the Europeans. You want that side strengthened as soon as possible so that you may go from strength to strength and become so securely entrenched that there will be no place left for the native in the political structure *unless you please to give it to him.*[26]

The functions of the Native Authorities, which was the legal name given to the tribal authorities, were administrative, judicial, and financial. The system was governed by two principal enactments, the Native Authority Ordinance of 1926 and the Native Courts Ordinance of 1929. The first, which broadened the scope of the Native Authority Ordinance of 1923, listed the duties and obligations undertaken by the Native Authorities as part of the machinery of government. The most important of these, recited in Section 4, was the general duty of the chief "to perform the obligations by this Ordinance imposed and generally to maintain order and good government among the natives residing or being in the area over which his authority extends." Section 6 dealt with the obligation of crime prevention. In order to carry out these obligations the Native Authorities were given special powers over and above the powers that were vested in them by virtue of native law or custom. In addition, the inherent or traditional powers posessed by the Native Authorities over a wide range of other matters were recognized by the Ordinance.

Lord Hailey points out that it was in this respect that the form of indirect administration put into practice in Tanganyika differed most sharply from that in other areas. Not only native administration, but actual native authority, was allowed for. The Ordinance pointed out, however, that although the Native Authorities might exercise individual responsibilities, they did so under the supervision of administrative officers of the government. The Native Authorities were further empowered under Section 15 to make rules, which were enforceable in the native courts, for the "peace, good order, and welfare" of Africans within their jurisdiction.[27]

The first important duty of the Native Authorities was to carry out a number of administrative functions. These consisted of maintaining law and order, collecting the hut and poll tax, keeping a census of their people and of livestock, reporting outbreaks of human and animal diseases, and maintaining roads other than trunk roads.

In accordance with Cameron's plan, a portion of the hut and poll tax collected by the Native Authorities was returned to them by the government and made up the bulk of their revenue. In some cases it was augmented by native court fees and local dues, such as ferry and market fees. To administer these funds each Native Authority had its own treasury. Originally fixed at 10 per cent, the rebate on the hut and poll tax gradually increased until it ranged from 20 to 33 per cent. From the total hut and poll tax of £632,330 collected in 1935, the native treasuries received £145,324 as a rebate, and after other local receipts were added in, their total revenue for 1935 amounted to £186,723. Most of this money, some 68 per cent in 1935, then went to pay the costs of tribal administration, which included the salaries of the chiefs, their deputies, the subchiefs, and the village headmen.[28] The remainder in each Native Authority constituted a Common Purpose Fund, which was used for the benefit of the entire community. It went for hospitals and dispensaries, schools, agricultural and veterinary instruction centers, wells, cattle dips, roads, afforestation, antitsetse bush-clearing, and other similar projects. W. M. Macmillan, a British historian who traveled through Tanganyika in 1930, credited much of the activity he found there to the fact that Cameron kept his administrative officers "on their toes," since, of course, the progress being made in each district depended to a large extent on the character of the officer in charge.[29]

By 1929, 166 native treasuries existed in the territory. Each tribal unit, no matter how small, was given its own treasury. Since the average annual income was only £180 per treasury, some of the smaller tribal units found it impossible to make any substantial improvements.[30] For this reason there was a gradual tendency toward centralization. One of the first groups to pool their resources were the nine independent tribes of the Sukuma people living in the Shinyanga subdistrict south of Lake Victoria. In all they numbered about 120,500. The Sukuma saw that with a united Common Purpose Fund much more could be done to improve conditions in the area. Consequently, the nine chiefs, after discussing the matter with the British authorities, established a confederation of the nine tribes and a common treasury. A similar union of the Sumbwa people took place in the Tabora district. Although such amalgamations were considered desirable, the administration did not urge such unions against the wishes of the people.[31]

The second important duty of the Native Authorities was to administer justice, a function that they performed through the native courts. The general powers of these courts were set out in the Native Courts Ordinance of 1929, and the precise jurisdiction of each court was defined in a warrant specially issued to it. The general jurisdiction of the courts was in the following areas:

(1) Native law and custom, as long as it was not repugnant to justice or morality or inconsistent with the provisions of any law in force in the territory.

(2) The provisions of any rules and orders made under the Native Authority Ordinance.

(3) The provisions of any law that the court was empowered to administer by the law itself or by special order of the Governor.

The right of appeal existed first from the lower native courts to the higher courts of the particular Native Authority, and then on up the chain-of-command in the civil service. District officers exercised close control over the native courts and rendered periodic reports to their provincial commissioners, who supervised the whole system. Any crime that a district officer judged too serious to be tried in a native court could be reserved for the ordinary courts.[32]

During the first year that the Native Authority Ordinance was in effect (1926), only five such authorities were gazetted.[33] The administration, however, persevered in its efforts to determine the traditional sources of authority and to establish the boundaries of each authority's jurisdiction. Since the law defined Native Authorities as "chiefs or other natives or any native Council or groups of natives declared as such by Government," various forms of authorities were established.[34] In some cases the Native Authority was a paramount chief (usually with lesser chiefs under him), who had direct control over the native treasury; in other cases it was the tribal council, consisting of petty chiefs, or headmen belonging to the same tribe, and having a common treasury.

Cameron emphasized that the Native Authority should be the person who was the *de jure* ruler, whoever he might be; for in his opinion the essence of true indirect administration was "the allegiance of a people to a tribal head freely and spontaneously accorded without external cause."[35] Particular care was taken to find "the authority which according to tribal tradition and usage has in the past regulated the affairs of each unit of native society, which the people of the present generation are willing to recognise and obey."[36] Cameron insisted that his administrative officers establish as Native Authorities only those persons recognized by the people as their rulers, no matter what opinion the officers had of them. He summed up his feelings as follows:

At this stage, it is far more important that we should as far as possible build up the authority of the Chiefs in order that the people of this country should take a proper place in the political future of Tanganyika than that we should seek a standard of excellence in the native which in the circumstances, it is quite unreasonable to expect that we should find.[37]

Unless native standards fell below a certain abnormal minimum in regard to the protection of life and freedom from oppression, European standards of efficiency were not to be forced upon people content with their own standards. The important thing was that Africans should share in the administration.

In a dispatch to the Secretary of State for the Colonies in June 1930, Cameron reported that "the policy of indirect administration has been warmly approved by the unofficial members of my Legislative Council as the best policy for the country." The opponents of the policy had abandoned their direct attack and were now asserting that the policy was being applied too rapidly. Cameron pointed out to the Colonial Secretary that "if the system were applied in a more attenuated form it could not be said to exist at all." For the most part what had been done during the five years he had been Governor was "little more than to regularize a native social system that was already in existence and in many places still in operation."[38]

At first Cameron feared that the areas under indirect administration might be less progressive than those under more direct rule; but it soon became clear that the opposite was the case.[39] There were, of course, some failures, but they were few. An attempt to establish the system in the coastal region failed, partly because people of different tribes and customs were living together in one locality, and partly because there had been a general breakdown of indigenous institutions. An attempt to use the village community as the administrative unit in the Dar es Salaam district was also unsuccessful. In other coastal areas, Native Authorities were ineffective without the continuous support of the district administration.

In general, however, the introduction of indirect administration in Tanganyika went very well. Lord Hailey wrote in 1938: "There has been a progressive integration of the traditional native institutions into the general administrative system, as is shown by the growing use of rules and orders issued by the native authorities to secure the purposes of government."[40] That the Africans themselves liked the new system is shown by their willingness to institute improvements with funds from the native treasuries.

An interesting insight into African opinion is given us by Chief Towegale of the Wabena people. Chief Towegale visited Dar es Salaam in 1934 and was there entertained by an African who had risen to be an assistant secretary in the Secretariat. Impressed, Towegale went back to his people convinced that the government's policy was not aimed at preventing Africans from advancing themselves, and that if the African now held an inferior position in the body politic, it was the result not of his color, but of his own limitations. He subsequently spread this conviction among the tribal elders, and as a result the Wabena were determined to show what they could do. They built new roads, markets, and brick buildings, and—most important of all—they developed "the will to learn to shoulder more and more responsibility." Moreover, Chief Towegale felt that even though he had to give up certain rights and to submit to certain limitations under the new system of government, these rights were unsuited to the type of ruler he wanted to be. He regarded the new government as enabling him to keep abreast of the times, anticipate the requirements of his tribe, and adapt his leadership to the changing needs of modern life.[41]

Cameron's system of indirect administration also met with the favor of the members of the Permanent Mandates Commission. At its eleventh session in 1927 the Commission said it was greatly impressed with the way in which the traditional tribal organization had been used to establish a system of native administration, and that it would continue to follow closely the system's further development. At its thirteenth session in 1928 the Commission noted its interest in the results of indirect administration in Tanganyika and the consolidation of tribal units into homogeneous organizations.[42]

Cameron preferred the term "indirect administration" to "indirect rule" and insisted that the latter, when applied to Tanganyika, was a misnomer. The Native Authority, in his opinion, was an organ of local government like any other, except that, being African, it was set up on a tribal basis.[43] The system of indirect administration, however, possesses an inherent danger, as Lord Hailey has pointed out—namely, "that its use may, by enlarging the position traditionally enjoyed by tribal or other authority, prevent our increasing the opportunities of self-government for the great majority of the population."[44] Cameron recognized the gravity of this danger, and it was his hope "that local government on a tribal basis will eventually develop into a form of local government of more normal character, probably on a representative basis."[45]

Although Cameron could not predict with any certainty what course political development would take in Tanganyika, he thought that regional councils for the discussion of common subjects among the chiefs of a particular area might be a useful next step. This in turn might lead to the institution of a Central Native Council for the discussion of matters affecting the African inhabitants of the territory as a whole. He further anticipated that "this Council might eventually become a General Native Council sending delegates to sit with delegates from a similar non-native Council for the transaction of the business which would ordinarily fall to a Legislative Council." The Legislative Council would then be composed of two General Councils with a joint Council above. Until such political development occurred, however, he felt that Africans should be appointed to the Legislative Council as soon as suitable representatives became available.

Summing up, Cameron wrote that the Native Authorities established by him "should be regarded as steppingstones; their success, or otherwise, to be gauged by the measure in which they may succeed in strengthening the fibre of the people they are designed to serve."[46]

Cameron's idea that indirect administration could be a preparation for representative government on the national level with equal participation by both Africans and non-Africans has been recently criticized by Sir Charles Dundas, who served as Tanganyika's first Secretary for Native Affairs. The substance of his criticism is as follows:

Twenty years passed and then the New Age burst upon Africa as on the rest of the world. But in those twenty years an ancient order had been sedulously resuscitated and it matched ill with the principles of the new order. For the essence of Indirect Rule was tribalism, and as such it was everything else but a preparation for democracy, the very basis of which is national unity. It must not be thought that tribal rule was equivalent to local government and in that way, a half-way stage to parliamentary rule. To the African his tribe is his nation, he has as yet no conception of larger grouping. The tribe has its own distinctive traditions, organisation, laws, language, even its own gods. In short, the tribe has all the attributes of nationhood and these were confirmed, even strengthened, in the practice of Indirect Rule. By its nature tribal rule also puts peculiar obstacles in the way of representative government, the same as those which make the institution of a Commonwealth parliament impracticable.[47]

In order to carry out a system of indirect administration Cameron found it necessary to revamp the administrative structure of the territory. On his arrival, Tanganyika was still divided into twenty-two administrative districts as originally established by the Germans. He found that there was little continuity of policy, and received permission from the Colonial Secretary to reconstruct the territory into eleven provinces. (A later Governor reduced the number to eight.) Each was headed by a provincial commissioner, who was responsible to the Governor for the general administration of his province. The provinces were divided into districts, each headed by a district commissioner responsible to a provincial commissioner. "In this way," Cameron said, "we built up a responsible Administrative Service which has done first-class work and become a great credit to the Territory."[48]

LAND POLICY AND NON-AFRICAN SETTLEMENT

Another important aspect of Cameron's policy was the alienation of land to non-Africans. Although primarily an economic matter, land policy in Africa has had tremendous political significance, a significance that Lord Hailey attributes to "the influence which it has exercised in determining the relations of the African people towards the Colonial Governments."[49] Looking back at the different land policies followed by the European powers in their African colonies and territories, he writes:

There is certainly no one feature of Colonial policy which has had an equal influence in determining the character of the relations between the indigenous people and a Colonial Administration. Whatever other reason may exist for the estimate made by Africans of the character of a Government, the fact that a considerable area of Native lands has passed permanently into the hands of non-Natives will always tend to colour any judgement that is formed of it. Nor will the emotion which this fact arouses permit of an objective assessment of the value which the use of the land by non-Natives has brought to the African community, however obvious this may be to the outside world.[50]

During the period of German administration, white settlement in the East African colony had been encouraged. By 1913 more than half a million hectares had been alienated; the total number of settlers was 882, the great majority being Germans.[51] Despite precautions for the protection of native rights, they were often neglected in practice. In the area around Mount Meru and Mount Kilimanjaro, dispossession was so extensive that the land left to the local tribes later became totally inadequate for their needs.

This area, which now forms the Moshi and Arusha districts, was not effectively occupied by the Germans until the 1890's. Finding that the tribes who lived there, the Chagga, the Meru, and the Arusha, had largely confined themselves to the upper lands carved out of the forest, the German settlers took up the areas below the tribal lands. In those days the native population was small owing to disease and tribal and clan warfare, and the people did not need the lower slopes traded away by the chiefs. Since the concept of absolute ownership of land was then unknown to the African, the German settlers obtained a title entirely different from what the chiefs thought they were giving them. At first there was no feeling of uneasiness among the African population, the danger of overcrowding not yet being apparent. Alienation continued until the ring of tribal land below the forest belt on the southern slopes of both mountains was virtually enclosed by an outer ring of nonnative land, for the most part held on freehold terms.

By the time the British took over, it was clear that these tribes, enclosed by an "iron ring" of nonnative property, were becoming congested. Eight former German farms on Mount Meru were returned to the Arusha and Meru tribes by the British, instead of being sold to new settlers. This gave some relief for the time being. On Kilimanjaro as well, some of the German farms were not re-alienated, but were turned over to the Chagga to provide temporary relief for their increasing population. In all, some 107 properties were acquired by the government for return to African use.[52] Nothing was done, however, to provide an outlet through the ring of alienated properties to lower, less congested lands for the mounting native population. No proper appreciation of the future land needs of these tribes existed; the majority of the German farms were re-alienated as demarcated before the British took over.[53]

The British, however, did restrict further alienation of the land until such time as land legislation could be enacted. In drawing up this legislation the Tanganyika government was guided by Article 6 of the Mandate Agreement. This article stated:

In the framing of laws relating to the holding or transfer of land, the Mandatory shall take into consideration native laws and customs, and shall respect the rights and safeguard the interests of the native population.

No native land may be transferred, except between natives, without the previous consent of the public authorities, and no real rights over native land in favour of non-natives may be created except with the same consent.

The Mandatory will promulgate strict regulations against usury.

The resulting legislation was the Land Ordinance of 1923, the text of which was as follows:

The whole of the lands of the Territory, whether occupied or unoccupied . . . are hereby declared to be public land . . . under the control and subject to the disposition of the Governor, and shall be held and administered for the use and common benefit, direct or indirect, of the natives of the Territory, and no title to the occupation of and use of any such lands shall be valid without the consent of the Governor.

In the exercise of these powers the Governor was required to "have regard to the native laws and customs existing in the district" concerned. Limited only by this provision, he could grant titles, in the form of certificates, giving a right of occupancy for not more than 99 years. Such titles could be granted to Africans as well as non-Africans, the former not being required to take out certificates of occupancy or to pay rent, and could be revoked under certain conditions defined in the ordinance. No area exceeding 5,000 acres could be alienated except with the approval of the Secretary of State for the Colonies.[54]

At its ninth session in 1926 the Permanent Mandates Commission expressed concern that the Land Ordinance made the validity of a title depend on its grant or recognition by the government, since this would appear to prejudice rights depending on customary occupation.[55] To meet this criticism a subsequent provision in the law recognized native customary rights as equally valid with those held under certificates of occupancy.

The practical significance of the Land Ordinance is that Africans were not confined to particular areas or native reserves, however generously defined, and that their existing customary rights to the land were recognized by the government. In addition, the Ordinance left intact freehold titles to land acquired before its enactment and did not preclude further alienation to non-Africans, although such alienation would not be on a freehold basis.

In undertaking the Mandate for Tanganyika, Great Britain pledged that she would "undertake to promote to the utmost the material and moral well-being" of the inhabitants. For the first five years of the Mandate, this was apparently interpreted to mean that Tanganyika should be an African state. Noting the tribes' suspicion on all questions connected with land (a reaction that was hardly surprising in view of the extent of previous alienations), the government was evidently in doubt whether circumstances justified an extension of European settlement. While home on leave in 1922, the Governor, Sir Horace Byatt, reportedly declared that the "future of the country lay in developing native cultivation only."[56] (Small additional amounts of land were alienated in 1923 and 1924, however.)

When Sir Donald Cameron became Governor in 1925, considerable pressure was being placed on the government by people wishing to settle in Tanganyika. The settlers who had purchased the former German properties were urging the government to develop the territory by adopting a policy of white settlement. They maintained that European settlement in East Africa should be encouraged as a counterbalance to the West African policy of developing predominantly African states.

Opinion on this matter was divided. Dr. D. Julius Richter of Berlin University writes that it was "a complicated question as to whether a larger percentage of Whites would be an asset or a liability in a land which is and will remain a 'black man's country.' "[57] Similarly, a conference of local administrative officers in 1924 expressed "doubts as to the advisability of alienating more land for non-native development," pointing out that it was already difficult to get African labor for non-African estates.[58] On the other side, the case for non-African settlement is presented by Charlotte Leubuscher: "A certain amount of white settlement is almost universally considered advantageous, because it helps to develop a country's resources, attracts capital, acts as an educational factor in relation to native methods of cultivation, and increases the wealth and tax-paying capacity of the population, native and non-native."[59]

Cameron's own opinion on the matter of non-African settlement was similar to that expressed in this last statement. He thought that if land were available and if European enterprise and capital wished to develop it, then it was "directly contrary to the interests of the country as a whole for the Government to refuse to admit that enterprise and capital." At the same time he pointed out that Tanganyika did not have the large tracts of land suitable for settlement that Kenya had; moreover, most of the areas that would appeal to settlers were "densely populated by the native inhabitants who, even already, have not in these areas adequate means of expansion as the population increases." When a message arrived from the Colonial Office that applications for land should be discouraged, Cameron replied that he believed "the forces to be too strong, that it is impossible to oppose non-native settlement in Tanganyika."[60]

The first of a series of East African governors' conferences was held at Nairobi in January 1926. Cameron went to Nairobi with some misgivings; he thought that the conference was premature, since none of the governors had yet been a full year at his post. Later he wrote: "There was to me something unreal in the whole proceedings, and when, at an early stage, one of the members moved that a labour law of a certain character should be introduced in each of the territories I thought that I was back in the Middle Ages."[61] The land question also came under discussion. The view of the conference was that wherever land was not in use, a sufficient area should be reserved for the needs of the tribes and European colonization encouraged on the rest. Since land policy had already stabilized elsewhere, the particular interest of these recommendations lay in their bearing on Tanganyika. Cameron agreed to them in general, but explicitly repudiated the policy of setting aside reserves, or special areas, for the African inhabitants, a policy he considered inadmissible under the Mandate.[62]

The principles to be followed in Tanganyika in regard to alienation of land were set out by Cameron in his speech to the first session of the Legislative Council in December 1926: "Non-native settlement should be encouraged wherever the climate is suitable and adequate areas are available without depriving the native population of sufficient land for its own use, provided always that transport facilities are available to evacuate the produce."[63] Cameron announced that he would consider applications for land in the Iringa district, where 40,000 acres had been made available for lease. Speaking before the Permanent Mandates Commission in 1927, he stated with reference to the land that had been alienated: "This land has been alienated, at all events from my point of view, in spite of the fact that Tanganyika is a country in which the interests of the natives are dominant and should remain dominant. We are proceeding on the basis that the European is the experimental factor and not the native."[64]

In 1930 the following provinces were closed entirely to further alienation: Lindi, Tabora, Mwanza, Bukoba, and Central. The government did this not on economic grounds, but with "a view to preserving racial homogeneity"; in these areas, applications would be accepted only from people who had sufficient capital to allow them to undertake such improvements as irrigation.[65]

In June 1930, the Secretary of State for the Colonies issued a declaration on native policy in East Africa, which stated in regard to land policy: "The first essential is to remove finally from the native mind any feeling of insecurity in regard to his tribal lands; and to keep available for all the tribes land of such extent and character as will fully suffice for their actual and future needs." It further declared that compulsory expropriation, however small in extent, should never be permitted "for the mere private or personal profit or other advantage of any individual whether of European, Indian, African or any other race."[66]

During Cameron's term as Governor, the total amount of alienated land steadily increased until a peak figure of 2,013,097 acres of agricultural holdings was reached in 1930. The amount in nonnative hands thus came to 3,125 square miles of the territory's total land area of 340,500 square miles and included some of the best land. This figure compared to 10,375 square miles alienated in Kenya from a total land area of 225,000 square miles.[67] After 1930, the world-wide economic depression caused a decrease in the demand for land, and for five years the surrender of holdings outpaced the alienations. The opportunity was taken at this time to return some of the surrendered farms in the Moshi and Arusha districts to the local tribes in an effort to relieve the land congestion that had developed. Some farms were purchased by the government for this purpose, and others were purchased by the Chagga, Arusha, and Meru peoples themselves. A large government scheme to relieve the growing congestion among the Chagga was never implemented owing to the outbreak of war in 1939. After 1935, the demand for land again increased. In 1937 a total of 155,793 acres were alienated,[68] followed by a further 62,778 acres in 1938.[69]

The total area alienated to non-Africans for agricultural and pastoral purposes amounted to 2,118,942 acres at the end of 1938. This was the highest figure so far attained and amounted to an increase of about 58 per cent over the figure of 1,339,643 acres alienated by the Germans by the end of 1913. However, this was still less than one per cent of the total land area of Tanganyika. At the end of 1938, nonnative agricultural enterprise was concentrated in four of the eight provinces: Eastern, Northern, Southern Highlands, and Tanga

Provinces, with a small area in Southern Province. Tanga Province, where much of the alienated land was taken up in sisal plantations, not only had the largest alienated area, but also the largest area held in freehold, because most of the plantations were held under titles first issued by the German government. Almost 90 per cent of the holdings in private occupation were in the hands of British, German, Indian, and Greek landowners.[70]

European immigration into Tanganyika decreased markedly because of the depression. Between 1921 and 1931, the European population had grown from 2,447 to 8,228; but from 1931 to 1938 it increased only another 1,117, or to a total of 9,345.[71] If the number of Europeans in Tanganyika had continued to grow at the rate of 1921–31 increase, and if further land alienation had proceeded apace, it is conceivable that the harmonious racial atmosphere existing in the territory might have been destroyed.

THE MOVEMENT FOR CLOSER UNION

Connected with the question of land alienation and white settlement in Tanganyika was the question of closer union in East Africa. Fearing that the Permanent Mandates Commission might interfere with the European colonization of the territory, the European settlers of East Africa promoted various schemes during the 1920's to deliver Tanganyika from the Commission's control. One of these was to alter the country's status from that of mandated territory to that of crown colony. Another, which had attractive administrative possibilities, was to establish a self-governing white dominion of East Africa.

This scheme originated with the plan formulated by Sir Harry Johnston and others following World War I for a federation or administrative union of Great Britain's East African territories. The Colonial Office was not long in expressing official interest in and support for the project. Winston Churchill, then Secretary of State for the Colonies, told representatives of Kenya and Uganda on January 27, 1922:

There is one other question I will touch upon. That is the scheme which has been in so many minds, to amalgamate the four countries of Kenya,

Uganda, Tanganyika, and Zanzibar. This would make a magnificent whole, and there is no doubt that many of the problems . . . which present themselves to-day in each of these four countries, can be solved on a higher plane and with greater advantage if there were a united superior organisation for the whole of those regions.[72]

The alleged advantages of such a federation were the elimination of administrative duplication and of competition in such matters as railway policy.

The driving force behind the federation scheme was the European community in Kenya. Following the appointment of Sir Edward Grigg as Governor of Kenya, the Kenya settlers began to promote the doctrine of white settlement throughout East Africa. Kenya's "missionary spirit" had its basis in the fear that if the Africans of Tanganyika and Uganda were not subjected to Kenya's native policy, white settlement in Kenya could not survive.[73] Lord Delamere, the leading settler in Kenya, sponsored three unofficial conferences of European settlers to drum up support for the establishment of a white dominion of East Africa. He declared that their purpose was to promote "the solidification of the white ideal,"[74] and to unite the settlers against the policies of the "West African school," which was already "predominant in Uganda" and "beginning to infect Tanganyika Territory and Nyasaland."[75] Lord Delamere was afraid that if the settlers of each territory presented their views separately to the Colonial Office, they would not be listened to. Only by concerted action could they gain a hearing. Accordingly, a series of unofficial conferences was planned so that the widely separated elements of the settler community could come to some understanding among themselves.[76]

The first conference took place in 1925 at Tukuyu in the Southern Highlands of Tanganyika. The main reason for its being called was that the idea of an East African federation was being pushed from London at the time, and Lord Delamere was afraid that this would lead to the spread of the West Coast policy. "The first thing we started to do," he said, "was to try and help to kill the spread of the West Coast policy in the East." This first unofficial conference was a great success.[77]

A second unofficial conference was held at Livingstone, Northern

Rhodesia, in September 1926, and a third at Nairobi in August 1927. Not until the third conference did Delamere openly support closer union. His opening address is unequivocal: "I believe that if we can get federation on our lines, then we can sit down in safety to pursue our economic research and our work for ourselves and our native people without bothering our heads about politics." He called on the delegates "to face the issue and decide on the necessary safeguards and fix the lines along which the countries of Eastern Africa are to advance in the future."[78]

Lord Delamere, however, had already decided what "the necessary safeguards" should be and had carried the Kenya electorate with him on this point at the recent general election. The one condition that he and his followers made for their support of the federation scheme was an elected majority on the Kenya Legislative Council. Without this, they feared that their interests would be swamped by a multitude of African concerns, Uganda and Tanganyika being regarded as too "native." Lord Delamere stated that it was "a vital necessity to any scheme of coordination based, for the present at least, on the radiation of civilization from Kenya that we should have a free Council here."[79] For most of the Kenya settlers, self-government was the main objective and federation a supplementary one. As Rothchild points out in his authoritative study of the movement for East African federation, the Kenya settler's interest in "closer union cannot be understood apart from the concurrent demand for a free hand in the local affairs of Kenya."[80]

The federation idea had a mixed reception in Tanganyika. Some Europeans welcomed it because they regarded federation as a means of encouraging outside capital investment. After Germany's entry into the League of Nations, the question was raised whether Britain ought not to relinquish the Mandate for Tanganyika in favor of Germany; as a result, potential overseas investors had been holding back in case the British Mandate should prove to be only temporary. If, however, Britain joined an East African federation, doubts about her permanency in the area would be dispelled. Other Europeans supported the idea because they were suspicious of Colonial Office control, and federation was viewed as a means of rectifying this situation. Their desire to be free of control increased whenever it seemed likely that the Labor Party might be coming to power in Britain. Public meetings supporting federation were held at Arusha and Iringa. And, finally, there were some Europeans who doubted whether the time was yet ripe for closer cooperation between the East African territories.[81]

The Indians in Tanganyika on the whole opposed federation. In a debate in the Legislative Council, the two Indian members gave the following reasons for their opposition: (1) A closer union should not be imposed solely because it was desired by the English settlers; the Africans as the great majority of the population should be consulted. (2) If federation came about, there was a danger that Kenya's racial policy would be applied in Tanganyika. (3) Only the settlers in Kenya would gain anything from federation.[82]

The first attempt by the British government to determine whether an East African federation should be established was the East Africa Commission of 1924 headed by William Ormsby-Gore. After spending three months traveling through Nyasaland, Kenya, Uganda, and Tanganyika, the Commission reported that though the need for greater understanding and cooperation was manifest, the time was "still far off when such cooperation could be brought about by the imposition of federal government over the whole territory."[83] The federation proposal continued to be discussed, however, owing to the fact that L. S. Amery, a leading advocate of closer union, became Colonial Secretary in 1925.

The question next arose in London in May 1927, when Amery discussed the matter with several of the East African governors. Sir Donald Cameron's memoirs describe the conference as a one-sided affair in which he was forced to play "a lone hand" in opposition to the proposals that were presented. He later recorded that if the views presented had been accepted, "it seemed clear to me that the work that I was doing in Tanganyika in the field of local native government . . . would certainly have been terminated at no distant date." Elaborating on the position he had taken, Cameron wrote:

If the natives of Tanganyika must be left a place, and a large place, in the political structure of their own country, . . . I am entirely unable to see how the Territory can be brought within the same political system as Kenya, where . . . the leaders of the European unofficial community declare that the Africans of Kenya must never at any time have any political rights in the parliaments of that country, such as they might be.[84]

In the end, nothing emerged from the Colonial Office conference except a decision by the British government to send out another commission to look into the possibilities of East African federation. This commission, headed by Sir Edward Hilton Young, reported its findings the following year to Parliament. Although it considered the time was "not yet ripe" for establishing a federation involving drastic changes, it recommended certain first steps toward an eventual union between Kenya, Uganda, and Tanganyika, a union that would be brought about by "the growth of confidence based on practical experience." It suggested that native policy be put under the control of a central authority and be made consistent throughout East Africa.[85]

The Hilton-Young Commission was followed by the dispatch of a one-man commission appointed to investigate on what lines a scheme for closer union might be administratively workable. Amery gave the job to his right-hand man, Sir Samuel Wilson. As a concession to settler objections to the Hilton-Young recommendation of a consistent native policy controlled by a central authority, Sir Samuel recommended the appointment of a High Commissioner exercising legislative and administrative control over certain major services, but leaving all other matters, including native policy, to the local legislatures.[86]

In the meantime a national election had been held at which the Conservatives were defeated, and a Labor government was now in office. With respect to the question of closer union, Lord Passfield, the new Secretary of State for the Colonies, chose a course that steered between the recommendations of the Hilton-Young Commission and the Wilson Report. In June 1930, he issued a White Paper on closer union, which recommended the application of a consistent native policy throughout East Africa, but suggested that this common policy be implemented by territorial authorities rather than by a central authority.[87]

In a companion White Paper, *Memorandum on Native Policy in East Africa,* Lord Passfield accepted the recommendation of the Hilton-Young Commission that "the paramountcy of native interests" should be established as the official policy of the British government in East Africa. The relation of the government to the native population was declared to be "one of trusteeship." The obligation of promoting native interests, however, was to "be regarded as in no way incompatible with the common duty of any Government to promote the development of the resources of its territtory and the prosperity of its inhabitants, including the immigrant communities within it."[88] This was not enough for the Kenya settlers. They were aghast that a White Paper suggesting union be attached to a second one advocating the paramountcy of native interests. Moreover, they were particularly irritated by the recommendation that the official majority on the Legislative Council be continued and by the support given, in the paper on closer union, to the ideal of a single electoral roll.[89]

Despite the inconclusiveness of these discussions, the matter was not yet dead. The Labor government now took the step of submitting the whole issue of closer union to a Joint Select Committee of Lords and Commons. That the controversy was at last brought into the open was largely due to Sir Donald Cameron, who had made his opposition to closer union clearly known. As an attachment to the Wilson Report, he had called for the establishment of "a highly authoritative Committee or Commission" in England, so that "those persons who are in opposition to the principles recommended by the Commission . . . should have an opportunity of stating their views publicly before such an authoritative body." He wrote later that his intention was "to do everything in my power to drag this business out of the atmosphere of secret counsels and finesse which had surrounded it for so many months."[90]

The Joint Select Committee sat and took evidence through most of 1931. It considered the proposals for closer union laid out by Lord Passfield and the opinions of the Governors of Kenya, Uganda, and Tanganyika in regard to these proposals. Cameron had already presented his views in a dispatch to the Secretary of State, which read in part:

It is the duty of this Government to record the considered opinion that regarded from the point of view of the interests of Tanganyika alone no constitutional change involving Closer Union with Kenya and Uganda is necessary. . . .

It will take a number of years for the advancement of the natives to reach a point at which they can, through their leaders and under official guidance, speak for themselves as a part of the community, and it seems to my Government to be indisputable that during the whole period of training under the British government the latter must make no disposition in the political field which would impair its power to give effect to any decision it might have to take in order to comply with the spirit and the letter of the Mandate; a proposition which no one would think of questioning if there were no non-natives in the Mandated Territory. . . .

If the British European inhabitants of Tanganyika aspire to higher political power in order to attain dominance before the natives are able to stand by themselves—as they do aspire—then, I say, that is not a legitimate aspiration and cannot be realised so long as the Mandate exists. . . .

It will be said that in considering the political future Tanganyika cannot be regarded as a separate unit apart from Kenya. I do not admit this so long as Tanganyika remains under Mandate; and it is possible that if she were left alone under the Mandate, instead of being drawn into the affairs of others for extraneous reasons, Tanganyika might grow into a model "mixed State" which would have a great influence on the shaping of affairs in East Africa.[91]

The Joint Committee heard evidence from delegations representing every shade of official and nonofficial opinion, and every racial community on the East African scene. The views of the Africans of Tanganyika were presented by three African witnesses. All three expressed the fear that union with Kenya and Uganda would facilitate domination of the Africans by the Europeans of Kenya. Furthermore, Tanganyika settlers, testifying before the Joint Committee, saw little advantage to themselves in a European unofficial majority on the Kenya Legislative Council. It became evident as the hearings progressed that there were wide differences of opinion between the various territories and also between the communities within each territory. The Joint Committee concluded that each group was mainly interested in the affairs of its own particular territory and that any major move toward closer union would be inopportune. But it did encourage continued economic cooperation between the territories through the regular conferences of the Governors of Kenya, Uganda, and Tanganyika, and through a joint secretariat, which it urged should be created. Thus the door was closed firmly on closer union for more than a decade to come.[92]

Looking back on the movement for closer union, Rothchild finds that although federation was encouraged for economic reasons, its real impetus lay in its potential as a security device.

This is made quite clear by the change of heart on the part of the settler community when federation was proposed without any provision for a European elected majority on the Kenya Legislative Council. When the settlers recognized that responsible government was out of the question for a long time to come, they came to look upon federation as a symbol of insecurity, thereby negating the reason for their initial support.[93]

The Permanent Mandates Commission of the League of Nations followed with interest the discussions on closer union in East Africa. Not until 1933, however, after Great Britain had submitted the decisions of the Joint Select Committee, did it deliver an opinion on the matter:

With reference to the expression "the time is not yet ripe," the Commission considers that a political or constitutional union of the mandated territory with the neighbouring territories cannot be carried out as long as the present mandate is in force.

It also considers, due regard being had to the provisions of Article 10 of the mandate, that any measures tending during that period towards the *de facto* establishment of such a "closer union" should be avoided.[94]

Such measures of administrative unification as were taken up after 1933 were subjected to close scrutiny by the Mandates Commission, but these were not numerous. The customs union between Kenya and Uganda, created in 1917, was extended to Tanganyika in 1933, and in the same year the postal service of the three areas was combined.

POLITICAL DEVELOPMENT DURING THE 1930'S

After the debate over the future of Britain's three African territories had come to an end in 1931, political development in Tanganyika took on a slower pace. The next few years, until the outbreak of war in 1939, were devoted to following through the policies begun during the six years of Sir Donald Cameron's governorship.

Cameron's departure from Tanganyika was much regretted. When he left the country in February 1931 to become Governor of Nigeria, a number of chiefs traveled to Dar es Salaam to say their farewells, some of them coming from as far away as Bukoba Province—a mark of respect that was quite unprecedented. One of Cameron's administrative officials later wrote him:

I must confess that even I am amazed at the spontaneous expressions of regret and sorrow at your departure which have been made to me. In earlier days in this Territory a few of the more enlightened natives in my District were dimly aware that a Bwana Governor existed somewhere, but they had never seen him and he was as remote from them as the Deity Mungu. Now your words to Chiefs and others at barazas are quoted in every village and all the natives mourn your departure.[95]

Although many significant things have happened in Tanganyika since 1931, Cameron's achievements have not been forgotten. According to Lord Twining, a recent Governor of the territory, it was Cameron who laid the foundations of multiracial policy in Tanganyika.[96] Julius Nyerere, the leading political figure in Tanganyika today, has repeatedly singled out Cameron as the only British Governor who did not administer the country as if it were a colony and who did not exploit the fear instilled into the people by the Germans.

The years preceding World War II in Tanganyika were dominated by the argument over the future status of the territory. Following Germany's entry into the League of Nations, the question of the permanency of Britain's Mandate over Tanganyika continually led to a feeling of insecurity among the British settlers. Although Amery, the Colonial Secretary, had stated earlier that the Mandate was in no sense a temporary tenure or lease from the League of Nations,[97] the fears of the British settlers only increased as the number of German settlers in the country continued to rise. Articles appeared in the British press vigorously opposing the suggestion that Tanganyika should be returned to Germany in an attempt to pacify Hitler. One article claimed that if Britain were to return Tanganyika to Germany, the Africans in Tanganyika would consider it nothing short of betrayal; it commented on the strong preference among Africans for

Britain's policy of indirect administration as against the former German policy of Direct Rule.[98] In the Governor's address to the Legislative Council in 1938, Sir Mark Young referred to the "anxiety and apprehension" that had developed in the territory as a result of people's fear that British rule was in jeopardy, a fear not shared by him. He went on to say that the "prevailing uncertainty" was having "a noticeably retarding effect" upon the economy.[99] The outbreak of war in 1939 finally put an end to the matter.

It may fairly be asked whether the fact that Tanganyika was a mandated territory under League of Nations supervision made any difference in the policies undertaken in Tanganyika by the British government. Many observers think that it did make a difference. Buell points out that whereas ordinarily the British Colonial Office is responsible only to Parliament—a situation in which "it is much easier for it to give in to an interested minority on the spot than to disinterested sentiment in England"—in Tanganyika it was supervised by the Permanent Mandates Commission, whose one job was to enforce the provisions of the Mandates; consequently, the possibility of criticism from a world-wide forum caused the British government to make certain that policy in Tanganyika conformed to the provisions of the Mandate.[100] In September 1936, the Labor Party in Britain paid an indirect compliment to the Mandates Commission by calling for an extension of the mandate principle over other British colonial territories.[101]

According to Sir Philip Mitchell, a former Governor of Kenya, an important aspect of the supervision of Tanganyika by the Mandates Commission was that it contributed to good race relations in the territory:

Perhaps it has been well that material development has not been too rapid or too great, for it has afforded time for the territory to develop human relations between all the races that live there—African, Arab, European and Indian—which are already a model for its neighbours of what such relations can be and seem likely to provide the foundation of a prosperous and happy future for the country. For this not a little of the credit belongs to the terms of the Mandate, under which all forms of discrimination have been illegal from the first, except such protective discrimination as backward people must have until they are able to stand on their own feet.[102]

Under these terms a color bar was illegal, although it did in fact exist socially, educationally, and to a certain extent economically. Nevertheless, interracial tension in Tanganyika remained at a low level between the two World Wars. Margaret Bates believes that the Mandates Commission helped to make this possible by acting as "a scapegoat on whom the responsibility might be put when protests from British settlers, businessmen and politicians became intense. Officials simply could, and did, say that a given policy was made necessary by the terms of the mandate, and local agitation, while still vocal, was dissipated." She remarks that it is in this respect that comparisons with policy in Kenya in the interwar period become most striking.[103]

There was one further benefit that Tanganyika derived from the terms of the Mandate: Article 7 provided that in economic matters the mandatory should accord equality of treatment with its own nationals to nationals of other states that were members of the League of Nations. This provision permitted the growth of a heterogeneous population, which proved to be an important factor in the later political development of the territory.

With the outbreak of war in 1939 the formative period in Tanganyika's history was brought to an end. This statement is corroborated by the findings of the East Africa Royal Commission of 1955. Among the important historical facts that the Commission regarded as having shaped the Tanganyika of today, only one took place during the period of German colonization, namely, "the reduction of the African population, its redistribution and the encroachment of the tsetse fly resulting from the decimation of the population." All the others occurred during the period of the Mandate:

The slow tempo of outside investment of capital and non-African settlement caused largely by political uncertainty as to the future of the country between the two wars; the fact that neither a "White Highlands" policy nor a "tribal reserves" policy has emerged; and that, subject to varying degrees of interpretation, a consistent policy of considering African interests to come first has been pursued since the beginning of the British Mandate.[104]

4

THE TRUSTEESHIP SYSTEM
AND CONSTITUTIONAL REFORM

Throughout World War II and until the end of 1946, Tanganyika continued to be administered under the terms of the Mandate. Although Chapters XII and XIII of the United Nations Charter approved at the San Francisco Conference in 1945 had provided for the establishment of a system of international trusteeship under the United Nations, this did not come into effect for nearly another two years. At the first part of the First Session of the General Assembly, which met in London in January and February 1946, Great Britain announced her intention of placing her mandated territories of Tanganyika, the Cameroons, and Togoland under the International Trusteeship System. In making the announcement, Ernest Bevin, the Secretary of State for Foreign Affairs, said: "The people of the territories themselves and the world at large should be left in no doubt that the continuity of British administration will be maintained until the ultimate objective of the trusteeship system, self-government or independence, as the case may be, is attained."[1]

This move was not well received by a group of British settlers in Tanganyika who, worried about their future status, wanted the British government to make the territory a crown colony and thereby end international control. In an attempt to calm their fears, the British Colonial Secretary declared in the House of Commons in March

1946 that "the placing of Tanganyika under trusteeship would not in any way affect, either now or in the future, the status of British subjects resident in the territory."[2]

The last meeting of the Assembly of the League of Nations took place at Geneva in April 1946. On April 18 it adopted a resolution recognizing that the League's functions with regard to mandates would cease upon the termination of the League itself. The resolution noted that the mandatory powers had expressed the intention of continuing to administer the mandated territories in accordance with the terms of the respective Mandate treaties "until other arrangements have been agreed between the United Nations and the respective mandatory Powers."[3] It thus recognized that the Trusteeship System did not automatically apply to the mandates, but that new terms for each territory would have to be made.

The first draft of the terms of trusteeship for Tanganyika was presented to Parliament in June 1946. A revised draft was published in October and, in accordance with Article 85 of the Charter, was filed with the Secretary-General of the United Nations for presentation to the General Assembly at the second part of its First Session, which was held later that year in New York. The draft agreement was examined clause by clause by a special committee, which made still further modifications at the suggestion of member states. The agreement was finally approved by the General Assembly on December 13, 1946, and differed only slightly from the revised text published in October.[4] With regard to the trusteeship agreements for former British mandated territories, Ivor Thomas, speaking to the General Assembly on Dec. 17, stated:

It is because the Trusteeship System is entirely in accordance with our policy that we have voluntarily, I emphasize the word voluntarily, offered to place all our African Mandate territories under the Trusteeship System. We shall look forward to the operations of this system with confidence that it will be a most valuable part of the machinery of the United Nations, and will give great hope to millions of dependent peoples in all parts of the world.[5]

Following the approval of these and other trusteeship agreements, the Trusteeship Council, the principal organ of the Trusteeship System, was set up. The first meeting of the Council was held in March 1947 at New York.

The Trusteeship System of the United Nations has several notable points of difference from the Mandates System of the League of Nations. As far as Tanganyika is concerned, the most important of these is contained in Article 76, which states specifically that Trust Territories are to be developed "towards self-government or independence." Under the Mandate the final destiny of the territory was left uncertain; the trust was defined by the Covenant only as "the well-being and development" of "peoples not yet able to stand by themselves." By Article 6 of the Trusteeship Agreement, Great Britain, as the Administering Authority, undertook to "develop the participation of the inhabitants of Tanganyika in advisory and legislative bodies and in the government of the Territory, both central and local, as may be appropriate to the particular circumstances of the Territory and its people."

Other important modifications are as follows. Under Article 87 of the Charter, the Trusteeship Council, unlike the Mandates Commission, has the power to initiate periodic visits of inspection to all trust territories. Furthermore, under the same article, the Trusteeship Council may "accept petitions and examine them in consultation with the administering authority." The Charter also requires each administering authority "to ensure that the trust territory shall play its part in the maintenance of international peace and security," whereas the Mandate had forbidden the fortifying of Tanganyika or the raising of troops for other than local defense. The "open door" provision found in the Mandate is replaced by a clause in Article 76 of the Charter that subordinates equality of economic treatment for all members of the United Nations to the "political, economic, social, and educational advancement of the inhabitants of the Trust Territories."

The Mandate provision supposedly limiting the type of administrative union that could be applied to Tanganyika is modified somewhat in Article 5 of the Trusteeship Agreement. Great Britain had asked for a free hand to place Tanganyika under any form of union that she considered to be in the territory's interest. Therefore the Trusteeship Agreement states that the Administering Authority shall be entitled to constitute Tanganyika into a customs, fiscal or administrative union or federation with adjacent territories under his sovereignty or control, and to establish common services between such territories and Tanganyika where such measures are not inconsistent with the basic objectives of the international trusteeship system and with the terms of this Agreement.[6]

Another modification, although it is uncertain whether it was intended as such, is the use of the word "inhabitants" instead of the Covenant's expression "peoples not yet able to stand by themselves" (Article 22). As previously quoted, Article 76 of the Charter states that one of the basic objectives of the Trusteeship System is "to promote the political, economic, social and educational advancement of the inhabitants of the Trust Territories"; and in Article 6 of the Trusteeship, Great Britain undertook to "develop the participation of the inhabitants of Tanganyika . . . in the government of the Territory." The Trusteeship Agreement, however, is not consistent in its terminology. Article 8, which refers to the framing of laws relating to the holding or transfer of land, stipulates that the Administering Authority "shall respect the rights and safeguard the interests . . . of the native population." It has therefore been argued that "inhabitants" does not mean just the native population, but includes the immigrant population as well. A statement in 1952 by Oliver Lyttleton, the Secretary of State for the Colonies, indicates that this was the view of the British government:

Her Majesty's Government interpret the Trusteeship Agreement and Article 76 of the United Nations Charter as imposing on the Administering Authority an obligation to provide for the full participation of all sections of the populations, irrespective of race or origin, in the progressive development of political institutions and in the economic and social advancement of the territory. Each section of the population must be enabled and encouraged to play its full part in the development of the territory and its institutions in complete confidence that the rights and interests of all communities, both indigenous and immigrant, will be secured and preserved.[7]

It was later claimed that this was the basis of the administration's postwar policy of multiracialism as opposed to the earlier objective of establishing a primarily African state.[8]

THE EXPANSION OF TERRITORIAL GOVERNMENT

Tanganyika's position at the end of World War II was completely different from the state she found herself in at the end of World War I. Whereas in 1918 the economy had been left broken following four years of hostilities in the country, in 1945 it was buoyant and expanding. Between 1940 and 1945 the value of sisal exports more than tripled, and the value of coffee exports doubled. Moreover, during these years an important new item of production appeared. Following Dr. John Williamson's discovery of the Mwadui Mine near Shinyanga, the annual output of diamonds increased regularly from a value of £12,600 in 1940 to a value of £638,383 in 1945; and diamond production was to have an even greater effect on the territory's economy after the war. Also during the war years, government revenue steadily increased, and the growing demands upon the territory's railways put their operation on a firm foundation for the first time.

The country's chief contribution to the general war effort was the provision of manpower to the armed forces. Troops from Tanganyika played an important part in the Somaliland, Burma, and Madagascar campaigns. But in spite of these wartime experiences, the return of the ex-servicemen to their homes after the war failed to produce the amount of political activity that had been expected.[9] Unlike the many African countries whose nationalist movements can be traced back to the war years, Tanganyika did not become politically active until nearly a decade later.

Political competition between various racial groups has been a characteristic of multiracial societies in eastern, central, and southern Africa. Lord Hailey has pointed out, however, that during the postwar period in Tanganyika, "when political issues began to occupy a more important place in the Territory, they never provided the same occasion for interracial discord as in Kenya." He attributes this in part to the different nature of the European and Asian communities in the two territories.

In Tanganyika the Europeans formed a far less homogeneous group; they represented a number of different nationalities, and they had not the advantage of occupying a compact block of country such as the Highlands in which most of the Europeans of Kenya were concentrated. The Asian community of Tanganyika was smaller in number than that of Kenya and it was also more scattered and was less efficiently organized.[10]

In 1945, shortly after the end of the war, an amendment to the Tanganyika Constitution enlarged the membership of the Legislative Council to 15 officials and 14 nominated unofficials, with the Governor remaining as President. Of the unofficial seats, seven were allotted to Europeans, including a European representative of African interests, three to Asians, and four to Africans. The names of the first two Africans appointed were announced in November. Both were chiefs, and both were young, well-educated men. One, Chief Abdiel Shangali, was a Christian from the Chagga tribe, and the other, Chief Kidaha Makwaia of the Sukuma tribe, was a Moslem and a graduate of Makerere College in Uganda. The two other unofficial African members were not named until much later, Chief Adam Sapi being appointed in June 1947 and Juma Mwindadi, an African schoolmaster in Dar es Salaam, in April 1948.

Although Indian unofficial representation was not increased by the amendment, one Indian unofficial member, Abdulla Karimjee, had been appointed only a year before. His family were owners of a firm that had been in Tanganyika more than a hundred years. On taking office he announced that he intended to do his best for the African population, "who have always been here and therefore have the first right to the country." He pointed out that the Indian population qualified as citizens by residence and by the part they had played in the development of the country, and he said that he hoped to contribute to interracial understanding.[11]

With the appointment of Mwindadi, the fourth unofficial African member, in April 1948, the composition of the Legislative Council came to be an example of what Lord Hailey calls "balanced representation." He contrasts this with a second arrangement, which he calls "equal representation." The two terms stand for two different approaches of the British government to the question of the relative representation to be accorded to the racial communities of East Africa:

"Balanced representation" involves assigning to one community which is considered to have predominant claim a measure of representation equal to that accorded to all other communities taken together. "Equal representation" would, on the other hand, accord the same numerical representation to each community.

Thus in Kenya and Tanganyika "balanced representation" took the form of granting to the Europeans, who were numerically the smallest of the major communities, representation in the Legislative Council equal to that accorded to Asians, Arabs, and Africans taken together. In Uganda, however, "balanced representation" meant that African representation equaled that accorded to Europeans and Asians together.[12]

The fact that the African and Asian communities, together about 99.9 per cent of the total population, were accorded representation only equal to that of the European community was criticized by the United Nations Visiting Mission to Tanganyika in 1948. Colonial officials in London replied that population strength could not serve as a criterion for representation on the Legislative Council. The Visiting Mission then raised the question of increasing Indian representation on the Council, but was told that this was not possible, since the Europeans were making a far greater contribution than the Indians to the development of the country.[13]

The African representation on the Council was far from being purely nominal. Following their appointment in 1945, Chief Shangali and Chief Makwaia took an active part in debates. Admittedly, they tended to raise questions relating exclusively to their own people (thus following the example of the Indian members), but they also showed an interest in broader issues. In many cases their questions implied a certain dissatisfaction or impatience with existing policies,[14] and, as Sir Edward Twining has pointed out, they were able to state their views with considerable force. He describes a situation that arose in the Council shortly after his arrival in the territory in 1949: "Government was introducing a bill which was very dear to its heart, but one of the African members made a speech opposing the bill, which was not only acclaimed as being the best speech made in the Council for ten years, but contained such powerful reasoning that Government had to withdraw the bill."[15]

The Tanganyika Executive Council was reorganized at the beginning of 1948. Its membership continued to consist of the Governor, as President, seven official members, and four nonofficial members appointed from the Legislative Council. (In 1948, three of the nonofficial members were Europeans and one was an Indian.) Experience in World War II, however, had shown that the existing structure of the Executive Council was unequal to the strain of a greatly expanded volume of business. In particular, the concentration of responsibility in the hands of the Chief Secretary was a serious bottleneck, since heads of departments communicated directly with him on all matters requiring reference to higher authority. It was therefore decided that administration should be decentralized and the Executive Council remodeled on the order of the "member system" already instituted in the other British African territories. The various departments of the government were arranged in groups, and each group was placed under the direction of a member of the Executive Council, who was then directly responsible to the Governor. The work of the Chief Secretary was thus greatly reduced, allowing him to pay closer attention to matters of major policy.

After the new plan was carried out, the official members of the Executive Council were the Chief Secretary, the Member for Law and Order, the Member for Finance, Trade, and Economics, the Member for Agriculture and Natural Resources, the Member for Lands and Mines, the Member for Labor, Education, and Social Welfare (the title was later changed to the Member for Social Services), and the Secretary for African Affairs. The official membership increased to eight in 1949, when the post of Member for Development and Works was created. In 1950, another new post, Member for Local Government, absorbed the duties of the Secretary for African Affairs.[16]

The annual report on Tanganyika to the United Nations for 1948 contains a comment on the political consciousness of the African people at that time. It noted that "the interests of the great majority of the indigenous population are still largely confined to purely local and domestic matters," but went on to say:

Nevertheless the signs of an awakening political consciousness are be-coming increasingly apparent. In most of the rural areas it is still circum-scribed but the increasing interest being taken by the younger generation in local government affairs is significant and important . . . The way is clear for the more rapid development of representative local govern-ment bodies. A sense of responsibility in local tribal affairs is the first step towards an interest and acceptance of responsibility in inter-tribal and territorial affairs. Some of the native authorities already have this wider vision, but as regards the indigenous population generally the display of any real interest in extra-tribal affairs and politics is at present largely confined to those who have forsaken rural life and occupations for those of the towns. Among such will be found many who do not hesitate to express their personal views and opinions, but they cannot at this stage be regarded as truly representative of the great mass of the people.[17]

The report of the 1948 Visiting Mission was somewhat critical of the attitude among government officials that progress in Tanganyika would be slow, and it expressed the hope, shared by articulate Afri-cans, "that evolution will be quicker than is thought possible." The Mission reported that in conversations with educated Africans it "was greatly impressed by the quality of their minds, their general and reasonable understanding of local affairs and requirements, and their appreciation of territorial problems."[18]

While the Visiting Mission was in the country, it received "numer-ous requests" from the African population for an increase in African membership in the Legislative Council. In London the Colonial Sec-retary told the Mission that the Administering Authority did indeed intend to afford Africans greater participation in the central organs of the government, including the Legislative Council, but that such progress could only come with further educational advancement. The Mission also received many complaints from African organiza-tions and communities "that the African members on the Legislative Council were not representative of the Africans of the Territory and as a consequence were in touch only with their own people, some-times only a section of their own communities, and were not respon-sive to the needs of the majority of Africans."[19] In particular, the Tanganyika African Association submitted a petition to the Visiting Mission, asking that the right to vote be instituted in the territory. The Association was the original African political organization in the country, created in 1929. However, since it was both political and social in character, it was not a purely nationalist organization. The Visiting Mission was told by members of the Association that it had 39 branches throughout the territory and a total membership of 1,780.[20]

Summing up, the report of the 1948 Visiting Mission urged that African representation in the Legislative Council be increased in the near future "toward the goal of one African member from each of the eight provinces." It recommended that this increase should not be accompanied by a proportionate increase in the nonofficial representation of the other two communities "so that in the resulting nonofficial representation there would be a majority of African members." It also agreed with the views expressed by many Africans "that the present African members are not truly representative of all the Africans of the Territory." The Mission suggested the introduction of an electoral system to correct this situation and, further, that Africans might "be accorded seats on the Executive Council as well." Its final observation on political advancement in the central government was as follows:

It appears to the Mission that the overwhelming majority of the Africans are not yet capable—and *under existing conditions* will not be capable for some considerable time to come—of assuming full political responsibility. Therefore, the Mission considers that the Administering Authority might now give urgent consideration to the formulation of appropriate measures for accelerating the development of the inhabitants of Tanganyika towards self-government or independence.[21]

These observations of the Visiting Mission, as well as its comments concerning economic, educational, and social matters, raised a storm of protest in Great Britain. This was due partly to some incorrect or misleading statements in the Mission's report and partly to the British government's sensitiveness about international intervention in its administration of Tanganyika. With regard to the government's attitude, Margaret Bates writes: "This tendency to regard trusteeship problems as imperial, and therefore domestic ones, is widely held in Britain; international discussion results in hurt feelings and loss of prestige even when—in fact, particularly when—the administration may have vulnerable spots." She goes on to point out that "much of the agitation aroused over the report of the 1948 visiting mission . . . may be ascribed to this feeling of possession and dislike of outside interference."

The dispute was heightened by the fact that this was the first Mission sent to Tanganyika and by the fact that the report was released by the United Nations before British observations on it had been received.[22] The controversy tended to obscure some favorable impressions of the Mission, such as its statement that it had everywhere found freedom of political expression and its high regard for the government officials it had met in the territory. However, there is probably some truth in the assessment that both sides were to blame for the strong feelings aroused, that the Mission was "suspicious and dogmatic," while the British government proved "peculiarly touchy." The Mission's report, however, gave much encouragement to African organizations in Tanganyika.[23]

Commenting on the Visiting Mission's report, the British government began by saying that it realized the Mission could not become fully familiar with the territory in the six weeks it had had at its disposal. With regard to the view that African representation on the Legislative Council should be increased, British officials stated that it was difficult "to find Africans who can participate usefully and effectively in the deliberations of the council and who are at the same time truly representative of the masses of the people." Moreover, they did not think that this problem could be solved by introducing an electoral system, as the Mission had suggested. They felt that any attempt to do so at present "would almost certainly result in the appointment of representatives of sectional interests, much less in touch with and responsive to the needs and wishes of the mass of the people than the present carefully chosen members." The aim of government policy was declared to be the introduction of popular representation, first at the level of the tribal council, to be followed at the district and provincial levels, and eventually at the national level. The Administering Authority considered this to be "the only basis on which sound political development can be assured."[24]

The recommendations of the Visiting Mission were noted with

interest by people in Tanganyika. On July 5, 1949, a number of the leading members of the European, Asian, and African communities in Dar es Salaam published in the *Tanganyika Standard* a memorandum stating that, in spite of more than twenty-five years of British trusteeship, no significant progress had been made toward representative government in the country. The memorandum called for the abolition of the system of nominations to local and central legislative and advisory bodies, and the adoption of an electoral system.[25]

Three months later, in October 1949, representatives from the British and Greek communities met at Dodoma in Central Province to form the Tanganyika European Council. The organization announced that its purpose was "to serve European settlement and interests, and work for the advancement of all peoples of the Territory under British leadership." The Council's chief support came from the European settlers of Northern Province, where a provincial European Council was already in existence.[26]

CONSTITUTIONAL REFORM, 1949–55

In December 1949, Governor Twining established the Committee on Constitutional Development, consisting of the Member for Law and Order as chairman, the Member for Local Government, and all the unofficial members of the Legislative Council. It was given the following terms of reference: "To review the present constitutional structure in the Territory, both local and territorial, and to make recommendations for future constitutional developments in the Territory."[27] During its investigation, the Committee met bitter opposition from the European settlers of Northern Province. They thought that the government intended to establish multiracial Provincial Councils, like the one already functioning in Lake Province, which would then act as electoral colleges for the appointment of unofficial members to the Legislative Council—a course of action that the Governor had suggested previously.[28] The settlers had opposed this plan because they feared it would mean the swamping of the Europeans.[29]

Some of the European settlers in Northern Province approached Kenyan settler groups for support in opposing the Committee's investigations. This caused Europeans elsewhere in the territory to speak out against the settlers of the north. At the opening of the Southern Highlands Provincial Council, Brigadier W. E. H. Scupham, an unofficial member of the Legislative Council, said that an overwhelming majority of the people of all races with whom he had discussed the matter deplored the behavior of the European settlers in Northern Province. Speaking on the same occasion, Governor Twining said that he was more than ever convinced that Tanganyika's future depended upon the successful partnership of the three main races. He continued:

We are fortunate in Tanganyika in having developed a very good atmosphere of mutual respect and understanding between the three races. Anyone who attempts to undo this by reckless or provocative actions, especially when they have made no effort to ascertain the true facts, is doing a grave disservice not only to Tanganyika, but to the community they claim to represent.[30]

Despite the public clamor, the Committee completed its investigations by the end of 1950, a year that saw "more political activity than any previous year in the Territory's short history."[31] On March 12, 1951, the Committee submitted its conclusions and recommendations to the Governor. In a covering letter, the chairman, Charles Mathew, pointed out that racial discord had never marred relations between the three main races during the thirty years that Tanganyika had been under British administration. He mentioned that the Committee wished to emphasize "the importance of this fact and in framing its recommendations for political development it has been at some pains to avoid impairing these relations, even though the pace of our political development may be slowed down."[32] Throughout its deliberations the Committee attempted to consider "the best interests of the inhabitants of the Territory as a whole, bearing in mind that this term includes the Europeans and Asians no less than the indigenous peoples."[33]

Among various recommendations dealing with the structure of the government both at the territorial level and lower, the Committee proposed that the unofficial membership of the Legislative Council should be increased from fourteen to twenty-one, with each of the three main racial communities receiving seven seats:

We do not consider that it is in the interests of any one community to strive for a dominant political position, as this could not fail in the long run to react to its own disadvantage. We are convinced that the only solution which is equitable and capable of obviating feelings of distrust and lack of confidence and of laying a sound foundation for the political development of the Territory is the equal distribution of unofficial seats on the Legislative Council.

With regard to the official membership of the Legislative Council, the Committee reported that responsible opinion favored the official majority, and it recommended that this be maintained. It suggested "that consideration should be given to the appointment of an African member of the Executive Council." And, finally, it considered that the establishment of the new Legislative Council, "combined with a form of elective representation," should not come about until three years after its recommendations for regional or local government institutions had been put into effect.[34]

After receiving the Committee's report, Governor Twining suggested to the Colonial Secretary that an objective of five years should be set for implementing the Committee's recommendations regarding the Legislative Council.[35] He also announced that he had accepted the recommendation to appoint an African to the Executive Council. Accordingly, Chief Kidaha Makwaia, a member of the Legislative Council was appointed as an unofficial member of the Executive Council.[36] Further action on the report was put off until the views of the various racial communities could be ascertained.

When the report was published in August 1951, the second United Nations Visiting Mission was in the process of touring the country. It thus had a unique opportunity of recording public reaction. "Immediately after the publication of the report, a considerable amount of opposition to the Committee's proposals, and in particular to the proposal for parity of representation in the Legislative Council, was reported in the local Press."[37] Members of the Tanganyika European Council at Arusha, Dar es Salaam, and in Southern Province informed the Visiting Mission of their opposition to the proposals. The Mission summarized their views as follows:

The European community had, up to the present, played a predominant role in the introduction of civilization and in the development of the Territory; the Asian and African communities were still politically immature; the present proposals were unduly favourable to the Asian community; what was needed for the development of the Territory was a period of political stability to enable economic development, which was the prime necessity at the moment, to be carried out in an atmosphere of confidence; the European unofficial members of the Legislative Council who had signed the report were not representative of their community, and consequently further consideration of the report by the Legislative Council should be postponed until a system of elections had been introduced for the European and Asian membership of the present Council.[38]

This was not the opinion of all Europeans in Tanganyika, however. Sir Eldred Hitchcock, the leading figure in the territory's sisal industry, was quoted as saying: "It is my view that an imposed white leadership is today an anachronism and will surely defeat its own objects. Leadership, whether by Europeans, Asians or Africans, will emerge on its own merits."[39]

Since it took some time for the Committee's proposals to reach the tribal areas, the Visiting Mission received little comment from tribal Africans. The Chagga Cultural Association at Moshi, however, did express the opinion that Africans were entitled to greater representation in the Legislative Council by reason of their numerical preponderance, but said that it was prepared to accept the Committee's proposals as the best terms obtainable at present.[40] A memorandum presented by the Association to the Visiting Mission stated that the organization "would strongly oppose any selfish demands for leadership by one racial group," and that "leadership, if any, must exist on its own merits for the interests of the Territory as a whole and not to perpetuate rule by a section of a race that has shown selfish disregard of democratic principles.[41]

The main representation by Africans on constitutional matters was made by the headquarters of the Tanganyika African Association, which the Visiting Mission regarded "as representative of educated African opinion." The Association expressed the view that the Committee on Constitutional Development had made "a genuine attempt to strike a blow at racialism," but it was not satisfied with the proportion of unofficial seats proposed for Africans. Nevertheless, acceptance of the Committee's proposals was not entirely out of the question if parity of representation in the Council was only a temporary phase.[42] A memorandum presented to the Mission by the Association made the following comments on the political situation in Tanganyika:

The word "inhabitants," we understand, has now been interpreted to mean everyone living here, African, Asian and European. This is an unfortunate interpretation. . . If one community of the immigrant races think there is another half-century before we can take our part side by side with them in the Government of this country, then they have the choice of either marching slowly with us or going elsewhere. The greatest political tragedy that could ever happen in this country is the granting of full political rights to immigrant races and denying them to us. . . We are willing to share this right with the immigrant races on a basis of partnership, but we are not, and never shall be, willing to surrender what we have come to regard as our rights, and allow our interests to be relegated to an inferior position.

The Tanganyika European Council . . . while talking of racial harmony . . . first makes fantastic claims . . . then floods the press with remarks that can hardly be said to promote racial harmony. We feel that the members of the Tanganyika European Council have a right to band together for their common interests, but there is no doubt that they are becoming too narrow-minded and sectional.[43]

Asian opinion was expressed through branches of the Asian Association in many of the principal towns. Though there was definite support for the Committee's proposals, the Association informed the Mission that it advocated the election of all non-African representatives to the Legislative Council on the basis of a "common roll," whereby all European and Asian voters would be registered on a single electoral roll. Eventually, it thought that a common roll should be introduced for all communities.[44]

After hearing the views of the territory's main racial groups, the Mission concluded that the Committee's proposal "for equal representation of the three main races on the Legislative Council represents a useful step as an interim measure," but that it would soon "be possible to depart from the principle of communal representation" and suggested that "the use of a common electoral roll with appropriate qualifications might form a bridge between the proposed system and a more representative one." It mentioned that there was "already support for this view among important sections of each community," but did not go into further detail.[45] It is interesting that the proposals of the Asian Association and the 1951 Mission for establishing a common electoral roll were not the first to be made in this respect. As far back as 1928, Raymond L. Buell had suggested that when the time came for elected representation in Tanganyika, a common roll not subject to a discriminatory education or property test should be used.[46]

The report of the 1951 Mission to Tanganyika was not made available to the public until the following year. In contrast with the public reaction to the report of the 1948 Mission, this report "was received with scarcely a ripple in Tanganyika itself."[47] Commenting on the 1951 report, the Administering Authority referred to its "notably objective nature" and welcomed it "as a clear and balanced study of conditions and problems in Tanganyika and as a helpful and encouraging document."[48]

The report was discussed by the Trusteeship Council at its Eleventh Session in June 1952. Sir Edward Twining, the Governor of Tanganyika, appeared before the Council on June 20 to make the Administering Authority's opening statement. He said that he was disturbed by a leitmotiv running throughout the report: "The need for speed is urged and the impression is left that events are moving too slowly." The government of Tanganyika, he remarked, had this sense of urgency too. He and his officers at time felt impatient and frustrated, but they had to contend with forces beyond their control. "Of all the problems with which I am faced in Tanganyika, this one of increasing the speed of progress is the most intractable." Twining went on to say that many Africans were afraid that a passion for speed might destroy the things they cherished before they were replaced by something better. African leaders had frequently urged him not to move at a pace faster than the people could take, and these considerations must be kept to the fore: "We intend to build a lasting structure and we must move surely, even if slowly. I, myself, believe that, as we proceed, our tempo will gather momentum and this view is borne out by the remarkable progress that has been made during the past few years."[49]

Following Twining's statement, Sir John Lamb, the special representative for Tanganyika, answered questions put to him by members of the Council concerning the Committee's proposals. He explained that the recommendation concerning parity of representation in the Legislative Council was an attempt to introduce "the principle of partnership." This principle was based not on a count of heads, but on a more equitable criterion: the contribution to the territory of each of the racial communities. Therefore, the nonindigenous section of the population, upon whom the economic development of the territory largely depended, was "surely entitled to a large share in the government of the country."[50]

On June 25, 1952, Oliver Lyttleton, the Colonial Secretary, announced that the British government had accepted the two main recommendations of the Committee on Constitutional Development: i.e., equal representation of the three main groups in an enlarged Legislative Council and the retention of an official majority in the Council. The government also accepted the Committee's suggestion that a Special Commissioner be appointed to examine matters arising out of the report.[51]

Professor W. J. M. Mackenzie of Manchester University was accordingly appointed Special Commissioner, with the task of considering, among other things, the most appropriate system for election of unofficial members to the Legislative Council. Mackenzie made two trips to Tanganyika as part of this study; his report appeared in 1953. It began by pointing out that a citizenship qualification would not be appropriate in Tanganyika because of the variety of nationalities found there. He therefore recommended that the franchise should be based upon birth, or residence in the territory during three out of the four years preceding the election. He recommended that there should be no discrimination on grounds of sex or race and that the franchise should be extended to all persons over the age of 21 who had paid their taxes. He rejected an income, property, or educational test, on the grounds that the franchise should have the widest possible basis, and that if such a test were imposed, a large proportion of the

African population would inevitably be excluded for many years to come. He concluded that the ultimate goal should be a system of common roll elections with safeguards for minority representation, but that such a system was not practicable in the greater part of Tanganyika in the near future. For although there was already a section of the African population that did not "think tribally," it would be some time before the general sentiment of one tribe could be truly represented by a member of another tribe, and if an electoral system were introduced, a member of the largest tribe would almost always win.[52]

While Mackenzie's recommendations were under consideration, a change was made in the structure of the Legislative Council under the terms of the Tanganyika (Legislative Council) (Amendment) Order in Council, 1953. By this action the Governor would no longer sit as President of the Legislative Council; in the future a Speaker would preside over the sessions of the Council. It was stipulated that the Speaker must be neither an official nor an unofficial member of the Council and would possess no vote. Although the Governor could no longer participate in the Council's debates, he still enjoyed the right to address the Council at any time when it was in session. Furthermore, he continued to possess the power to give assent or refusal to any bill passed by the legislature, or to reserve it for the signification of the Crown. Under this new arrangement, Brigadier W. E. H. Scupham was appointed Speaker by Governor Twining in November 1953. On November 17, the Legislative Council was presided over by the Speaker for the first time.[53]

During the previous month, the Legislative Council had debated Professor Mackenzie's recommendations concerning the machinery of constitutional development. Members of all races spoke in favor of proceeding slowly with constitutional reform.[54] In May 1954, Sir Edward Twining announced the government's intention of introducing the reconstituted Legislative Council within twelve months. At that time it was proposed that the membership of the Council should be increased to 55, the unofficial bench of 27 members consisting of one representative from each of the three main racial groups in each province and in the capital city of Dar es Salaam, which was to be established as a separate constituency.

In December the Governor announced a decision to increase the unofficial membership still further to a total of 30, the three additional members, one of each race, to be chosen by him to represent such interests and areas as he saw fit. In order to maintain an official majority, the government side of the Council would be increased to 31, not all of whom would hold Government posts. Conditions were not yet considered favorable for the introduction of elections, and unofficial members would therefore continue to be nominated by the Governor in consultation with representative bodies.[55]

The reforms proposed by the Governor in December 1954 were put into effect by the Tanganyika (Legislative Council) (Amendment) Order in Council, 1955, on March 17, 1955. Previously the Colonial Secretary had stated that the reconstitution of the Legislative Council, when it came into effect, would be "designed to last for a considerable period and until the time comes for the main communities in Tanganyika to consider a different system of representation."[56] Beginning in 1955, then, the unofficial membership of the Legislative Council came to be an example of what Lord Hailey calls "equal representation." The "balanced representation" favoring the Europeans, which had existed on the unofficial side since 1948, was at an end.

The Executive Council was also reorganized to conform with the parity principle of representation, and in November 1954 the unofficial membership was increased to six: two Asians, two Europeans, and two Africans. I. C. Chopra, an Asian, and Chief Adam Sapi, an African, were appointed as the two new members; both retained their seats in the Legislative Council as well. The government side of the Executive Council consisted of three ex officio members and five nominated official members. The Governor remained President of the Council.

5

GOVERNMENT
UNDER THE TRUSTEESHIP

During the early 1950's, while the country was working out its constitutional reforms, interracial relations in the territory as a whole remained good. According to one report, in spite of some discord between the various groups, there was more racial harmony in Tanganyika than in any other African territory with a large immigrant population.[1] The 1954 Visiting Mission remarked that it often heard the term "multiracial society" used with "obviously good intentions," but that it was not in fact applicable to the situation in Tanganyika.

The people of Tanganyika comprise not one society but three. In economic and social development the paths of the African, Asian, and European are widely separated. The difference in their economic activities extends even into fields of production in which more than one racial group plays an important part. The social conditions of the population vary more strikingly between the three racial groups than within each one of them. With some exceptions, the modes and standards of living, the everyday interests, and the social and political organization of the three groups differ markedly.

The Mission concluded that the territory was "a long way from achieving that degree of integration . . . which is essential if the Asian and European settlers as well as the Africans are to belong fully to the future self-governing state."[2]

With respect to political organization, the annual report for 1954 stated that "no developments in the formation of political parties in the generally accepted sense have yet taken place." As far as the European political organizations went, the Tanganyika European Council "continued to represent a body of non-official European opinion."[3] To the 1954 Mission the Council appeared to be "largely dormant if not disorganized." The transfer of the Council's headquarters from Arusha to Dar es Salaam had resulted in a loss of support for the Northern Province branch. The Mission reported that this branch was "apparently defunct, . . . the once extreme views of some of the European farmers . . . having been subdued by the more general acceptance by the European community of the parity formula, and also by the tension which had gathered in the intervening years on both sides of the Kenya-Tanganyika border." Thus, whereas the previous Mission had encountered strong opposition to the parity formula for the Legislative Council from European settlers in Northern Province, the 1954 Mission did not receive a single protest in this connection from any section of the European community. The Mission noted that "the only political issue of importance . . . now actively interesting any substantial number of non-official Europeans is the question of election rather than the nomination of future members of the Legislative Council."[4]

Among the Asian section of the population no organized community of interests transcending the religious and social differences between the principal Hindu and Muslim components existed. The Asian Association of Dar es Salaam presented the Visiting Mission with a pamphlet entitled *The Right Road for Tanganyika,* which set out the Association's point of view on future policy for Tanganyika. The ultimate goal was described as a "non-racial, secular state." The election of the new members of the Legislative Council was urged; elections on a purely communal basis, however, were opposed on the grounds that they would tend to create racial hostility and to hinder the development of a common citizenship. It was proposed that each voter of each race should have three votes; the voter could then vote for a candidate of each race to represent his constituency. The existing nominated members of the Legislative Council were accused of being completely out of touch with public opinion, and furthermore (this applied especially to the Asian members) of frustrating the introduction of Asian elections.[5]

The 1954 report noted that there were numerous local associations of a political nature among the African population, of which the longest established were the Kilimanjaro Chagga Citizens Union and the Bahaya Union, "the membership of each of which probably exceeds that of the one territorial association."[6] This territorial group was the former Tanganyika African Association, reconstituted during the year as the Tanganyika African National Union. The 1951 Visiting Mission had reported that the Association had about 5,000 members, but that a large proportion of these were government employees and teachers, its influence among tribal Africans being small.[7] During the next two years it showed few signs of life. At the end of 1952 it was without a president, and no meetings were held during the second part of the year.[8]

In 1953, Julius Nyerere, the man later to become the first Prime Minister of Tanganyika, was elected President of the Association. He decided that it should drop its social functions and be reorganized along more definite political lines. The next year was spent in drawing up a new constitution and in seeking the support of the tribal authorities for the new organization, so that it might become a genuine political party with branches in all parts of the territory, not just the larger towns. In July 1954 the Tanganyika African National Union came into being. "Racial equality in the eyes of the law" was established as its objective; this, however, was qualified by the statement that in order "to be democratic it must be individual as opposed to communal racial equality," a distinction that stressed the organization's differences with the government's parity representation policy. The Union also gave as its aims self-government and independence.[9]

Julius is one of twenty-six children born to Chief Nyerere Burito of the Zanaki tribe, one of the territory's smallest tribes. After receiving his early education in Roman Catholic mission schools, Nyerere attended Makerere College in Uganda. From 1949 to 1952 he attended the University of Edinburgh, and returned to Tanganyika with a Master of Arts degree. At that time he was 30 years old. He became a teacher in a Roman Catholic school at Pugu, about twelve miles from Dar es Salaam. The distance did not keep him from renewing his ties with the Tanganyika African Association, and in 1953 he was made its President.

As already stated, the next year was spent in building up support for the new organization, the Tanganyika African National Union, Nyerere being assisted in this task by the Party's unpaid organizing secretary, Oscar Kambona. Nyerere has sometimes been asked how he ever managed to achieve unity in the face of so many conflicting tribal loyalties. He has always replied that, on the contrary, his organization was helped by the fact the African population is divided into 120 tribes. "The more tribes we have, the better," he explains; if there were only five tribes, there might be serious clashes. "My own tribe is 35,000 people; my brother is the chief. If my brother wanted to be a nuisance, he couldn't be much of a nuisance."[10]

By 1954 the Union had grown so much that Nyerere was forced to choose between his teaching career and politics; he chose the latter. He stuck to his decision even though the government tried to lure him away from politics by offering him the prestige and security of a district officer's post. He rejected this offer out of a conviction that his duty was to lead and organize his people. Even though the Union has become a wealthy organization of more than 1,000,000 members, Nyerere has remained scrupulously honest and demands the same high standard of conduct of all the organization's officers. Those who have misused funds have been handed over to the police and imprisoned.[11]

When the 1954 Visiting Mission came to Dar es Salaam, the central committee of the Tanganyika African National Union, or TANU as it came to be called, took the opportunity of presenting the new organization's views to the Mission. The committee, led by Nyerere, asked for assurance from both the United Nations and Great Britain "that this territory, although multi-racial in population, is primarily an African country and must be developed as such." The committee said that TANU, like the other groups, had accepted the principle of parity representation in the Legislative Council, but only "as a necessary and convenient expedient and not as a permanent state of affairs." They expressed the view that future changes in the composition of the Council should enable the largest racial community to have the largest number of seats. As for the manner of selection of the unofficial members of the Council, they felt that at least the members representing Dar es Salaam should be elected. Until suffrage was extended elsewhere, the various organizations could submit lists of names from which the Governor could make the final selection. In conclusion, the committee emphasized that the African population valued their status as a Trust Territory.[12]

During a visit to the new local government training school near Morogoro, the Mission sounded out the views of twenty chiefs in attendance there. When asked what they thought of the new constitutional developments and particularly the principle of parity representation, one chief promptly answered that he did not think it right: "The Africans have the largest population, and so they should have the majority of seats"; the others agreed. Although some of the chiefs felt that the Africans were not yet educated or interested enough to vote in large numbers, most appeared to favor election rather than nomination of members to territorial and local councils.[13]

LOCAL GOVERNMENT

These changes in territorial government were not the only signs of political progress in the ten years following World War II. Great advances were made also at the local, district, and provincial levels. Although the return of servicemen to their villages after the war did not have as marked an effect as might have been expected, it did lead to some new developments in local government. The fact that so many people had had their outlook enlarged by travel during the war helped to bring about a democratization of the Native Authorities, hitherto unrecognized advisers of the chiefs gradually being made an integral part of local government bodies. This trend was particularly noticeable in 1948 and 1949, when it became increasingly common, though by no means standard, to substitute the title "Chief in Council" for "Chief" in referring to the Native Authority.[14]

Government policy regarding local government remained essentially the same as that instituted by Sir Donald Cameron more than twenty years before. In 1952 it was restated as follows:

The underlying principle has been to leave the conduct of local affairs to those who under established indigenous constitutions are the recognized tribal authorities and command the respect and confidence of the people, while at the same time taking every possible step to hasten the change over from the traditional to a modern system of administration.[15]

This process of evolutionary change began during the period of the Mandate, when the chiefs of some of the smaller tribes banded together to form a federation or council of chiefs to act as the primary Native Authority for a certain area. One such amalgamation was a federation of nine Sukuma chiefdoms, but it never really got off its feet because of the divergent interests of the parties concerned. This federation did not include all the Sukuma people, and in 1942 the question of a formal union of all the Sukuma chiefdoms was broached. Eventually, in October 1946, a union of the seven Sukuma federations of chiefs took place—i.e., a union of the 51 chiefs of the Sukuma people. Except for two islands in Lake Victoria, this federation, known as the Sukumaland Federation, occupied the entire land area of four districts of Lake Province and included an estimated 1,000,000 people in 1950. Its headquarters was established at Malya in Maswa District. The Sukumaland Federal Council was gazetted as a supreme Native Authority, all other Native Authorities being subordinate to it. The Council deals with matters of policy and local legislation and controls the amalgamated treasury of the tribe.[16]

Another important council of chiefs, also established in 1946, was the reorganized Chagga Council. The Chagga have often been recognized as one of the most progressive tribes in Tanganyika. Until 1946, however, their council "was conspicuous mainly for its contentious debates and its inability to arrive at any joint decisions." This was no doubt partly due to the fact that the nineteen Chagga chiefdoms were all treated with equal standing though they varied greatly in size. Not only was this system ineffective as an agency of local administration, but there was wide dissatisfaction among the more advanced elements of the Chagga at the position accorded to the chiefs. In 1948 the reorganization of the Chagga into three main sections, each gazetted as a separate Native Authority, recognized the natural divisions of the people. Each of these sections had a Superior Chief, who was assisted by a deputy selected by the people of the section. Each Superior Chief had a council of advisers that included some representatives chosen by the people. The new Chagga Council consisted of the three Superior Chiefs, each aided by nine of their advisers. Further reorganization during the following years resulted in the people's being able to take a more direct part in the management of the tribe's financial affairs.[17]

Except for the Chagga Council and the Sukumaland Federation, the other native administrations visited by the 1948 Mission appeared generally "to be weak and unprepared for progressive development toward self-governing institutions." The government, however, announced its intention of correcting this situation in a memorandum given to the Mission by the Secretary for African Affairs: "The establishment of a stable and efficient—and to some extent integrated—system of local government is an essential first step [toward self-government], and will occupy all the Government's efforts and attention for a long time ahead." This statement did not deter the Mission from criticizing the Administration for "an apparent void" of long-range plans for political development in Tanganyika.[18]

The British government reacted with some heat to the criticisms of the Visiting Mission. As part of its observations on the report, the Administering Authority wrote:

The development of democratic political institutions among the indigenous inhabitants must inevitably be gradual if they are to rest on a solid and lasting foundation. . . . If primitive African peoples are to play their part willingly and confidently in political advancement towards the ideals of a free democracy, the first stage of the advance must be erected on the foundations of their own political conceptions and traditions, which must be modified and adapted to the new order by a steady process of education and guidance.

. . . It is quite impracticable and would serve no good purpose to formulate definite plans at this state for the "precise manner" in which these developments shall take place.[19]

The Visiting Mission also expressed concern over what it regarded as "the tendency of Native Administrations, even in the form of federations, to develop in isolation from each other." It feared that this "might result in a separatism and provincialism inimical to the unity necessary for political advancement."[20] Sir Donald Cameron, it will be remembered, had pointed out this danger many years before. The Administering Authority attempted to reassure the Trusteeship Council that this was not the case:

On the contrary, the development of tribal federations and amalgamations is one of the most important steps in the process of bringing Native Administrations into closer relationship with one another. Disconnected tribal units must be welded together before the different tribes can be brought into closer relationship and be more closely integrated with the central government.[21]

As a means of counteracting what it considered to be divisive tendencies in the existing Native Authority system, the Mission proposed that multiracial district and provincial councils be established and also an African territorial council. It suggested that the members of these councils should be elected directly by the people, or if this were not possible, through an indirect electoral system.[22] Some representative African area and district councils were already in operation in different parts of the territory. The Administering Authority recognized that the first step toward a sound system of local government was to secure popular representation in the tribal organization; but until such a system had been consolidated, popular representation on higher-level councils was not thought to be practical. With respect to the establishment of multiracial provincial councils as proposed by the Mission, the Administering Authority stated that this was already government policy.

Such a council is now being set up in the Lake Province and is to serve as a guide and to provide the necessary experience for similar action in other provinces. The aim is to establish councils of this nature in all provinces, but the speed at which this can be done must necessarily be governed largely by local conditions. . . .

Provincial councils will at first necessarily be largely consultative and advisory but the importance of expanding their executive and financial responsibilities is fully appreciated.[23]

The Mission's suggestion of an African territorial council was rejected for the time being.

Tanganyika's first Provincial Council was inaugurated at Mwanza, in Lake Province, in June 1949. It was composed of official and unofficial members from the European, African, and Asian communities. The following November, Governor Twining recommended that similar councils with "some form of popular support" and considerable local financial responsibility be established in all the provinces. If they functioned satisfactorily, he suggested that they might become electoral colleges for the appointment of unofficial members to the Legislative Council, a proposal previously made by the Visiting Mission. The Governor pointed out that such councils would put into practice the two most important factors necessary for political advancement in Tanganyika, namely, interracial cooperation and "building from the bottom."[24] A second Provincial Council, similar to the Lake Province one, was established in Southern Highlands Province in March 1950.

Below the provincial level, African local government developed somewhat unevenly from one area to another during this period. The Native Authorities varied greatly in size and in the extent of their development. Where possible, attempts were made to change the traditional tribal system of rule into more modern forms of local government at the district level and below that at the divisional level. Progress made in grafting popular representation onto the existing institutions was summed up as follows in 1950:

The degree of popular representation tends to rise from the lower to the higher levels of government. Many village councils have been formed, commoners being selected by popular acclaim. Sub-chiefs in charge of village groups are increasingly accepting people's members on their councils. All chiefs' councils now include a certain number of elected members, while at the District level the chiefs sit together with commoners in the all-African District Councils.[25]

In all but a few areas, the move to associate popular representation with the Native Authorities was well in advance of public opinion. Many of the chiefs were in agreement with the government's aim of greater democratization; "progress is limited not so much by overt opposition from vested hereditary interests, therefore, as by apathy and ignorance on the part of the people."[26] However, it was encouraging for "officers combatting apathy and ineffectiveness to find that live interest in the new institutions often follows their creation."[27] Governor Twining predicted in 1951 that the forms of African local government being instituted would come to "play a very valuable part in African life." He found it heartening "to find examples of Native Authorities becoming local government bodies dealing effectively, not only with tribal matters but with the affairs of migrant Natives, who in some instances outnumber the local tribesmen."[28]

In 1951 the Committee on Constitutional Development, in its recommendations regarding Tanganyika's future political development, proposed the creation of County Councils in which Africans, Asians, and Europeans should be represented. It suggested that these councils, which would cover an area of several districts, should deal with matters that were of common interest to all races. The Committee felt that County Councils would be more genuine local government units than Provincial Councils, and suggested that some of the functions of the Native Authorities might be transferred to them; it was not proposed, however, that the councils should exercise control over the Native Authorities. Finally, it was the Committee's opinion that the creation of County Councils would promote interracial cooperation:

In our opinion inter-racial cooperation is easier of achievement in dealing with local affairs than those of central government. Racial relationships are less complicated and people know each other better. We consider therefore that the establishment of these councils would stimulate interracial cooperation and afford facilities for the political education of all races.[29]

One of the tasks assigned to Professor Mackenzie on his appointment as Special Commissioner was to review the Committee's proposals for interracial local government. He concluded that the recommendation for the creation of County Councils was sound. He felt that there were a number of areas in which such councils could be started almost at once on the lines proposed by the Committee, provided that an ordinance were so framed that the composition and powers of the councils could be varied a good deal to suit local circumstances. He listed eight areas in which he considered councils should be formed immediately and specified that they should have a majority of African unofficial members. He further recommended that the whole territory be divided into county areas, but that this scheme be realized gradually, in step with economic and social development, since he viewed rapid political development with some trepidation: "Relations between races and communities in Tanganyika are at present good; but there is a general lack of political experience and there is a real danger that good relations might deteriorate if there were to be rapid political development."[30]

Mackenzie's proposals were accepted, with modifications, and in 1953 the Legislative Council enacted the Local Government Ordinance. It came into effect the following year. The Ordinance provided for the constitution of County and Local Councils, the Local Councils being intended gradually to replace the Native Authorities. They were to be composed of nominated or elected members, or a combination of them; no specific reference was made to traditional status as a qualification for membership, nor was membership limited to Africans. Section 3 of the Ordinance was added in committee at the request of unofficial members of all three races: "Before any authority is established under this ordinance the member shall have satisfied himself from such enquiries as he has made or has caused to be made that there is among the inhabitants of and residents in the area concerned a general wish that the authority should be established."[31]

Under the new Ordinance, the first Local Council was established at Newala in December 1954. It took over full executive responsibility in the area at the local government level. The Council was composed of 7 official members and a maximum of 35 other members nominated by the Provincial Commissioner, Southern Province. The Newala Local Council was the outgrowth of an experiment in interracial cooperation in rural local government begun the year before. The district council, which was already in existence, co-opted a European settler, two European mission representatives, and two Asian traders. A second Local Council was established on Mafia Island in

July 1955. Its composition was similar to that of the Newala Council, and it also contained representatives from all three racial communities.

The first County Council, the South East Lake County Council, was established in May 1955. It covered eight districts, including the five Sukumaland districts, the total area containing a population of one and a half million Africans, 9,000 Asians, and 1,200 Europeans.[32] The Council consisted of 54 members, including representatives of the three racial communities. At the end of 1954 a similar council was under consideration for Southern Highlands Province. All such councils were intended to be interracial bodies. According to the 1954 annual report on Tanganyika, "it is the policy of the Government to encourage the setting up of these advanced councils wherever public opinion has shown that it desires and supports such changes."[33]

So far our discussion has dealt with what may be generally classified as rural area councils, rather than with urban area councils. Obviously some form of local government was needed in the cities and towns, which usually were not included in the area governed through the Native Authority system. At the end of 1951 there were 30 Township Authorities in the territory and one Municipal Council, in Dar es Salaam, a common factor to all being some degree of interracial participation in local government.

Township Authorities usually consisted of a number of officials and a varying number of unofficials nominated by the Provincial Commissioner. The Dar es Salaam Municipal Council, created on January 1, 1949, consisted of 24 appointed members, 7 members from each racial community, and 3 Europeans representing government interests. Each year the members elected the city's mayor from their own number.[34]

The report of the Committee on Constitutional Development also included recommendations concerning urban local government. These were as follows: that the Township Authorities include fewer official and more unofficial members; that nonracial elective representation be introduced in the urban areas, particularly in Dar es Salaam; that legislation be enacted to enable the townships to progress by stages to financial and political autonomy, six townships being named as already qualifying for this status; and that Dar es Salaam develop into an all-purpose local government body independent of the County Council system. [35]

Subsequently, the Local Government Ordinance of 1953 included a provision enabling local government bodies to achieve an autonomous status known as Town Councils. The first Town Council was established at Tanga in August 1954 and consisted of 24 members, 8 representatives from each racial community. Three more Town Councils, all of them interracial bodies, came into existence at Lindi, Arusha, and Mwanza on January 1, 1955. As for the Township Authorities, in most cases they contained an unofficial majority by the end of 1954. Membership was interracial, Africans either having equal representation, or, in a number of cases, being in the majority.

Progress in developing the machinery of African local government in the rural areas continued during these years. In 1951, in response to requests by members of the Chagga tribe, the Governor appointed a committee of 5 Europeans and 26 Africans who were widely representative of the tribe to make recommendations on local government. As a result of their recommendations, the Chagga Council and all subordinate councils were considerably enlarged to provide for greater popular representation. The Chagga Council contained 19 ex officio, 16 directly elected, 6 indirectly elected, and 6 co-opted members.

In accordance with another recommendation, the Council then nominated candidates for election as Chief of the Chagga. The Chief was to be the keystone of the Chagga political system, the symbol of the unity of the Chagga tribe, and the principal liaison between the Chagga Council and the government. The four candidates were the three divisional chiefs and one government servant, Thomas Marealle, a grandson of a leading chief who had died in 1915. Marealle, supported by the Kilimanjaro Citizens Union, won the election and was duly installed as Chief at the official opening of the new Chagga Council early in January 1952. Chief Marealle was one of the official guests at Westminster Abbey for Queen Elizabeth's coronation.[36]

During 1953 the Nyamwezi people of the Kahama, Nzega, and Tabora districts joined in the Nyamwezi Federation, which possessed a strong representative federal council and an executive committee.

Also in 1953 a new constitution for the Meru chiefdom was drawn up in consultation with the people. This provided for a representative council, with the Mangi (Chief) as chairman, and an executive council for the conduct of day-to-day business. The selection of the Mangi was to be by secret ballot, with special provisions for voting by illiterates. During 1953 a central school was opened at Mzumbe in Eastern Province for training Native Authority staff.

The organization of African district councils continued throughout the territory. By the end of 1952 they had been organized in almost all districts of Central Province, "although here, with rare exceptions, the councils have been brought into being to stimulate public interest in local government and not to meet a popular demand."[37] During the next two years, many of the district councils co-opted nonofficials from all races. It was hoped that the future statutory County and Local Councils would grow from these councils. Seventy-seven local government bodies of various kinds, all with interracial membership were in operation by the end of 1954.[38] Elections for members of district, divisional, and other councils were widespread throughout the territory.

INTERTERRITORIAL ORGANIZATION

Another aspect of Tanganyika's political development during the years 1945–54 was its ties with Kenya and Uganda through interterritorial organizations. Formal relations between the three territories continued to be developed by means of the Governors' Conference and its permanent Secretariat until the end of World War II. The coming of the war had shown a need for greater cooperation between the territories; the East African Production Supply Council and a number of other bodies were accordingly set up to coordinate the economy and the manpower of the East African countries. By the end of 1944, "the process of collaboration in many fields had resulted in an organic growth which, based on the Secretariat of the Governor's Conference, was in effect a form of central administration for a large group of subjects."[39]

It was felt, however, that the organization was incomplete; both the railways and the customs departments were outside it. Futher-more, the central administration that had grown up had no consti-tutional existence. It was therefore proposed in 1945 to attempt some measure for dealing with services common to the three territories without reopening the question of political union.

It became clear, however, that a forum for public discussion, in the nature of a central legislative body, would be a necessary feature of any machinery if it were to work successfully. Tentative proposals were put forward at the end of 1945 in Colonial Paper No. 191 as a basis for discussion. It was emphasized that the proposals were in no sense a step toward political union of the three territories, but were designed for closer economic coordination in the future development of East Africa. "After considerable debate and controversy and fol-lowing a visit from Mr. Creech Jones, then Parliamentary Under-Secretary for the Colonies, public opinion of all shades in East Africa came to be very much more favourably disposed towards the whole conception."[40] Revised proposals containing modifications to meet the objections of certain groups in East Africa were published in Colonial Paper No. 210 in early 1947, and were accepted by the Legis-lative Councils of the three territories. Accordingly, by the East Africa (High Commission) Order in Council of December 1947, the East Africa High Commission and Central Legislative Assembly came into being, with effect from January 1, 1948.

The question of representation on the Central Legislative Assem-bly had been the main source of controversy in East Africa during the two years that the proposals were under consideration. Originally it was proposed that the Assembly consist of 12 official members and 18 unofficial members, 6 of whom would be European and 6 Asian, together with 6 members to be nominated by the Governors of the three territories; it was hoped that as many as possible of the last group would be Africans. This proposal for equal representation of the races was welcomed by the leaders of the Asian and African com-munities, but strongly opposed by the Europeans. The government was forced to modify its position. The proposals in Colonial Paper No. 210 were thus accepted by the Europeans, but opposed by the Asians and Africans. "Official sources repudiated the suggestion that the principle of 'equal representation' had been abandoned, but the fact remains that the European leaders felt able to assure their followers that the European unofficial numbers in the Legislative Assembly would in practice be found to equal in number the representatives of other races."[41]

The High Commission, consisting of the Governors of Kenya, Tanganyika, and Uganda, had its headquarters in Nairobi, Kenya. The Central Legislative Assembly normally met in Nairobi, but was free to hold occasional meetings in Uganda or Tanganyika. It consisted of seven ex officio members who were officers in the service of the High Commission, three nominated official members, and thirteen unofficial members. With the consent of the Assembly, the High Commission could legislate with respect to a defined range of interterritorial services. It was responsible for administering the railway, harbor, post and telegraph, and customs and excise services, as well as the joint research and scientific services. Thus the Commission did not deal with political issues or control domestic policies; in fact, it was effective only with the cooperation of the three territorial governments.

European opinion in Tanganyika regarding interterritorial reorganization was divided. Some followed the Kenya settlers' example of categorical rejection of the original proposals made in 1945. Others were willing to accept the proposals as a basis for discussion. The latter group, moreover, resented the action of the European elected members of the Kenya Legislative Council who had sent the Tanganyika members a message attacking the proposals as "a grave menace to the future of the British European communities of these territories." Speaking on behalf of his European colleagues, an unofficial member of the Tanganyika Council deplored consideration of the scheme from a racial viewpoint.[42]

Although Africans in all three territories at first suspected the proposals in Colonial No. 191 of being the old bogey of closer union in disguise, Africans in Kenya and Uganda did eventually give their grudging support—after repeated assurances that the proposed reorganization was strictly economic in nature. Africans in Tanganyika, however, remained opposed to the proposals, regarding them as a trap to bring Tanganyika under the control of the Kenya settlers.[43] They therefore demanded greater assurances regarding African representation on the Central Assembly and on the boards and committees of the High Commission.[44] Indian opinion in Tanganyika mirrored that of the African community in respect to Colonial No. 191. Indians "were utterly opposed to anything which they considered might extend or strengthen the Kenya 'settler influence' in East African affairs."[45]

The picture changed considerably with the publication of the British government's revised proposals in 1947. In Kenya and Uganda, Africans and Indians who had been willing to go along with the initial proposals now found themselves in firm opposition to the new version; Europeans in Kenya who had found the proposals unacceptable favored those of Colonial No. 210, since they realized that this was the best they were going to get. In Tanganyika, Asians and Africans, joined by Europeans from the south, were amazed at Creech Jones's new proposals.

By his action Labor's Colonial Secretary had seemed to them to heed the entreaties of the settlers more than those of the less impassioned and less vocal multitudes of Kenya, Uganda and Tanganyika. Now the trend seemed clearly against them, and the Africans, Indians and their European allies acted hastily to regain their lost momentum. Each of these communities pilloried Colonial 210 in swift succession.[46]

The revised proposals were discussed in an Extraordinary Meeting of the Tanganyika Legislative Council held on April 15 and 16, 1947. I. C. Chopra, an Indian member of the Council, opposed in principle any union or amalgamation of any of the Tanganyika services with those of Kenya. He felt that Tanganyika had sufficient resources to exist independently of Kenya. Another Council member, V. M. Nazerali, supported Chopra's arguments and called the Council's attention to the categorical rejection by the Indian Association of Colonial No. 210. Chief Abdiel Shangali and Chief Kidaha Makwaia, the two African members, asked that consideration of the proposals be postponed because their constituents had not had enough time to become fully acquainted with the modified version. The following day the Chief Secretary stated that it was not possible to grant postponement, and later that day a motion favoring the acceptance of the revised proposals was carried by a large margin. All the official members and all the European members supported the motion, although some of the European members had reservations; the Asian members voted against the motion, and the African members abstained for the reason already stated.[47]

After Colonial Paper No. 210 had been brought into effect, public opinion in Tanganyika at first remained opposed to the closer ties with Kenya. An acute apprehension about the interterritorial organization on the part of articulate sections of the African and Asian communities and "an almost unanimous opposition" to it were noted by the 1948 Visiting Mission.[48] Public opinion, however, gradually changed, and in 1951 the Tanganyika Legislative Council voted unanimously to renew the life of the Central Legislative Assembly. This change of attitude was partly attributable to a statement made by James Griffiths, the Secretary of State for the Colonies, in December 1950 concerning the future course of political development in East Africa: "I have come to the conclusion that it will be best to pursue the matter, for the time being at any rate, separately in each territory rather than on a general East African basis."[49] Public opinion was also shaped by the fact that the interterritorial organization had adhered closely to its economic tasks during the four years. Doubt continued to persist, however, as to the intentions of the Kenya Europeans, particularly because of their economic predominance and their attitude on race relations.

In 1953, serious concern arose over a statement by the new Colonial Secretary, Oliver Lyttleton, that apparently modified Griffiths' earlier pronouncement. The Federation of Rhodesia and Nyasaland had recently been brought into being in the face of strenuous objections from the African population of Nyasaland and Northern Rhodesia, and Africans and Asians in Tanganyika feared that the same thing might happen to them. Referring to the establishment of the Central African Federation, Lyttleton had stated: "Nor should we exclude from our minds the evolution, as time goes on, of still larger measures of unification and possibly still larger measures of federation of the whole East African territories."[50]

According to the 1954 Visiting Mission, opinion was still against any form of political federation with Kenya. Representatives of the Bahaya tribe asked for an assurance that Tanganyika would "not be federated till there is a desire and a specific demand and full consent of all the people of the Territory."[51] The Asian Association stated: "We believe that as long as our neighbours have not learned to have an equitable racial policy, no closer economic or political association can be a benefit to Tanganyika." The Association was dubious also about the economic benefits to Tanganyika of the existing interterritorial organization.[52] The apparatus by that time, however, was beginning to become a permanent fixture. Few complaints were raised at the second extension of the Central Legislative Assembly in 1955, an indication of public confidence.

European intentions to create an East African Federation aroused the uneasiness of the United Nations. Although Article 5(b) of the Trusteeship Agreement permitted the Administering Authority "to constitute Tanganyika into a customs, fiscal or administrative union or federation with adjacent territories under his control," such a move was required to conform with the objectives of the Trusteeship System. The establishment of interterritorial machinery in 1948 was criticized by nonadministering members of the United Nations in the Trusteeship Council and the General Assembly on two counts: first, that the move implied a political association with Uganda and Kenya that would ultimately destroy Tanganyika's status as a trust territory; and second, that the British government should have consulted the Trusteeship Council before establishing the administrative union. The British representative replied to these criticisms by "pointing out, first, that inclusion in the East Africa High Commission involved no change in Tanganyika's political status, and secondly, that, since the Trusteeship Agreement specifically permitted administrative unions, prior consultation with the Trusteeship Council was unnecessary."[53] In the end, the General Assembly endorsed an observation of the Trusteeship Council that an administrative union "must remain strictly administrative in its nature and its scope, and that its operation must not have the effect of creating any conditions which will obstruct the separate development of the Trust Territory . . . as a distinct entity."[54] The Trusteeship Council created a Standing Committee on Administrative Unions to watch further developments.

The 1948 Visiting Mission noted that the interterritorial organization, though not a purely administrative union since it possessed certain powers of legislation as well, appeared to be, nevertheless, "short of a complete political union." It added: "It would indeed be a political union if it possessed full powers of legislation and administration over any or all common services. At present the organization does not possess such full powers."[55] In its comments on the Mission's report, Britain assured the Trusteeship Council that "the operation of the Inter-Territorial Organization does not, and will not, prejudice the determination of the ultimate status of Tanganyika."[56]

Since 1948, the Trusteeship Council has become somewhat reconciled to the interterritorial organization. Discussion in the Council has become concerned more with the economic effects of the interterritorial machinery and less with the political effects. The East African Industrial Council, which has the power to regulate the establishment of certain industries in Tanganyika, has been particularly criticized. The Council considered that this body might prejudice economic development in Tanganyika and thus slow down the territory's progress toward self-government.[57] According to the 1951 Mission, "the inter-territorial arrangement on the existing basis is operating to the advantage of Tanganyika but . . . should be kept strictly within its present limits."[58] The 1954 Mission noted that there had been "a good deal of criticism of various aspects of the High Commission system by various sections of the non-African commercial community in particular." Much of this criticism concerned the industrial licensing system. However, the Mission concluded that there was "no clear evidence to prove that the present arrangements operate either to the advantage or the disadvantage of Tanganyika."[59]

LAND PROBLEMS

During the period 1945–54 certain aspects of the Tanganyika government's land policy became important political issues in the territory. In 1954 the Visiting Mission noted: "The land and its use and tenure comprise, in the African mind, the outstanding political and economic issue of the day; and the alienation of land in the past, and fears and suspicions as to what the future may hold, form the most delicate and sensitive side of that issue."[60] This impression was confirmed by Governor Twining, who considered land to be "probably the most sensitive subject in the African mind."[61]

The government's land policy with regard to alienation for non-African cultivation remained much the same following World War II as during the period of the Mandate. The basic law remained the Land Ordinance of 1923. The obligation to protect native land rights assumed by Britain in Article 8 of the Trusteeship Agreement was, except for the change of a few words, the same as that assumed in Article 6 of the Mandate Agreement.

Policy with regard to the future alienation of land to non-Africans was set out by Lord Hall, Secretary of State for the Colonies, in a letter to the Governor of Tanganyika in February 1946: "The needs of the African inhabitants of Tanganyika must have priority and land should not be allocated for non-native settlement . . . unless it can be shown that the land in question is not required for native occupation and is not likely to be required in the foreseeable future." With these provisions in mind, it was announced that schemes for nonnative settlement would be considered, since "a limited amount of non-native settlement . . . is likely to be conducive to the economic development of the Territory."[62] A statement by the Tanganyika government in 1953 reaffirmed the above policy, and a further stipulation provided that there should be no question of the best land being allocated for non-African settlement at the expense of the African population.[63]

Although the average density of population is very low in Tanganyika, there are some areas where pressure on the land exists. According to a statement made by the Administering Authority:

The various contributory causes include encroachment by the tsetse fly, rapid increase in population, both human and stock, and primitive systems of land usage resulting in soil exhaustion and erosion. In one or two cases the position has been aggravated by the extent of land alienation during the period of the former German administration.

The statement further noted that the situation in Arusha and Moshi districts of Northern Province was "complicated by extensive land alienation."[64] As already mentioned, attempts had been made during the Mandate period to alleviate the land congestion in these districts. In 1946 the government appointed the Arusha-Moshi Lands Commission, with Justice Mark Wilson as Commissioner, to formulate a comprehensive plan for the redistribution of alienated and tribal lands in these districts. Recommendations were to aim at "improving the homogeneity of alienated and tribal lands respectively; affording relief to congestion of the native population in tribal lands."[65]

Wilson spent the second half of 1946 making a personal survey of the land problem in the Arusha and Moshi districts. He found that there were some 250 alienated holdings totaling approximately 183,-000 acres in Moshi District and 220 holdings totaling approximately 141,000 acres in Arusha District. After asking African and European farmers and local government officials for their views about what should be done to alleviate the land congestion on Mount Kilimanjaro and Mount Meru, Wilson drew up his recommendations. They covered both immediate and long-term policy. As a means of affording some immediate relief for the congested areas, he recommended that certain alienated lands, including former German properties seized at the outbreak of World War II and some of the surplus land held by missions, should be acquired and made available for tribal occupation. Although the Chagga and certain local government officials strongly advocated the return of all alienated land on the southern slopes of Mount Kilimanjaro, Wilson took the view that even if this were practicable, it would not solve the problem in the long run. He therefore recommended opening up new land below the European holdings on both mountains to provide room for tribal expansion.

Although the Commission's terms of reference called for recommendations aimed at "improving the homogeneity of alienated and tribal lands," Wilson did not consider any wholesale redistribution of tribal and alienated lands to be practicable. He admitted that homogeneous grouping of land would have certain advantages, but was doubtful whether that "ideal" should be pursued in Tanganyika.

Should not the Government of a mandated or trust Territory avoid doing anything which contributes to the perpetuation of tribal, racial and colour divisions? Should it not rather so arrange matters that all who live in the Territory within the King's peace can live side by side and be treated equally under the law as inhabitants of the Territory irrespective of their native or non-native origin? Should not the same social amenities be allowed and the same anti-disease measures be applied to all? Is it necessary or desirable to segregate races each of which has something to contribute to the welfare of the other and the common good?[66]

In Arusha District, however, Wilson did recommend certain adjustments aimed at creating a homogeneous area of non-African settlement; these recommendations were made in order to accommodate a government plan to establish a dairying industry in the area.

The 1948 Visiting Mission reported that the opposition of some Africans to Wilson's proposals was, in the main, based on his recommendation that some of the German farms should be re-alienated to European use. The African Association of Arusha and the Chagga Council both thought that these farms should be returned to the Africans; the Arusha group proposed that the Africans pay for them on an installment basis. The Mission therefore recommended that, as a general policy, all former German estates be placed under African ownership. The Administering Authority opposed this recommendation for the following reason:

The estates in question include some of the most productive sisal and coffee plantations in Tanganyika, run on European commercial lines, and their transfer to tribal occupation in the present stage of development of African agricultural practice and technique would inevitably lead to the loss of the advantages of large-scale production methods, a decrease in output and a drop in exports, with consequent adverse repercussions on the Territory's financial position.[67]

Noting the concern of Africans at the expansion of European settlement in Tanganyika, the Mission also proposed that "European colonization should be curtailed and the strictest control exercised to keep it at the barest minimum consistent with the development of the Territory and the present and long-range needs and interests of the African inhabitants."[68] The Administering Authority did not consider this proposal to be "a truly realistic appreciation of the position." It went on to say:

. . . there are large areas in Tanganyika which are capable of development within measurable time only by non-indigenous effort, areas where there is no present pressure of indigenous population and where there will be no such pressure for many years to come. It is also an indisputable fact that, unless every practicable step is taken to promote the development of the Territory, its capacity to finance much-needed expansion in education, health, social welfare and other social services must be affected adversely.[69]

In 1948 the government began to reallocate to selected applicants many of the German farms seized at the outbreak of World War II. In all cases freehold titles were extinguished, and Rights of Occupancy were granted for an initial term of 33 years with the possibility of renewal. This process of re-alienation was completed in 1951. Alienation of land other than former German properties was also resumed in 1948, and in 1950 grants for 99 years were again permitted, except in the congested areas of the Moshi and Arusha districts. The additional acreages of land issued under Rights of Occupancy amounted to 42,975 acres in 1948, to 71,959 acres in 1949, and to 124,368 acres in 1950.[70]

By the end of 1951 the total area alienated to nonindigenous persons, including companies and various missionary bodies, amounted to 2,284,434 acres. Of this area, 1,333,487 acres were held in leasehold and 950,947 acres in freehold.[71] This compared with the 1948 figure of 1,846,278 acres for the total area of alienated land, of which 1,058,240 acres were held under freehold title and 788,038 acres under Rights of Occupancy.[72] The amount of land held in freehold decreased during the three-year period owing to the fact that the German farms, formerly held under freehold title, were re-alienated under Rights of Occupancy or returned to African use. Out of a total area of 123,000,-000 acres suitable for agricultural purposes, 1,846,278 acres had been alienated by 1948, and 4,487,722 acres were under indigenous cultivation.[73] Therefore, in the territory as a whole there was no shortage of agricultural land, except in a few places where too much alienation had occurred; however, the figures do show the large role played by nonindigenous cultivation in the agricultural economy.

The recommendations of the Arusha-Moshi Lands Commission were approved, with certain modifications, by the British government in 1949, and most of them had been put into effect in Arusha District by the end of 1951. Here, a total area of 11,190 acres of formerly alienated land was acquired for tribal occupation. In addition, a new area of some 159,000 acres adjoining the Meru tribal lands on the lower slopes of the mountain was being opened up for settlement. In Moshi District the Chagga had been provided with some 4,500 acres of land that either had been made available from former German estates or had been compulsorily acquired by the government for this purpose in exchange for other lands.[74]

New alienations of land on a leasehold basis continued during the years 1952–54. Long-term Rights of Occupancy over agricultural and pastoral land granted in 1952 involved a total area of 731,632 acres; this figure included 334,728 acres allocated to the Overseas Food Corporation during the previous five years in connection with the notorious groundnut scheme, the final grant and registration of this land not being completed until 1952.[75] Further alienations for agricultural purposes totaled 186,691 acres in 1953[76] and 91,672 acres in 1954. Long-term Rights of Occupancy over agricultural and pastoral land on register at the end of 1954 involved a total of 2,180,166 acres.[77] This figure, added to the 730,000 acres held under freehold at the end of 1954, gives a total of 2,910,166 acres alienated in the territory.[78] This compared with a total alienated area of 1,846,278 acres in 1948 and 2,284,434 acres in 1951. During this period, land held under freehold decreased by about 30 per cent. The total number of holdings under Rights of Occupancy at the end of 1954 was 1,476, the main nationalities being British (443), Indian or Pakistani (274), and Greek (247).[79]

The 1954 Visiting Mission emphasized "that where the problem of land is at its most acute in either the political or economic sense, or both, the alienations cover some of the best land in the territory, the greater part of it taken in German times and in some cases ex-

tended since then." The recent course of land alienations had caused
many Africans to feel apprehensive about the future; some of them,
however, used alienation of land to non-Africans as "a scapegoat for
land problems which do not directly stem from it." In any case, land
alienation on the slopes of the northern mountains had created "real
economic problems" and had "at the same time created political fears
and suspicions not only there but also in Mwanza, Tabora, Tukuyu,
Dar es Salaam and wherever else African political leaders have a
following."[80] For example, the TANU branch at Musoma told the
Mission that immigration was against the wishes of the African people and should be stopped, with the exception of government officials.
A spokesman stated: "We do not mind the officials; we don't like
settlers."[81]

The land problem continued to be at its most acute in Northern
Province. According to the 1954 Mission, factors increasing the pressure on the land were a rate of population growth among Africans
that was higher than the Tanganyika average, African interest in
cash crops, the accumulation of land by some individual African
farmers, and the influx and settlement over the years of Africans
alien to the area. "But the factor which seemed to the Mission to be,
in the African mind, the most critical, is that of European settlement."
Alienation in Arusha District had been so extensive that "the amount
of land alienated to a few hundred persons is larger than the amount
available for settlement by Africans, who now number perhaps
120,000." In Moshi District, among the Chagga, the Mission did not
consider the immediate problem to be so acute.[82]

The Chagga themselves, however, were worried about the future
because they expected their population to double within another generation, and therefore additional land would be needed. For this
reason the Mission admitted that the Chagga probably had the greatest
problem in the long run. Opinion among these tribes was that all
alienated land on the southern slopes of Mount Kilimanjaro should
eventually be returned to them. The Mission recorded concern also
among the Arusha about 1,000 young men for whom no land was
available; the tribal council accused the government of having alienated land without paying proper attention to the rate of increase in

population. The Arusha and the Masai both complained that the government was alienating land without consulting the tribal authorities.[83]

The Mission also reported that the Meru tribe was highly incensed over the recent establishment of a large European dairying industry. This scheme, already mentioned in connection with the Wilson Report (p. 115), had necessitated the alienation of 78,000 acres of land. In late 1951 about 1,000 members of the tribe had been forcibly evicted from two farms (covering some 5,345 acres) that were inside the area to be included in the dairying scheme. The evicted families were moved 35 miles away, to new land that had recently been opened up by the government. Finding this land not to their liking, they returned to other tribal lands and took up residence there. A representative of the Meru Citizens Union twice took the case to the United Nations in 1951, first to the Trusteeship Council and later to the Fourth Committee, but was unable to get the United Nations to force Great Britain to restore the two farms to the evicted families.

Two years later, at the time of the Mission's visit, the tribe was still insisting on the return of the two farms. The matter had grown all out of proportion. The Mission noted that "the eviction case is . . . widely known and talked about—and for the most part with sympathy for the Meru—among more educated Africans from one end of the Territory to the other."[84] The Meru case had become "a by-word among politically conscious Africans . . . not so much for the sake of the Meru people as because of the doubts which their case has raised as to the whole meaning and intention of non-African, and especially European, settlement in the Territory."[85]

The Mission discussed the matter with the Governor and his senior officers, and was told that whenever farms bordering on the lands occupied by the Meru became available in the future, the government would, "in allocating these lands to Africans, take into consideration the needs of the Meru." Although the Mission welcomed this statement, it remained seriously concerned about the rift that had developed between the African farmer and the European settler, and declared that it was "a matter of urgency to effect a reconciliation of the Meru people with the Government." It added: "Two dominant impressions left with the Mission are the understandably enormous importance that the African attaches to his land, and the danger to peace that springs from its disregard."[86]

In conclusion, the Mission made the following observations. It stated that the government's land policy did not "take sufficient account of the political and economic realities of the situation in Tanganyika . . . or of the trends in land policy which are already appearing." It accused the government of having underestimated the Africans' capacity for modern development.

It believes that this under-estimation, even if there were no other reasons, serves largely to explain why too much land has been alienated for either the economic or the political good of Tanganyika, and why African resistance against alienation is so serious a political matter at present.[87]

With regard to the land problems of the Chagga, Meru, and Arusha peoples, the Mission considered that "the existence in their midst of an unusual number of large farms owned or occupied by a few hundred individual non-Africans but capable of being farmed intensively and well by some thousands of Africans is an anomaly in the economic sense and a serious condition politically." The Mission welcomed a statement by the Governor that it was unlikely that much more land would be alienated for individual European agricultural settlement. However, it considered that this kind of alienation should be stopped altogether, since it was "politically undesirable and economically of doubtful advantage." The Mission also considered that the terms of leases should be limited to 25 or 30 years (instead of 99 years), after which time they would be subject to renewal. It felt that the government should give the assurance "that when leases are revoked or expire for any cause the land will revert automatically to the Africans." These last three proposals did not have the support of the Mission's chairman, J. S. Reid, who felt it was premature to discuss these issues, since they were being considered at that time by the Royal Commission on land and population questions in East Africa.

The Mission concluded its observations by urging the government to intensify its policy of reacquiring alienated land for African use and to carry out an extensive public inquiry, with full African participation, into the matter of land redistribution.[88]

A DECADE OF POLITICAL EVOLUTION

In summing up Tanganyika's over-all progress toward self-government or independence during the postwar decade, the 1954 Visiting Mission recorded that it was "impressed by the Government's general flexibility of approach, its willingness to experiment, and its desire to consult public opinion" in carrying out a transfer of authority and responsibility for local affairs to the local level. At the level of central government, although greater participation of nonofficials was beginning to take place, progress was "more gradual." Nevertheless, the Mission noted "that a constitutional structure exists which can be regarded as the nucleus around which democratic institutions of self-government can evolve."

At both levels the Mission had reservations about the rate of progress and about the government's policy with regard to the representation of African and non-African sections of the population.[89] Although the territory still had no suffrage law, the Mission pointed out the following:

The Government has accepted as a general principle that the ultimate goal should be a system of common roll elections with safeguards for minority representation; its announced policy is to proceed gradually in this matter until there is a general demand for elections, which it expects to arise (and is at present encouraging) in urban areas first, then in the new county areas, and finally in territorial constituencies represented in the Legislative Council.[90]

The Mission had "no doubt of the Government's intention eventually to supplant the nomination system by an elective one," and it considered that the government's policy at the local level bore witness to this.[91]

These comments by the 1954 Visiting Mission support the position taken by Margaret Bates in 1955 that "the Tanganyika government and the Colonial Office should be given credit for trying to achieve" the objective of self-governing political institutions called for by the Trusteeship Agreement. She points out that the British government often felt the criticism of its policies was unfair in that progress which had been made was not recognized. Since the Trusteeship Council is composed of official representatives of the United Nations members, rather than independent experts serving in their individual capacities as in the case of the Permanent Mandates Commission, political factors were increasingly brought to the fore. With reference to Tanganyika, Miss Bates notes that "anti-colonial feeling in the United Nations has frequently been more vigorous than in the territory itself, which has remained politically placid."[92] The first genuinely nationalist political organization, the Tanganyika African National Union, was established only in 1954. From the beginning it exhibited a remarkably reasonable attitude toward the colonial administration. It is significant that in its discussions with the Visiting Mission TANU's central committee considered ignorance and poverty, not lack of self-government, to be the most pressing of the problems facing the African population.[93]

The problem of political evolution in Tanganyika at this time was as much a human problem as anything else. The pace of political development in the future depended in large measure upon a parallel growth in racial understanding. F. M. van Asbeck has stated that "the beginnings of political reform and reconciliation in a multi-racial society lie in humane relations between people of different race."[94] Referring to this statement, A. K. Datta wrote in 1955: "The 'cold war' between racial groups . . . may not be settled by a more human attitude to one another, but it certainly leads to an atmosphere of détente, thereby providing an opportunity to all concerned to find a basis of understanding."[95]

The report of the 1954 Visiting Mission left no doubt that Tanganyika was far from having achieved racial harmony. On the other hand, the racial problem was not nearly so acute in Tanganyika as in some other parts of Africa.

In early 1955 Miss Bates reported "a growing feeling of nationality in the territory," which resulted in "pressure for the creation of a Tanganyika nationality as such." For the first time, racial groups were willing, to some extent, to give up their special positions.[96] As for the European community, the 1954 Mission stated that nowhere in the territory did it "hear from any organized group any assertions of special European rights of the kind heard by the previous missions."[97]

The stage was thus set for the six-year period of increased political activity that was to follow. As E. R. Danielson, superintendent of the Lutheran Church of Northern Tanganyika, had remarked to the 1954 Mission, these years were to be the crucial period for the development of a genuine multiracial society in Tanganyika. And, as Danielson further predicted, it was the Europeans, as a race, for whom the adjustment to a nonsegregated, nondiscriminatory society proved to be most difficult.[98]

6

POLITICAL DEVELOPMENTS
1955–1958

"U.N. Mission Proposes Timetable for Tanganyika" was the chief headline of Dar es Salaam's *Tanganyika Standard* on the morning of January 26, 1955. The article began:

In a lengthy report published today, the United Nations Visiting Mission which toured Tanganyika for five weeks last year outlines its impressions and puts forward several drastic recommendations, particularly relating to political development.

The mission looks forward to a Legislative Council with a majority of Africans on the unofficial benches at the end of three years from the commencement of the "parity" period, and self-government within 20 or 25 years.

The chairman of the mission, Mr. J. S. Reid, from New Zealand, disagrees with the majority view that constitutional progress should be speeded up and approves, in general, the present cautious approach of the Government.

The article went on to summarize the Mission's observations relating to Tanganyika's political advancement. Two other headlines of articles appearing on the front page of the same issue read, "U.N. Timetables Unacceptable to U.K. Government" and "Sir Eldred Hitchcock Condemns Report and Calls for Rejection."

Such was the initial reaction in Tanganyika to the 1954 report. During the next few weeks the Mission's proposals were applauded vigorously by some and condemned just at vigorously by others. A month later the dispute was carried to the chamber of the Trusteeship Council itself.

The most controversial of the Mission's proposals concerned a timetable for political development in the territory and a statement regarding the ultimate form of government for Tanganyika. The Mission expressed the view that "no stability is possible unless it is made clear that the goal is the government of the country mainly by Africans" and it reported that "among a number of the better-educated Africans who are in a position to influence public opinion there is a desire for a more definite sense of direction than they now have regarding the future development of the territory." The Mission considered that the doubts and uncertainties of Africans who viewed the government's multiracial policy as endangering their conception of Tanganyika as an ultimately African state should be resolved. If they were not resolved, they were bound to spread. In that case "doubt may become suspicion and uncertainty become frustration." According to the Mission, this could be prevented "by providing an outlet for legitimate aspirations. . . . Nothing is at once more inspiring and constructive than planned political development towards the ultimate goal within the foreseeable future."

The Mission was of the opinion that a more definite series of targets aimed at self-government would "induce an atmosphere of understanding and confidence in which the country should be able to move rapidly and smoothly ahead." It noted that it had already expressed its belief that Ruanda-Urundi, "a relatively less-developed country," would become self-governing in 20 or 25 years.

Applying the same criteria and bearing in mind the striking development in Tanganyika during the last eight years, and despite its unevenness, the much larger area of the Territory, and its widely dispersed population, the Mission believes that self-government is within reach of the people of Tanganyika much earlier. It must be borne in mind that other factors may well intervene, internally or from the outside, which will speed up the progress towards self-government. The point is that, even at the present pace of development, the people can be developed to become self-governing within a single generation.

Therefore the Mission believed that it should be possible to set intermediate targets and target dates for phases of political development leading to complete independence perhaps somewhat before 1975, and not later than 1985. The Mission added to this statement by recommending the establishment of a substantial African majority on the unofficial side of the Legislative Council at the end of three years from the commencement of the parity legislature.

The chairman of the Mission, J. S. Reid, disassociated himself from these proposals, stating that they were "ambiguous." He noted that the Administering Authority's obligation to bring the inhabitants of Tanganyika to self-government or independence as soon as possible was contained in the Trusteeship Agreement, and "no doubt was expressed to the Mission in respect of the determination of the Administration to achieve that." But he felt it was neither possible on the evidence available nor helpful to the people to attempt at that time to set a limit for the attainment of self-government or independence in terms of years. In addition, he did not support the proposal that there should be an African majority on the unofficial side of the Legislative Council after three years, although he concurred in the progressive increase of African representation as early as possible.

Other recommendations of the Visiting Mission concerned the composition of the new Legislative Council, particularly the representation of the three racial communities. The Mission raised the question of "whether the same arguments and influences which justified the idea of parity in 1951-52 are still as valid today. The fact should not be ignored that it was evolved at a time when European political organization was at its strongest and African organization weaker." In support of its recommendation that the official majority should be maintained while African representation should be increased on the unofficial side of the Legislative Council, the Mission said it believed that "the official majority can and should be used as a kind of protective umbrella under which a more realistic form and ratio of representation can be established without raising any fears that legitimate non-African interests may be damaged by either political immaturity or premature demands on the part of the Africans."

The Mission also noted "a strong sentiment among the more politically conscious sections of the population in favour of immediate elections to the Legislative Council." Accordingly, it urged the introduction of the elective principle at both the local and the central levels of government; in this way the next few years would "offer at least an opportunity for electoral experimentation, whether it be with direct or indirect elections, some form of common roll elections, or a combination of both." The Mission supported this recommendation as follows:

So long as racial distribution of seats is maintained, and a measure of control is retained by the Government, there seems to be no real obstacle to making the means of suffrage available to all those who wish to use it. There may be apathy and confusion at first, but it is better to teach these lessons in democracy earlier rather than later when the councils will assume heavier responsibilities.

Reid considered that the government's policy of encouraging the people to accept an electoral system should be continued. He felt that the time had not yet arrived for the election of nonofficial members of the Legislative Council, but that steps toward that end could be taken by inviting nominations from the local authorities, which were already representative in character.

The Mission, pointing out that the government had agreed in principle that the ultimate objective should be a system of common roll elections with safeguards for minority representation, stated: "Every effort must be made to develop conditions under which no special protection of minorities will be necessary—in other words, to develop a single Tanganyika society in which the rights of individuals, and not of communities, will form the foundation of its institutions." Reid saw no reason to object to "any normal electoral procedure to give adequate representation to minorities."

With respect to the general political situation, the Mission noted that political activity was most pronounced among the Africans. The only organization considered by the Mission to be a "national movement" was the newly organized Tanganyika African National Union. The Mission remarked that its was impressed with "the quality of the leaders of the movement" and by "their moderation and sense of realism."[1]

The recommendations of the Visiting Mission were severely criticized by the European community in Tanganyika. Mason Sears, the American member of the Mission, has described reaction to the Mission's report as follows:

The forecast of independence perhaps somewhat before 1975, but not later than 1985, was considered revolutionary, and immediately precipitated strong reaction, even resentment, among European administrators and business men throughout East Africa. They considered the estimate to be totally unrealistic, claiming that it was far too short a period to enable a territory like Tanganyika to prepare itself for self-government.[2]

A leading resident, Sir Eldred Hitchcock, condemned the report as being "shot through with preconceived notions which are unrealistic and even dangerous to Tanganyika." He believed that if the Mission's recommendations were adopted by the Trusteeship Council, they "would throw Tanganyika into chaos such as its best friends and worst enemies could not wish."[3]

The *Tanganyika Standard,* the leading daily newspaper, also objected to the Mission's main recommendations, terming them "irresponsible and mischievous." It held that the Tanganyika government's political policy had overwhelming support both in Tanganyika and in Great Britain; "moreover, it has been agreed to consistently by the Trusteeship Council, a fact which the Mission seems to have overlooked." It claimed that the Mission had chosen to ignore the fact that "the great majority of the African population are solidly behind the Government in its present policy."[4]

The British government had not yet completed the final version of its observations on the Mission's report at the time the report was published. It became known, however, that the government strongly opposed the Mission's main recommendations. The government's objections were supported by *The Times,* whose editorial made the following comment: "The sweeping but imprecise proposals of the report published today by the mission which toured the territory last Autumn will not help. Many items in the report, for all its facts and arguments, bear little relation to the realities."[5]

On February 10 the Tanganyika Legislative Council unanimously passed a resolution recording the Council's "deep regret at the procedure adopted by the Trusteeship Council in the publication of the recent report on the Territory by the United Nations visiting mission." Several members expressed resentment over the fact that the report was published in New York before the Tanganyika government had a chance to compose replies.[6] V. M. Nazerali, an unofficial member of the Council and a leader of Tanganyika's Ismaili community, called it "a crude report" and claimed that its main emphasis was political advancement, while such important items as education, economic development, and social welfare took second place.[7]

African reaction to the Mission's report, although slow in developing, was the most dramatic. The Tanganyika African National Union delayed official comment until it could obtain a copy of the report. Once this had been accomplished, TANU realized how favorable the Mission was to its position. It also realized that some step would have to be taken to let the Trusteeship Council know of African support of the report, since all published comment up to that time in Tanganyika had been unfavorable to it. TANU accordingly decided that it would try to raise enough money to send a representative to New York to testify before the Trusteeship Council, a move that would, in addition, attract African attention throughout the territory to the new organization. In just a few days some £600 had been collected in Dar es Salaam and other parts of the territory. TANU's Central committee then announced that Julius Nyerere, the organization's president, would represent TANU at the Trusteeship Council's debate on the Visiting Mission's report, which was scheduled for the end of February 1955.

On the eve of his departure for New York, Nyerere, in an interview with the *Tanganyika Standard,* said that Europeans, Arabs, and Indians then in Tanganyika, although they were actually foreigners, were welcome to remain and help the country prosper. He considered that they were fully entitled to stay, since it was their home and their country of adoption; they would never be regarded as enemies. Nevertheless, he said that he was going to point out to the Trusteeship Council that Tanganyika was primarily an African country. With regard to future settlement in Tanganyika, Nyerere stated that government civil servants, missionaries (in their capacity as teachers), and businessmen bringing in capital were welcome, but that there was no more room for settlers.[8] The *Standard* commended TANU's "more moderate view," and went on to say:

T.A.N.U.'s original policy of demanding control of affairs with the least possible delay, seems to have been modified to a considerable extent. The same appears to be the case in respect of T.A.N.U.'s attitude towards the Europeans and Asians in the country and its admission of the valuable part the Administrating Authority is playing in the development of the country.[9]

On the day that Nyerere left for New York the Tanganyika Unofficial Members' Organization, a body composed of all the unofficial members of the Legislative Council, announced that it was sending a multiracial delegation to New York to testify against the Visiting Mission's report. The delegation would consist of Sir Charles Phillips, the Organization's chairman, Liwali Justino D. Mponda, and I. C. Chopra.

The observations of the British government on the Visiting Mission's report were published on February 22, 1955. The Administering Authority charged that the Mission had not been careful "to search out and give proper consideration to the views of the less articulate sections of the people and of those who had no special reason for putting forward their opinions." The Mission was criticized for giving greater emphasis to the views of TANU's central committee than to the "views of responsible and well-educated Native Authorities." Britain also claimed that there were "many inaccuracies and wrong assumptions" in the Mission's report, and went on to say that "this accumulated substructure of error tends to vitiate the whole report and in particular to deprive its recommendations of any claim to authority." Even if the errors were not present, the Mission's recommendations with regard to political development would still be "entirely unrealistic." Furthermore, the Mission's proposals would tend to create an atmosphere of financial insecurity, which would "imperil the economic stability of the Territory, retard its economic progress and threaten the basis of those social services which now exist."

"It is not therefore surprising," commented the Administering Authority, "that very few of the recommendations and proposals of the Mission have proved to be acceptable." With regard to the Mission's controversial recommendation that a timetable be fixed for Tanganyika's future political development and that a date be established by which time the territory would be granted self-government, the British government stated:

The declared policy of the Administering Authority is that constitutional development of Tanganyika should be by stages, the ground being consolidated and the future reviewed in the light of the experience gained before each important stage is undertaken. The rigidity of a fixed timetable would be inimical to the harmonious development of political institutions corresponding to consecutive stages of economic and social evolution. This does not mean that political and constitutional progress will be slow.[10]

The Trusteeship Council began its examination of the Visiting Mission's report at the end of February 1955. Sir Alan Burns made the opening statement for the Administering Authority. He said that the Mission, having seen only a small part of the territory and a fraction of its population, had reached conclusions and made proposals diametrically opposed to the policy of the Governor and his experienced advisers. He stated that Great Britain was ready and anxious to receive constructive criticism and advice from the Trusteeship Council, but his government would not be deflected from its considered policy "by criticism which is based on an insufficient knowledge of the facts and a lack of that experience which is so necessary." Sir Alan added that it was the Administering Authority's opinion that the report could result only in harm to the inhabitants of Tanganyika. He concluded: "I greatly regret that my delegation will be compelled to oppose virtually every major recommendation in the Visiting Mission's report."[11]

The special representative of the Tanganyika government, A. J. Grattan-Bellew, defended the British government's policy, which, he said, had met with considerable success and held justifiable hopes for good results if persevered in and carried on to fulfillment. With regard to the problem of developing a multiracial society in Tanganyika, Grattan-Bellew noted that the tendency to think of the Tanganyikan population as composed of three races overlooked the fact that the 8,000,000 Africans were divided into about 120 different tribes at many different levels of development and were "not yet in any sense of the word mono-racial." He pointed out that many of the tribes differed from each other to a greater degree than the educated sections of the Africans differed from the Europeans. And, finally, he observed that because of fear and distrust between neighboring tribes it was doubtful whether any one tribe would be prepared at that time to accept a member of another tribe at its representative.[12]

During the Council's discussion of the question of self-government, the United States delegate, Mason Sears, announced that the position of his government on this matter differed from the position he had taken when, as a member of the Visiting Mission, he had voted in favor of the recommendation; the United States, he stated, felt that a timetable was too rigid a measure for a territory like Tanganyika and could only be useful when the achievement of self-government was near. Another member of the Mission, Rafael Equizabal, the representative of El Salvador, stated that his government thought the setting of a timetable would be an inspiration and an incentive to the people. Some other members of the Council agreed with the British representative that a timetable for Tanganyika would be divisive politically and disastrous economically.[13]

During the course of the debate, the Council heard and questioned two Tanganyikans: Sir Charles Phillips and Julius Nyerere. Sir Charles told the Council that the unofficial members of the Legislative Council felt the Mission's report had laid undue emphasis on political questions and had failed to realize that the main objective of the Tanganyika people was to develop a prosperous country. In reply to a question, Sir Charles said that he opposed the establishment of a target date for self-government, since it would plunge the territory into political and financial chaos. A number of representatives questioned Sir Charles's right to give anything but a personal opinion on these matters; to which he replied that he was giving the opinion of the Unofficial Members' Organization, which considered itself to be representative of the Tanganyika people.[14]

Nyerere, on the other hand, supported the views of the Visiting Mission and said the assertion that the vast majority of Tanganyika's inhabitants opposed them was false. He said the Tanganyika Unofficial Members' Organization could not claim to represent public opinion, since the members of the Legislative Council had been appointed in their individual capacity and thus were not in fact representative of public opinion. He described TANU's purpose as being the preparation of the people of Tanganyika for self-government and independence. As a first step toward this goal, his organization sought to see the elective principle established and African majorities on all representative public bodies.

With respect to the changes to be made in the composition of the Legislative Council, Nyerere said that TANU accepted parity of representation only as a transitional stage toward a more democratic form of representation. He asked for a categorical statement from the Trusteeship Council and the Administering Authority that the future government of Tanganyika would be primarily African; until that assurance was given, parity of representation would continue to inspire false hopes in the non-African and false fears in the African. Such a statement would not mean that self-governing Tanganyika was to be governed by the Africans alone; TANU had never advocated this, but sought simply to obtain a due share of responsibility for the Africans in accordance with accepted democratic principles.

In conclusion, Nyerere expressed his hope that the future Tanganyika would be nationally homogeneous, although racially heterogeneous; he said that he regarded Asians and Europeans who had made Tanganyika their home as much Tanganyikans as Africans born in the country. After self-government had been achieved, they should be entitled to equal rights as fellow citizens. At first, however, he thought it might be necessary to provide certain guarantees of protection for the minorities until the goal of a nationally homogeneous state had been realized.[15]

On March 24, following the general debate on the Visiting Mission's report, the Trusteeship Council adopted the text of the chapter dealing with Tanganyika in its annual report to the General Assembly. The Council made no recommendation concerning a target date for self-government, the following statement being adopted instead:

The Council expresses the hope that the experience gained in the next constitutional stage will point the way towards an early and progressive increase in African non-official representation in the Legislative Council and towards the attainment as soon as possible of the Charter objective of self-government or independence.[16]

On his return home from the United Nations session, Nyerere addressed a gathering of about 10,000 people in Dar es Salaam. He gave this account of his mission: "I did not go to America to bring you self-government immediately, but I went there to ascertain whether the possibility is there. By hard work, either in our own lifetime or that of our children, we shall achieve it."[17] Once again he stated that non-Africans were welcome to stay on in Tanganyika after the territory achieved self-government. The following week a correspondent of the *Kenya Weekly News* commented that Nyerere's words "may have relieved the minds of some who have been worried by the apparent threat of his Union to racial harmony." However, the correspondent strongly questioned Nyerere's assertion that Great Britain did not oppose an African government for Tanganyika after the achievement of self-government:

It is believed that this is extremely questionable and that Britain is NOT prepared to say at this stage any such thing—surely the attitude of the Administering Authority is one of complete reserve and a refusal to try to peer into the distant future and the kind of government Tanganyikans will elect to rule them when self-government is in reach.[18]

POLITICAL DEVELOPMENTS, 1955–1957

Tanganyika's new constitution came into effect on April 1, 1955, with the promulgation of the Tanganyika (Legislative Council) (Amendment) Order in Council of 1955. The enlarged Legislative Council held its first meeting on April 19, 1955. As agreed, the Council was composed of 31 official members and 30 unofficial members. The government side now consisted of 8 officials appointed by virtue of their office, 6 unofficial members of the Executive Council, and 17 nominated members, some of whom were civil servants and other leading nonofficial members of the territory's three racial communities; the government side was made up of 21 Europeans, 6 Asians, and 4 Africans.

The representative side consisted of ten members from each of the three racial groups. Each constituency, of which there were nine, had three representatives, one of each race. These members were not responsible solely to people of their own race, but to all the people of their constituency. In addition to the 27 unofficial members representing constituencies, three other unofficial members, one of each race, represented the general interests of the territory.

All members of the Legislative Council were appointed by the Governor. For the first time women members sat on the Council; there were three of them, again one from each race. The Council was also distinguished by the fact that it contained more nonwhite members, 30 in all, than any other legislative body in Africa outside of the West African colonies.[19] From these figures showing the racial composition of the Council, it can be seen that in spite of equal representation of the races on the unofficial side, the total membership consisted of 31 Europeans and 30 non-Europeans. Therefore not only did the government retain an official majority on the Council, but European members remained in the majority as well.

In his inaugural address to the Council, the Governor, Sir Edward Twining, commented on parity of representation on the unofficial side: "It ensures equal representation of all three races, and diminishes the possibility of domination by any one race. It provides the best means for representatives of the three races on which Tanganyika so much depends to examine the problems of the territory together on an equal basis." He urged members not to look at problems from a communal point of view, since he felt this might inhibit, rather than promote, progress. He repeated the statement made by the Secretary of State for the Colonies in 1952 that the changes in the Council's membership were designed to last "for a considerable period." Twining also spoke on the question of race relations, a matter that had recently caused the Administering Authority to be criticized by the Trusteeship Council:

Tanganyika is correctly described as having a multi-racial society. The three races have learned to grow up together and to understand their different roles. Inter-racial relations have improved out of all recognition during the last few years and I doubt whether there is any country—certainly in the African Continent—where they are better.[20]

The first year of the new Legislative Council's life was marked by a spirit of cooperation that existed between all members, irrespective of race. The Council acted to eliminate forms of racial discrimination still existing in Tanganyika, such as prohibitions on African consumption of intoxicating beverages. During the session of the Council held in early September 1955, on no issue did the members of one race line up against the members of another race. Despite this, *The Times* (London) reported that because of the rapid pace of political development in the territory "few people expect this experiment in multiracial government to last for long." On the other hand, it found that the Governor continued to exert "considerable influence," that "he is a benevolent but strict father to all races and peace seems assured as long as he is there."[21]

The publication of the Visiting Mission's report and the inauguration of the new Legislative Council were the two most important political events of 1955 in Tanganyika. Another important feature in the second half of the year was the growth of TANU. Making the most of the prominence it had received when Julius Nyerere presented its views to the Trusteeship Council, TANU launched an extensive campaign to build up its organization throughout the territory. Its efforts were remarkably successful, and by the end of the year, twenty TANU branches had been established. These were concentrated chiefly in the Dar es Salaam area, urban centers on the Central Railway, and in Lake, Northern, Tanga, and Southern Provinces.[22] Among the new members were several thousand women, which led to the creation of the TANU Women's Section. Speaking to a crowd of 7,000 in September, Nyerere called for the election of unofficial members to the Legislative Council, at least in Dar es Salaam, without delay.

Althouh TANU's political activity evoked mixed feelings from the European community, observers outside the territory were impressed by the organization's moderation and by its leadership. A publication of the Fabian Colonial Bureau considered TANU to be "unique" in Africa:

The movement has so far avoided all the stridency, intolerance and demagogy which have normally marked such nationalist movements. They have held huge mass meetings in Dar-es-Salaam without the slightest disorder or even mob emotion. They have maintained friendly relations with the other races. They are prepared to see a gradual evolution towards their aims and demand only that the final aim of democracy shall be stated.

The publication criticized the government for classifying TANU's "intelligent and constructive African leaders as 'agitators,' " when it should have been encouraging the growth of such a nationalist movement.[23] The Fabian writer John Hatch, following a visit to Tanganyika in 1955, expressed similar views concerning political developments. He wrote that Tanganyika Africans had contributed "a generous measure of intelligence, constructive thought, and perhaps above all, tolerance and good humour to the East African scene." He noted that the general atmosphere of Dar es Salaam was one of "tolerance and lack of tension."[24]

TANU's domination of the political scene was short-lived. Its success in building up an African nationalist movement led to the creation of a multiracial political party, the United Tanganyika Party (UTP), set up by the unofficial members of the Legislative Council in February 1956. The manifesto setting out the Party's beliefs and aims stated that the tempo of events both within and without the territory made it imperative that a nonracial political party be formed. The manifesto further stated that "the evolution of Government in Tanganyika should be a developing process directed towards full self-government within the Commonwealth, in which all races will take their part." The Party considered that the existing Constitition "should continue until such time as the main races are more nearly formed into one whole as responsible citizens of Tanganyika." With regard to a suitable franchise for Tanganyika, the Party pledged "to resist all proposals which would lead to the domination of one racial group over the others or the subjugation of one group by the others."[25] Among the signatories of the manifesto were Sir Eldred Hitchcock, Chief K. Makwaia, V. M. Nazerali, and T. W. Tyrrell. In all, 28 unofficial members of the Council supported the new Party. The two remaining members, both Africans, were already members of TANU.

TANU was not long in attacking its new political rival. Despite its multiracialism, the UTP was accused, in a statement issued by Nyerere, of hoping to "entrench and perpetuate racialism" through the continuation of a Legislative Council based on parity. Because of superior voting strength, Nyerere said, European and Asian members of the Council could ignore the wishes of the vastly larger African population. He charged the UTP with advocating a form of partnership similar to that practiced in Central Africa "and not a democratic partnership which recognises the basic rights of the individual irrespective of his or her colour or creed."[26]

Replying to Nyerere's charges, the UTP pointed out that whereas TANU based its appeal on exclusive African nationalism, the UTP was a party open to all, whatever their race. The statement claimed that TANU's real complaint was that it would no longer be the only political party active among the African population. The *Kenya Weekly News* commented as follows: "All these preliminary skirmishes between the two parties-in-embryo are but manoeuvers for position in the preliminary stages of the political battle ahead—the battle between multi-racialism (and all that implies) and straightforward black nationalism.[27]

The Trusteeship Council's annual examination of conditions in Tanganyika took place during these same months. Grattan-Bellew, the special representative of the Tanganyika government, told the Council that because of the lack of racial problems Tanganyika was better described as a nonracial than a multiracial state. He said that the parity principle of representation on the Legislative Council had so far been "completely satisfactory" and that the system, which had been designed to last for a long time, was likely to outlive the life of the new Legislative Council.[28]

When the Trusteeship Council considered the proposals of its drafting committee on Tanganyika, discussion turned on a recommendation for a series of target dates to be set for political, economic, social, and educational development in the territory. Sir Alan Burns, the British representative on the Council, announced that his government viewed this recommendation with "much disappointment." He said it implied that there was no difference between timed political development and timed economic, social, and educational development, whereas, in fact, the difference was profound. Development in the other spheres was fundamentally development of a physical nature, whereas timed political development would have to be "absolute guesswork," since there could be no physical or factual basis on which to calculate. The proposal was eventually adopted by eight votes to five with one abstention. In the course of the discussion, the United States delegate suggested that in light of conditions in Tanganyika intermediate targets might be of some value.[29]

When news of the Trusteeship Council's recommendation reached Tanganyika, it was harshly criticized by the press. And although TANU welcomed the recommendation, Nyerere issued a statement saying that Tanganyika Africans were not yet ready for self-government. He urged Africans to join with TANU in laying the foundations of possible self-government in 20 to 25 years' time.[30]

Opening the new session of the Legislative Council on April 25, 1956, the Governor, Sir Edward Twining, announced that the government proposed to introduce common roll elections in a few constituencies, probably in the first quarter of 1958. He said that in view of the existing system of parity representation in each constituency, the government proposed that each voter who had the necessary educational, domiciliary, or other defined qualifications should vote for three candidates, one of each race. A committee representing all three races and consisting of members of the Legislative Council was to be established to draw up proposals with regard to electoral qualifications and procedures.[31]

Nyerere had already informed the Governor that TANU thought

it would be improper for the Council to discuss the introduction of elections in the territory, since the UTP dominated the unofficial seats and held a few seats on the government side as well. Nyerere pointed out that these members were going to decide not only "whether or when we are going to have elections," but the voters' and candidates' qualifications as well; "that one political party should hold this unique position in the country and that without any mandate whatsoever from the people, is not a matter to be treated lightly." Had things remained as they were, he said, TANU would have been willing to let the existing Council live out its fixed life of three years, but now it strongly believed that an immediate election of representative members should be held.[32] Following the Governor's speech, Nyerere said that TANU would continue to demand universal adult suffrage, since there was no justification for the imposition of electoral restrictions.[33]

Throughout these early months of 1956 the UTP was busy lining up supporters. Brian Willis, formerly with the Conservative Party in Britain, was hired as the UTP's general director. In an interview with the *Tanganyika Standard,* Ivor Bayldon, the chairman of the Party's caretaker committee, stated that the UTP's most important aim was "unity"; he conceived of "unity" as cooperation between the non-African population and the Africans, the former assisting and encouraging the latter to take an increased share in the management of the country. Bayldon ended his remarks on his Party's policy as follows:

It must be frankly recognized that the Tanganyika Governments of the future will be largely African and that the speed at which they assume their responsibilities will depend on their progress and preparedness and mutual efforts to raise their educational and economic status. There can be no progress if standards are lowered, and the U.T.P. stands firmly by the principle that advances towards self-government must be fully responsible and that the highest standards of efficiency, honesty and integrity must be maintained.[34]

By the end of June the new Party had won the support of all but one of the European members of the Legislative Council.

On July 1 the Asian Association announced that after considering the fullest implications of the UTP's beliefs and aims, it was unable to advise its members to subscribe to them. The Association said that the new Party's support of the parity constitution would entrench racial differences and, furthermore, its franchise proposals ran counter to all democratic principles. Two other statements made by the Party were described as "mere platitudes, betraying mental reservations as regards the quality of man." The Association's announcement ended with the following words:

As stated in the past, belief in non-racialism and nationhood is a matter of conviction with us, and not of expediency. We take this opportunity of reiterating these principles and are prepared to join hands with others in taking practical steps to achieve the nationhood of Tanganyika, without presumptions, without reservations and without fear.[35]

Also at this time the UTP held its first territory-wide convention. On the opening day, July 2, Ivor Bayldon was elected chairman of the Party. In a speech to the convention he referred to "subversive activity" in the territory, but assured his audience that there was not the "remotest chance" of Tanganyika's ever being allowed to fall into "irresponsible hands," no matter how "lavish may be the wild promises held out by the nationalists." He accused the nationalists of acting like cheap imitations of American gangsters and of introducing a reign of terror. "They exploit every grievance, whether real or imaginary, in the interests of their own party. They encourage ill-will and stir up racial hatred." Bayldon appealed to Africans "sincere in their interest in the future of Tanganyika" to give the UTP a fair hearing, since the Party did not blame them but their leaders. He claimed that only inside the UTP could Africans realize their desire to play a leading part in the development of Tanganyika.[36]

An editorial in the *Tanganyika Standard* the following day said that the UTP "with its progressive and 'non-racial' outlook" merited "earnest consideration by all men and women who have the interests of the territory at heart." The *Standard* claimed that the Asian Association's opposition to the UTP was of "little consequence," since the Association was not "regarded with favour by a large proportion of the Asian community."[37]

Julius Nyerere, addressing TANU's second anniversary meeting a week later, said that although TANU had not been specifically mentioned at the UTP convention, it has been implied that some of its members behaved like "American gangsters." He stressed that although TANU was determined to obtain freedom for Tanganyika regardless of how long it would take, the struggle for freedom would be by lawful and peaceful means, since the way of the jungle was "not good for people claiming to be civilized."[38]

It is apparent that the attitude of the European in Tanganyika toward TANU had changed from one of indifference to one of fear during the two years that the organization had been in existence. However, it was not a fear so much of Nyerere as of TANU's officials and members at the lower levels. The *Tanganyika Standard* reported that many of its African correspondents seemed to be under the impression that self-government meant that all Europeans and Asians would automatically leave the territory and that all the land held by them would revert to African use. "The more ambitious see themselves as presidents, prime ministers, and ministers with fantastic salaries."[39] The *Kenya Weekly News* pointed out that Nyerere's overzealous supporters would be one of his chief problems: "Mr. Nyerere, with his cautious and moderate approach to the nationalist programme, is a force to be reckoned with increasingly and, if he can control the tail which, at times, is inclined to wag the body of his party, he may well go far and become a great name in Tanganyika."[40]

Continued reports in the press of statements by TANU officials and members that all Europeans and Asians would be forced to leave the country when TANU came to power accentuated the Europeans' fear of the organization. Nyerere repeatedly contradicted such statements, but to no avail. On one occasion he said those Africans who imagined that all members of other races would be thrown into the sea when self-government was achieved were being very foolish. He appealed to Africans not to fear the "immigrant races" because fear was the beginning of hatred. Similarly, he said Asians and Europeans should not fear the African population.[41]

Although Nyerere was never attacked personally, the press showed increasing enmity toward the nationalist movement. TANU members were accused of being "the only people in this territory who now advocate 'racial discrimination' . . . They stand for complete African domination with the avowed intention of getting rid of the 'whites' and 'browns' in their midst."[42] One editorial claiming that TANU's brand of nationalism was not doing the territory's race relations any good prompted the following response from Nyerere:

Your suggestion that contentment born of good health and prosperity is all that man should ask of life is as dangerously materialistic as if it had been cooked in Moscow. No, Sir, it is not religion, but your type of journalism which is the opium of the people. Man does not live by bread alone, religion says: but "our national Press" tells us this is all nonsense: man should ask for no more than good health and prosperity . . . Let me assure you, Sir, that on my part I would rather be a poor invalid in freedom, than a prosperous robust in servitude.[43]

In September an editorial noted that the "fear of extreme nationalism" was having "a most depressing effect on the general outlook in Tanganyika," causing "very real alarm" among members of the immigrant races who had made their homes there, and retarding the country's economic development. The editorial asked for "renewed assurance that the vital interests of all the inhabitants will be respected in an eventual government in which all races are fully represented."[44]

A few days later, in a speech before several thousand Dar es Salaam supporters, Steven Mhando, TANU's Executive Secretary, denied allegations that TANU wanted the Europeans and Asians to leave the territory upon the attainment of self-government. He declared that, on the contrary, TANU wanted all communities to stay and work together for the country's good, with equal rights for all. Mhando accused some elements of the local press of stirring up racial hatred. "If two or three hooligans speak nonsense," he said, "it does not mean that the whole nation has the same views."[45] The *Tanganyika Standard* welcomed Mhando's statement as evidence "that those in authority in T.A.N.U. appreciate the harm that can be done—and has been done—by sentiments of extreme nationalism that may sound impressive as political propaganda, but which, in the cold light of reason, are by no means practical politics."[46]

During the months following the creation of the UTP, the Party was often described as being simply a political version of the Capricorn Africa Society, an assertion that was repeatedly denied by the UTP. The Capricorn Society, a multiracial organization supporting racial cooperation, had from the first been viewed with disfavor by Africans in Tanganyika: they were suspicious of its proposed multiple vote franchise system based on education and other qualifications, and feared that in the end the professed racial partnership of the Society would prove similar to that practiced in Rhodesia. In order to alleviate the African's fear of outside ties, the local chapter of the Society re-formed as the Tanganyika National Society at the end of 1955; its aims were virtually those of the Capricorn Society except that they were given special application to Tanganyika. "One loyalty for all races to Tanganyika and self-government . . . within the British Commonwealth" became one of the new organization's basic principles; another urged "a common citizenship for all citizens of Tanganyika regardless of race, colour or creed." In spite of these aims, however, the National Society failed to gain substantial African support.[47]

African distrust of multiracialism carried over to the United Tanganyika Party as well. The UTP's proposal of multiracial government, even with eventual African domination, met with strong suspicion and opposition from certain sections of the African community. For example, S. K. George, an African member of the Legislative Council, asked how Africans could believe that the UTP's early promises would not later be discarded in light of what had happened in South Africa, Central Africa, and Kenya. "We in Tanganyika . . . are under the Trusteeship of the U.N.O. and believe in the protection of the Colonial Office of Her Majesty's Government until such time as we can stand on our own feet," he said.[48]

From the first, the leaders of the UTP realized that their most difficult task would be to enlist African support. They tried to gain backing by arguing that progress would come to a halt if TANU gained the upper hand in Tanganyika politics. Ivor Bayldon stated, "Once the African recognises the essential role of the immigrant and the opportunities which a multi-racial nation could provide for him the first important step towards economic progress will have been taken." He went on to say:

In seeking to establish itself on a popular basis the UTP has found that contact between the races . . . is smaller than had been popularly supposed. The "racial harmony" which has often been referred to in the past was largely the harmony existing between groups who lived in worlds of their own. There was little conflict because there was little contact.[49]

After six months the UTP had in fact made some headway, the African membership in the Party being greater than either the Asian or the European membership. But although a number of Africans in the rural areas had joined the Party, Africans in the cities continued to give their allegiance to TANU. The UTP's biggest branches, which were located at Tukuyu and Bukoba, had an almost wholly African membership and were run by Africans.[50]

During September, TANU's executive committee submitted to the government a memorandum entitled "TANU and the Constitution," which outlined the Union's constitutional proposals. The memorandum stated that "an obstinate Government in Dar es Salaam, presumably supported by the British Government, is refusing to take the only steps which can ensure gradual and peaceful development in Tanganyika towards self-government." This criticism was directed toward the government's refusal to consider a change in the constitution. The memorandum went on to remark that "this obstinacy can only lead to the discrediting of moderate statesmanship and the encouragement of extreme African nationalism on the one hand and non-African reactionarism on the other." If the government maintained its position, conflict between the Africans and the non-Africans was almost certain. "TANU is prepared to do anything in our power to ensure peaceful development. We are convinced the immigrant minorities will do the same."[51]

TANU's proposals for constitutional changes involved both the Executive Council and the Legislative Council. The memorandum stated that TANU was not opposed to the continuation of an official majority in both Councils, provided certain other changes were made. These included the abolition of the parity system of representation for unofficials in both Councils. TANU demanded a new system of representation in the Legislative Council that would make the African representative members equal in number to their non-African counterparts. It was proposed that there should be 16 seats for Africans, 8 for Europeans, and 8 for Asians on the unofficial side. TANU also demanded the election of representative members by means of a common roll on a universal adult franchise.

Addressing a press conference in London at the end of September, Nyerere said that if the present good relations in Tanganyika were to continue, it was essential that the British government should issue a definite statement of policy concerning future constitutional development. Nyerere announced that TANU was not prepared to participate in the forthcoming elections to the Legislative Council on the basis of the government's proposals. He also declared that TANU favored a timetable for Tanganyika's constitutional development which would provide for the ending of the trusteeship in not more than 25 years.[52]

Replying to TANU's demands, the Governor, Sir Edward Twining, said that although the parity system of representation did not provide the final answer, it would be "premature" to change it. He stated that it was the "Government's responsibility to make sure that we do not go too fast and that we consolidate each position before we move forward"; "the resulting collapse of the economy would be far too high a price to pay" for rapid constitutional changes.[53]

In December 1956, Nyerere appeared before the Fourth Committee of the United Nations General Assembly during its consideration of the Trusteeship Council's annual report. He called for a declaration by Britain that Tanganyika would be developed as a democratic state. He explained that such an announcement would be an assurance that Tanganyika would be primarily an African state, since 98 per cent of the territory's population were Africans. Instead of political development on a multiracial pattern, which based politics on racial representation, Nyerere appealed for development on a nonracial pattern, whereby a person's race would be irrelevant to his participation in the government of the territory. He mentioned that the Asian Association also favored a nonracial policy and a universal adult franchise, and noted that only a very small minority of the European settlers thought in terms of dominating the Africans. Asked when he thought Tanganyika should receive independence, Nyerere said it should be in about ten years' time. This was a reduction of fifteen years over his statement of two months before.

Nyerere made a profound impression upon the members of the Committee. The Yugoslavian representative commented that TANU's requests were "extremely moderate," and the Mexican representative complimented Nyerere for his "statesmanlike viewpoint."[54] After further debate the Committee drafted a resolution concerning political development in Tanganyika, which it submitted to the General Assembly for approval. It was subsequently passed by the General Assembly by a vote of 47 to 15 with 11 abstentions. In its final form the resolution recommended that the Administering Authority should consider making a statement on the policy it proposed to follow in Tanganyika and should include in it the principle that, in accordance with the aims of the International Trusteeship System, "the Territory shall be guided towards self-government or independence and shall become a democratic State in which all inhabitants have equal rights."[55]

The reaction in Tanganyika to Nyerere's appearance before the Fourth Committee was mixed. The *Tanganyika Standard* indicated its approval of what it termed Nyerere's "broadening outlook." It pointed out that apparently Nyerere was keeping in mind the assurances of the United Nations Charter to all inhabitants of a trust territory, assurances that it considered important and that "ardent followers of TANU are apt to overlook."[56] Although the vast majority of Africans found nothing wrong with Nyerere's statement, there were some who expressed disapproval. One prominent African wrote in a letter to the *Tangaiyika Standard* that Nyerere could not claim to speak for all of Tanganyika's eight million Africans, as he had done, but only for TANU's 100,000 members.[57] Derek Bryceson, one of the leaders of the Tanganyika National Society, described Nyerere's statement as "a masterpiece of studied inaccuracy."[58]

Finally, the issue made sufficient stir to cause the Tanganyika government to put out a leaflet answering certain charges Nyerere had made at the United Nations.[59]

When the substance of the Fourth Committee's draft resolution became known in Tanganyika, loud protests went up from the European community. The local press was especially indignant that the Committee had chosen to regard Nyerere's statement as representing the prevailing opinion of Tanganyika's eight million Africans. The *Tanganyika Standard* declared that TANU was an "extreme nationalist organisation," whose membership did not include chiefs, elders, and other prominent members of the African population.[60]

One result of the increased political activity in Tanganyika was a growth in national feeling on the part of the Europeans, who were no longer willing to support every aspect of British policy in the territory. This can be seen, for example, in their gradual acceptance of the idea of a timetable for political development. Toward the end of 1956 one observer reported that some Europeans were wondering whether "there would be any great harm in attempting some kind of conservative plan upon which to build up by stages from the foundations of local government through the higher levels of territorial government to the final edifice of complete independence within the Commonwealth."[61] Following Nyerere's statement to the Fourth Committee that TANU supported such a timetable, members of the European community suggested that Britain should "take the bull by the horns" and draw up a timetable for political advancement so that the government would no longer be open to criticism by the United Nations on this point—a measure that would have the additional advantage of removing one of TANU's most effective arguments for enlisting African support.[62] In June 1957, Brian Willis, the general director of the UTP, indicated that the UTP considered the question of a timetable to be "psychologically important," provided that it was "realistically based."[63]

The year 1957 was marked by an increasingly harsh policy on the part of the government with regard to TANU. In January an African at Korogwe was convicted of sedition for asserting that TANU now governed the country and that from now on TANU and not the

Native Authority would hear all cases. Shortly afterward the registration of TANU's Korogwe branch was revoked. In the same month a government order banning political uniforms was viewed by Africans as another attempt to suppress African national pride.

During February, the government refused to grant Nyerere permission to hold two open-air meetings because of the "inflammatory nature" of two speeches he had made to large crowds after his return from the United States.[64] This resulted in a protest by Nyerere against what he referred to as the government's "muzzling" of TANU. He admitted the government's right and obligation to keep order in the country, but denied that anything he had said, or that his organization had done, justified this action by the government. "We preach all over the country obedience to Government and respect for authority," he said.[65] In one of the speeches in question, the local press reported that Nyerere had attacked certain aspects of government policy, but had exhorted his audience "to be civilised," since it was the duty of all races to try to cooperate and live peacefully together in the country.[66] At that time, two weeks before the government placed restrictions on Nyerere, the *Tanganyika Standard* commented that Nyerere's address "could in no way be interpreted as some fiery, political outburst intended to play on the less rational emotions of his listeners."[67]

Nyerere's protest was to no avail. A ban against public gatherings organized by TANU continued for months; no restrictions were placed against meetings limited to Party members, however. Other government restrictions on TANU activities were to deny Nyerere access to Tanga Province and to refuse registration to several TANU branches. Not accepting the government's argument that open-air meetings were likely to inflame the uneducated mass of Africans, TANU accused the government in general, and Sir Edward Twining in particular, of deliberately trying to suppress freedom of speech, when such speech was critical of government policy.[68]

In May 1957, the *Kenya Weekly News* expressed the opinion that TANU could rightly be described as a moderate organization: "While certain people will disagree violently with its creed and policies, no one can seriously claim that it publicly advocates immoderate measures, or violence, or anything of the kind."[69] Two months later, however, following an attack on a policeman by an official of a TANU branch, the *News* sounded a note of alarm. It remarked that although the incident itself was trivial, criminal offenses by TANU officials were becoming too common.

No-one supposes that Mr. Nyerere supports or approves the hotheads or rowdies among his followers, but some pretty severe disciplining is going to be necessary in the Union if the whole movement is not . . . to become dubbed as irresponsible and dangerous and a threat to the peaceful development of Tanganyika towards independence.[70]

During May the Legislative Council debated and passed the Legislative Council Elections Bill of 1957. The bill provided for the election of representative members to the Council from four or five constituencies, the elections to be held in September 1958 and to be followed by the election of representative members from the other constituencies within twelve months' time. The staggering of elections was necessary for administrative reasons. In spite of TANU's opposition, the bill also provided for the continuation of the parity system of representation in the Council. Under the provisions of the bill each voter would be required to vote for three representatives, one from each race; if he did not vote for three, his ballot would not be valid. When the bill was passed on May 28, only two European members voted against it; all African and Asian members voted in favor.[71]

The bill provided for a common electoral roll, the possibility of using separate electoral rolls for each of the three races having been rejected on the grounds that such a system would heighten racial feeling in the territory. The franchise qualifications were derived from the report of the Franchise Committee. A voter was required to have reached the age of 21 and to have resided in the territory for three of the preceding five years. He was further required to possess one of the three alternative qualifications: educational training equivalent to Standard VII or higher; an income of more than £150 per annum; or experience in certain specified categories of office. This last qualification covered members or former members of the Legislative Council, members of local government bodies, chiefs and various types of headmen, and heads of clans or kindred groups. The qualifications for candidates were somewhat higher. Among them was the requirement that the candidate should be willing and able to take the oath of allegiance to the Crown should he be elected.[72]

The Trusteeship Council's annual review of developments in Tanganyika took place in June 1957. In addition to the special representative of the Tanganyika government, John Fletcher-Cooke, the Council was addressed by Nyerere and Chief Thomas Marealle II of the Chagga tribe. Nyerere again asked for a statement by Great Britain to the effect that Tanganyika would be developed as a primarily African state. In protesting the government's restrictions on TANU, he denied that he had said anything inflammatory in his speeches. He pointed out that despite the restrictions, TANU's membership had continued to grow rapidly and at that time numbered between 150,000 and 200,000. Between 1955 and mid-1957, the number of branches had increased from 25 to 48. In defending his party's exclusively African membership, Nyerere observed that this was a direct reaction to the ostracism practiced against the Africans prior to the establishment of the UTP. However, he stated that TANU was prepared to open its membership to representatives of all races who were sincerely anxious to promote African interests. He told the Council that TANU favored racial harmony in a democracy, and consequently did not favor the expulsion of aliens from the territory. He added that he would be willing to see minority safeguards for the non-African population.

Marealle's statement to the Council agreed substantially with Nyerere's. He criticized the attitude of the settlers and called on the nonindigenous elements of the population to recognize that Tanganyika was to become a primarily African state. He pointed out that, given the prerequisites of a realistic partnership basis, sound economic planning, and political stability, Tanganyika could be self-governing within 10 to 15 years. He also favored the drawing up of a timetable for the territory's political development.

Fletcher-Cooke, replying to Nyerere's charge that only a limited number of Africans would be eligible to vote under the recently enacted franchise qualifications, said that African voters would very likely be in a substantial majority. He supported the tripartite vote

by pointing out that it emphasized a national rather than a racial outlook, since a candidate would have to rely on a majority from all races
in his constituency. Referring to the ban on mass public meetings,
Fletcher-Cooke stated that the government considered there would
have been a grave risk of a breach of the peace if more speeches similar to those in the past had been permitted elsewhere in the territory.

In a final statement the representative of Great Britain, Sir Andrew
Cohen, emphasized that the Administering Authority recognized
that the majority of the population was African, and recognized also
the implications of that fact. He said that Britain's whole policy,
record, and national outlook, as well as the terms of the Charter and
of the Trusteeship Agreement, were a sufficient guarantee that the
political development of the territory would be democratic. The Africans' participation in both the legislative and the executive branches
of the government was bound to increase as their educational, social,
and economic progress continued. Sir Andrew concluded by saying
that his government was seeking to build a nonracial, rather than a
multiracial, society in Tanganyika.[73]

In its report to the General Assembly, the Trusteeship Council
noted that the introduction of the elective principle was "a significant
forward step and one which should have an important effect on the
political development of the Territory." The Council wished to
stress, however, "the desirability of progressively broadening the
franchise" and of establishing universal suffrage in the territory as
soon as possible. A review of the parity system following the 1958 and
1959 elections was also suggested.[74]

Commenting on the statements by Nyerere and Marealle to the
Council, the *Tanganyika Standard* found it "of the utmost importance" that "it is being generally recognized by the Africans in this
territory that we must have political stability based on a rapidly expanding economy, and that in that economic development the Europeans and Asians have a major role to play."[75] Owing to the Europeans' effort to build up an African leader whom they did not regard
as a nationalist, Marealle's views came in for particularly favorable
comment. They were praised as representing "all who have the true
interests of the territory at heart."[76] According to Brian Willis, the

general director of the UTP, "Chief Marealle has spoken as an African who is prepared to be a Tanganyikan. The non-African who wishes to stay here, and those who wish to settle in the future, must give a similar response." It was also Willis's opinion that the chiefs should "be brought forward to help shape the future of the territory."[77]

In accordance with an earlier announcement by the Governor, a ministerial system of government was introduced in Tanganyika on July 1, 1957, replacing the membership system, which had come into existence on January 1, 1948. The redesignation of the official members of the Executive Council as ministers reflected the growth of public business that had occurred during the ten-year period. The official side of the Council had been increased to nine members the previous year; it now consisted of the Chief Secretary, the Minister for Constitutional Affairs, the Attorney General, the Minister for Finance and Economics, the Minister for Social Services, the Minister for Local Government and Administration, the Minister for Lands and Mineral Resources, the Minister for Natural Resources, and the Minister for Communications and Works. Late in 1957 the unofficial side of the Council was increased to seven members by the appointment of Chief Thomas Marealle.

As another step in the preparation of Tanganyika for self-government, Sir Edward Twining announced the appointment of six assistant ministers drawn from the unofficial ranks of the Legislative Council. The assistant ministers now became ex officio members of the Legislative Council, with the duty of speaking for the departments assigned to them. They were not, however, members of the Executive Council, although they might attend meetings and take part in discussion when matters affecting their departments came before that Council. The Governor said that appointments would be made on a nonracial basis. Accordingly four Africans, one European, and one Asian were appointed. They were Derek Bryceson for Labor; Amir Yusafali Karimjee for Commerce and Industry; Chief H. M. Lugusha for Social Development; David P. K. Makwaia for Land; Chief John Maruma for African Education; and Chief Humbi Ziota for Agricultural Production.

Late in July 1957, the Tanganyika government lifted its ban against public meetings organized by TANU. The previous month several members of the Trusteeship Council had criticized the restrictions on TANU and, in view of the approaching elections of 1958, had urged Great Britain to permit a maximum amount of freedom of speech in the territory. Government bans against certain TANU branches continued in effect, however. TANU's first open-air meeting followed the lifting of the ban took place in Dar es Salaam on the first Sunday in August. The main speech was delivered by Nyerere, who attacked racialism and urged foreigners in the territory to regard themselves as Tanganyikans. He pointed out that the African population "would like to cooperate with all the foreigners," but that it would not "stand for different treatment than the treatment given to the foreigners."[78] The Tanganyika correspondent of the *Kenya Weekly News* commented that this was "fair enough" and added: "Unless one is unusually dumb and stupid, the declared objects of the two parties seem to be drawing ever closer together—indeed T.A.N.U. as represented by its chief has come more than half way across the gulf which once seemed to separate it from its rival."[79]

In an interview with the *Tanganyika Standard*, Nyerere stated that he did not wish to see politics develop along racial lines, and he felt that this might happen if, in the forthcoming elections, ten Africans nominated by TANU and ten Europeans nominated by the UTP were elected. "It might be to my advantage," he said, "but I do not want racial politics in this country." He therefore proposed that five constituencies should be single-seat constituencies.[80]

Instead of allowing the existing Legislative Council to run its normal course until March 1958, at which time it was to be reorganized, the Governor dissolved the Council in June 1957 and proceeded to appoint a new one. In an attempt to make the new Council more representative of African interests, he nominated Nyerere as one of the representative members for the Dar es Salaam constituency, Chief Marealle as an unofficial member on the government side, and Rashidi Kawawa, General Secretary of the Tanganyika Federation of Labor, as one of the three members appointed to represent general interests on the unofficial side. The six assistant ministers became ex officio members. The first session of the reorganized Council was held in September 1957.

The constitution of the Legislative Council was changed further by the Tanganyika (Legislative Council) (Amendment) Order in Council, 1957, which provided for the creation of a tenth constituency. The new constituency was formed by dividing the heavily populated Lake Province constituency into the West Lake and South-East Lake constituencies. When the representatives of the West Lake constituency took their seats at the December session of the Council, its membership was raised to 34 members on the government side and 33 members on the representative side. The government side was composed of 15 ex officio members, and 19 nominated members; its racial division consisted of 20 Europeans, 11 Africans, and 3 Asians. The representative side continued to be divided equally among the three races.[81]

In his address opening the new Legislative Council, Sir Edward Twining stated the government's position regarding a broadened franchise: "In introducing qualitative franchise on the basis of a common roll in Tanganyika we are taking a great step forward. This measure has yet to be tested in practice and must be given a fair trial." He announced that the five constituencies selected for the first round of elections in 1958 were Northern, Tanga, Eastern, Western, and Southern Highlands Provinces. After the second round of elections in 1959, he proposed to set up a committee of the Legislative Council to examine the desirability of making further constitutional changes, including the possible replacement of the Executive Council by a Council of Ministers. Twining explained that the principal need of the territory at its present stage of evolution was for political stability and economic development. He believed that if these conditions were fulfilled, the rate of progress toward responsible government and later self-government could not only be maintained, but probably be increased.[82]

According to the Secretary of State for the Colonies, Alan Lennox-Boyd, who visited Tanganyika in October 1957, the rate of Tanganyika's constitutional development was "if anything in danger of being too rapid rather than too slow." He stated that Britain had no intention of abandoning her trust, or handing it over to "irresponsible people" or "to any government under which responsible people of all races in Tanganyika would not feel secure." Furthermore, the British government would support "any measures" the Tanganyika government might feel were necessary "to deal firmly with bodies that claim in some parts of the Territory to have assumed the function of government."[83]

With another year to go before the territory's first elections, most people were still relatively unconcerned about politics. The two main political parties, however, were preparing for the struggle to come. Despite the fact that of its membership of 7,000 about 65 per cent were Africans and another 25 per cent Asians,[84] the UTP was still thought of by many Africans as the Europeans' party—a natural impression in view of the Party's aim of reserving a place in an independent Tanganyika for the non-African and its close relationship with the administration. In order to identify itself more closely with African aspirations, the UTP adopted the following new platform at its second convention in September 1957: a date for self-government, a radical change from the parity system of representation, and the creation of single-member constituencies. Accepting the fact that elections on the basis of color would eventually mean the eclipse of the non-African, the Party put its faith in the "concept of Tanganyikan nationality." It also favored a gradual advance to universal adult suffrage.[85]

The UTP was additionally handicapped by a lack of support from the European and Asian communities. Most European settlers paid only lip service to multiracialism, and only a few grudgingly gave their support to the Party. The Asians, although they had a greater stake in the future of the country, were far less alarmed by the prospect of African nationalism than the Europeans. Moreover, realizing that they might eventually have to live in Tanganyika under a nationalist government, they did not want to compromise their future by supporting the multiracial UTP.[86]

TANU, on the other hand, had been highly successful in building up support. According to Nyerere's statement to the Trusteeship Council in June, the Party's membership was between 150,000 and 200,000. The main backing came from detribalized Africans in the towns and cities, but it was becoming increasingly evident that the Union was building up a strong following in certain rural areas as well. Exploiting the friction between African and European over land, some TANU organizers promised that all the land held by Europeans would soon be returned to the Africans. Although such tactics did not have the approval of the Party's leaders, this "unofficial" nationalist land policy inevitably had more popular appeal than the UTP's stand in favor of long-term rights of occupancy— particularly in the congested areas.[87]

The Tanganyika government's reaction to the growing political activity was one of distaste. From the first Sir Edward Twining had been opposed to the formation of political parties out of a fear that they might force the territory to move ahead too fast for its own good. In a speech delivered to the Caledonian Society in early December, he deplored the turn politics had taken, claiming that the territory's good racial relations were being damaged.[88]

For some time, in an attempt to slow down TANU's drive toward self-government, Twining had been trying to maintain the support of the African tribal leaders for the government's policy. In 1955 he reported having heard rumors that tribalism was to be destroyed in Tanganyika, a development that he considered would be "disastrous to the great majority of the African population." Although the tribal system was undergoing change, he was against its being replaced "by some alien system" in which the African could not have the same confidence.[89]

Similarly, in a speech to the Legislative Council in 1957, the Governor referred to the important part played by the chiefs in the administration of the territory. He said that even with further change in local government, the chiefs "will remain the key men, and it would be a bad day for Tanganyika if it were otherwise."[90] Two weeks later Twining spoke to the Convention of Chiefs, consisting of 57 chiefs from all over the territory. In an attempt to stiffen their support of government policy, he warned them of the effects on them and their people if the nationalists, who did not have the proper respect for the Native Authorities or the chiefs, carried the day. "Most of their ideas," he said, "come from outside Tanganyika, put into their heads by people who do not have the true interests of the territory at heart." He expressed his conviction that disaster would follow if "such important—indeed fundamental—institutions as the tribal system and the office of chief" were discarded.[91]

From time to time there had been talk in government circles of bringing the traditional African leaders more into the central government; the first concrete proposal, however, came from the UTP. In its new statement of policy, the UTP called for the creation of a consultative second chamber to include in its membership people of all races who were outstanding citizens of Tanganyika. The Party considered that in view of the political advances being made in the territory, the authority and experience of the chiefs should be called upon to ensure a smooth transition from a tribal society to a Tanganyikan nationality.[92]

Registration of voters for the 1958 and 1959 elections took place during the last three months of 1957. The apathy shown by those eligible to register led to a debate at the December session of the Legislative Council on the matter of the compulsory tripartite vote. Nyerere moved that the requirement to vote for a candidate of each race be dropped. He reported that people objected to a system that might compel them to vote for someone they did not like simply in order to make their ballots valid. Alec Le Maitre, the European representative member from Tanga Province, supported Nyerere's motion on the grounds that compulsory tripartite voting would have the opposite effect of ensuring that the three races were truly represented in the Council; he said that many people would be forced to vote for someone about whom they knew nothing. Although fourteen representative members voted in favor of the motion, it failed to pass.[93] Two months before, the UTP had recommended that the tripartite vote be made optional, since it had little support among the general public.[94]

A week after the Legislative Council's debate, Nyerere resigned from the Council. He issued the following statement:

I came to the Council expecting a little of the spirit of give and take. That spirit is not there. . . . The Government has consistently, and for the most unconvincing reasons, rejected every proposal that I have made in the Legislative Council. Most of the proposals . . . have been compromises of those originally made by my organisation.

He concluded by accusing the government of opposition for opposition's sake.[95]

THE REPORT OF THE 1957 VISITING MISSION

The report of the 1957 United Nations Visiting Mission, which had spent nearly six weeks during August and September surveying the situation in the trust territory, was released in early January 1958. The Mission consisted of a chairman, Max H. Dorsinville of Haiti, and representatives of three other Trusteeship Council members, Australia, Burma, and France. The Mission's general conclusion was that "much ground has yet to be covered in a territory where the majority of the people still live under primitive conditions before self-government can be achieved." The report noted that political progress at the central government level was conditioned by many factors, especially economic and educational ones and the need to develop local government. All these factors involved the questions of a target date for self-government and a timetable for political, economic, and social development. The Mission stated that it appreciated the difficulties which had prevented the Administering Authority from making any formal declaration with regard to such matters and which had influenced it to adhere to the view that an empirical approach was necessary.

Referring to the territory's political progress, the Mission commented:

The fact that tensions have been kept to a minimum may be attributed to a desire of most of the political leaders of all races to work together for the common good, even when they do not agree on the means of achieving it, and to the moderating influence exercised by the Administering Authority in this difficult and delicate situation.

Nevertheless, it noted that many Europeans were apprehensive lest an irresponsible form of African nationalism should arise to disturb the territory's stability and orderly progress.

The Mission would stress its belief, however, that a majority of the non-Africans, no less than of the articulate Africans, accept as an ultimate objective that Tanganyika should become a self-governing State, the constitution of which would guarantee equal rights to all races without discrimination.

The Mission reported that although the Administering Authority had made several declarations, principally within the confines of the United Nations, clearly indicating that its policy was directed toward the creation of a democratic state with equal rights for all citizens, these assurances either had not been clearly understood or had yet to become widely known in the territory. It believed that "a clearer understanding by the people that the Administering Authority shares the ultimate objective of the political leaders would strengthen confidence generally in the Territory" and urged the dissemination of such information to all sections of the population.

The Mission found that many people in the territory wanted a more rapid rate of political development and, in particular, a form of representation that took better account of the numerical size of the three racial communities. The report noted TANU's rejection of the government's multiracial policy, "which treats the immigrant minorities as privileged groups, thus giving them political rights here which no such groups could enjoy in any democratic country." It was TANU's belief that the government's policy sought to give confidence to the wrong people. "Tanganyika being a plural society and the history of the plural societies in Africa being what it is," TANU said, "the African, much more than the immigrant minorities, needs an assurance about the future." The Mission found that opposition to the parity constitution was widespread among African groups in the territory.

The Mission further noted that although the UTP had formerly favored the retention of the parity system, it, too, now advocated an increase in African representation in the relatively near future. It differed from TANU, however, in that it favored a more gradual change toward the two parties' common goal of self-government on a nonracial basis with an African majority.

Although the UTP included Europeans and Asians among its membership, the Mission found that it did not express the view of all the Europeans and Asians. Many Asians were concerned lest the government's policy of rapid constitutional advancement endanger the territory's political stability. And some small Asian societies, such as the Asian Association of Dar es Salaam, supported TANU's demands. The Mission believed that a number of Asians and Europeans held doubts about the government's policy.

The Mission concluded that parity of representation for the three main races on the representative side of the Legislative Council was in accordance with the government's policy of fostering interracial partnership and progressing by gradual steps toward a nonracial form of government. With regard to the electoral system for the Council, three members of the Mission were of the opinion that the compulsory tripartite vote was undesirable; they also favored a liberalization of the electoral qualifications. The entire Mission hoped that it would be possible, after the 1958 and 1959 elections, to adopt a system of universal adult suffrage with a secret ballot.

Noting the tremendous increase in political activity over the past three years, the Mission emphasized the importance of cooperation between political parties and the administration. It expressed disappointment that "competition between political parties for popular support has led in some instances to the organization of various types of political opposition to such eminently advantageous government programmes as those of destocking, cattle-dipping, and soil and water conservation." It advised the political parties to "take care that healthy competition does not degenerate into opportunism," threatening the speed and thoroughness of Tanganyika's progress to self-government.[96] Referring to the allegation that irresponsible political activity was driving capital away from the territory, the Mission stated that on the basis of what it was told by the Tanganyika government and of its own observations "there was no evidence that political development in the Territory was having an adverse effect on the investment of outside capital."[97]

The report of the 1957 Mission was much more favorably received by members of all races than the report of its 1954 counterpart. The fact that the 1957 Mission devoted greater attention to economic development and the necessity of finding capital to carry out major development schemes for the benefit of the entire country made its report more appealing both to the British government and to the European community in Tanganyika. Nor did the Mission's statement that the territory was not yet ready for self-government pass unnoticed. The *Tanganyika Standard* called the report "the most constructive appreciation of political, economic and social conditions, ever recorded by a Visiting Mission."[98]

The observations of the British government on the Visiting Mission's report were presented at the twenty-first session of the Trusteeship Council. The Administering Authority noted the "objective nature" of the report and said that on the whole it gave "a fair and balanced account of the situation prevailing in Tanganyika today." With regard to the Mission's suggestions about electoral procedure, the British government was against introducing any change at the present late stage in the preparations for the elections. Bearing in mind that these would be the first territory-wide elections, the Administering Authority considered that the compulsory tripartite vote would encourage racial moderation on the part of all candidates for contested seats and that it therefore had sufficient merit to warrant its being given a fair trial. The British government was also unable to accept the Mission's suggestion that the voting qualifications should be liberalized, both because the franchise had not yet been tried and because any change would necessitate postponing the elections.[99]

The questions put to the special representative of the Tanganyika government, Fletcher-Cooke, during the Trusteeship Council's discussion of the territory chiefly concerned the forthcoming elections and the constitutional committee that was to be appointed following the second round of elections in 1959. There was general praise for Tanganyika's recent political development.[100] In its annual report the Council once again urged "the introduction of universal suffrage with the least possible delay." It also hoped that the composition of the constitutional committee would be "as representative as possible" and that there would be "substantial African representation" on it.[101]

During 1958, Tanganyika saw the creation of two African nationalist splinter parties. In February, Zuberi M. Mtemvu, a former provincial secretary of TANU, announced that he was forming the Tanganyika African Congress. In a long memorandum, Mtemvu stated that he was disgusted with the moderate political philosophy of Nyerere and TANU. He held that Tanganyika should not be primarily African but completely African, and alleged that Nyerere advocated equal rights for non-Africans in order to protect his European and Asian friends. Mtemvu denied, however, that his party had any intention of driving foreigners out of the country. He opposed the possibility of TANU's opening its membership to non-Africans and accused TANU and the UTP of being too much alike; the African Congress would be "extreme" and "radical." He advocated "internal self-government" for Tanganyika by 1962.[102] Mtemvu's bid to lead an extreme African nationalist party was largely unsuccessful. His narrow views alienated much African opinion. In May the Registrar of Societies announced that the Tanganyika African Congress's application for registration had been refused because of certain implications in its manifesto.

The second dissident nationalist group formed was the all-African Tanganyika Federal Independence Party, with headquarters in Tanga. The new party demanded separate independence for the territory's provinces. It also failed to gain a significant following.

At its annual conference in January, TANU decided not to boycott the elections, as it had threatened, but to put up candidates and encourage its members to vote. A resolution was passed calling on the government to increase the number of unofficial members in the Legislative Council. TANU said that it wanted responsible government with an elected majority and a majority of elected ministers in 1959. If the government refused this request, the Union would consider "more positive action."[103]

In a speech before an open-air meeting of 50,000 people at Dar es Salaam, Nyerere made it clear that such "positive action" would include an appeal to the United Nations. He warned that anyone advocating the use of force or mistreatment of non-Africans would be expelled from the Union. Although he did not specifically offer Asians and Europeans membership in TANU, he called on them to help the Africans achieve the country's freedom.[104] Some Asians and Europeans were already contributing to the Party's funds. Nyerere's address was editorially welcomed by the *Tanganyika Standard* as "realistic," and Nyerere was commended for the moderation and sound common sense "that has marked his recent approach to constitutional development."[105] An observer noted that this was a considerable shift in tone for the *Standard*: "Times change. A new extremist in Mtemvu appears on the horizon, and overnight an ex-extremist becomes a 'moderate.' Such is politics."[106]

Irresponsible action on the part of minor officials continued to plague TANU. Late in 1957 the TANU branch at Iringa was closed down by the government because its chairman had attempted to interfere with the government's cattle-dipping scheme there. TANU officially condemned the interference and expelled the man responsible for it. From other parts of the territory came reports that African members of the UTP were being subjected to intimidation by TANU supporters. Speaking on this subject at Arusha, Nyerere deplored such behavior and urged TANU members to act as responsible citizens.[107] In April 1958 the provincial commissioner of Lake Province attacked certain "irresponsible, self-seeking" persons for spreading rumors that Tanganyika was to have self-government before the end of the year, after which time no one would have to pay taxes.[108]

Geita District was the scene of considerable unrest during 1958. In March the Registrar of Societies refused to register the local TANU branch, and in May all further activities of TANU in the district were banned for a period of six months. Agitation continued, however, over the setting up of Geita's multiracial district council. Late in July nearly 1,000 Africans from Geita, protesting the establishment of the Council, descended on the provincial capital of Mwanza and camped in the town for several days. The police had to use tear gas on the crowd after appeals to the demonstrators to disperse had proved fruitless. The ringleaders of the demonstration were subsequently arrested.

Sir Edward Twining's term as Governor came to a close in June 1958. His successor, Sir Richard Turnbull, was announced earlier in the year. For the previous three years, Turnbull had served as Chief Secretary of Kenya, during which time he had gained a reputation of maintaining good relations with all the racial communities—a record that caused the *Tanganyika Standard* to describe the appointment as "a happy one." The *Standard* made special mention of Turnbull's "intimate contact with the Africans themselves and understanding of their problems."[109]

Twining made his last speech to the Legislative Council on May 6, 1958. He said that it was the policy of the administration to promote self-government with the utmost vigor; he therefore thought that those who wanted "to see self-government introduced without further ado" showed only a superficial knowledge of what self-government meant and what were its essential requirements. He came out strongly in favor of the proposed Council of State, commenting that "there would be considerable merit in establishing a Council in which the wisdom and experience of the traditional authorities would find expression." Further studies were to be made of the matter. He concluded his remarks as follows:

The Territory has a reputation for possessing people who have a great fund of good will and shrewd common sense. Let us hope that they will live up to their reputation and will finally achieve the goal in a spirit of tolerance and good will under the guidance of wise, experienced and sensible leaders whom the people of the Territory can trust.[110]

Twining left Tanganyika on June 16, 1958, after nine years' service as Governor. Despite certain political differences, he left with the good will of all three races. A year before, *The Economist* remarked, "Sir Edward Twining's imaginative paternalism has created a situation in which political experiment is possible."[111] That this political experiment in multiracial partnership had gone forward peacefully and without seriously disturbing Tanganyika's tradition of amicable

race relations is to Sir Edward's credit. Writing shortly after his re-
tirement, Twining made it clear he hoped Tanganyika would follow
a middle course in racial relations. "The sensible course would be for
no one race to dominate, but for the Africans, because of their numbers, ultimately to predominate." He distrusted TANU not so much
for its racialism as for its "strong emotional appeal to the Africans,"
which might cause events to move too fast for the territory's own
good.[112] According to one observer, this fear had caused his administration to become somewhat static: "Lord Twining had done much
in his earlier days to lay the foundations of a healthy racial pattern in
the country. In his last years he had become less imaginative, tending
to obstruct the growth of TANU."[113] Without the early foundations,
however, the last ten years in Tanganyika would not have been so
peaceful.

Sir Richard Turnbull was sworn into office on July 15, 1958. He
addressed the large crowd that was at hand, delighting the Africans
by repeating his speech in Swahili after giving it in English. This did
much to dispel the suspicion that surrounded Turnbull's Kenya background in the minds of many Africans. His broadcast to the territory
the following month went further in this respect. Commenting on
the confusion he had found in people's ideas about Tanganyika's
immediate future, he stated:

There are some people in Tanganyika who have been led to believe that
self-government is coming in 1959. This is not possible. Self-government
will come to Tanganyika in due course; this has been stated on numerous
occasions by representatives of the Government both in this country and
in the United Kingdom, and we are doing all we can to speed up the
process of preparing the people of the territory for self-government.[114]

As part of this program to speed up constitutional development,
Turnbull announced that the second round of the territorial elections,
previously planned for September 1959, was to be brought forward
to February 1959. In this way the committee that was to discuss the
next stages of constitutional progress could go to work that much
sooner. Turnbull thus showed that he was less cautious than his
predecessor, Twining having been opposed to any step that speeded

up the arrangements already made.[115] The decision was warmly welcomed by TANU. Its news sheet, *Sauti ya TANU,* remarked: "Well done, Sir. This alone shows your cleverness at visualising from far away. Now things will go along a right path."[116]

Turnbull was faced with a dangerous political situation in his very first month in office. In June, Nyerere had been served with a summons alleging criminal libel against the district commissioners of Musoma and Songea in the May 27 issue of *Sauti ya TANU.* There were three charges against Nyerere: first, that he had accused these officials of arbitrarily closing several of TANU's branches; second, that he had accused them of being a party to the fabrication of evidence produced in court; and, third, that he had published the following statement: "These same officials would have people committing perjury in court if only to vilify TANU. These same people who intimidate and punish innocence, cajole and reward crookery, have the temerity to invoke law and order."[117]

The trial took place in July; Nyerere pleaded not guilty to all three charges. He said he wrote the article in question in order to draw the government's attention to "serious discontent" in the Geita and Musoma areas.[118] Because of certain technicalities, the government withdrew its charges of criminal libel against the district commissioner of Musoma. The magistrate, L. A. Davies, subsequently convicted Nyerere on the remaining counts. Passing sentence, he said that the offenses were not only serious and scurrilous, but indefensible as well. He continued:

I have had no evidence before me that the accused had undertaken any serious investigation into the matters concerning Mr. Scott. The accused said in evidence that he knew that Mr. Scott had not closed down the TANU branch but had acted within the law in not having it registered. He [Nyerere] was not acting in good faith, but from motives best known to himself. He cannot satisfy me that what he wrote was true or that it was privileged.

Davies said that Nyerere was "an extremely intelligent man and a responsible and reasonable public official"; nevertheless, he had committed a "grave and mischievous indiscretion." Since it was not customary to impose a prison sentence in such cases, Nyerere was given the alternative of paying a £150 fine or spending six months in prison.[119] He turned down the opportunity to become a political martyr and paid the fine because, he said, he wanted to give the new Governor a chance to start his administration without embarrassment.[120]

7

TANGANYIKA APPROACHES
SELF-GOVERNMENT

TANGANYIKA'S FIRST ELECTIONS

During 1958, the United Tanganyika Party came upon hard times. In February it was announced that the Party had been forced to dispense with the services of its general director, Brian Willis, because of a shortage of funds. The Party's executive committee, headed by Sheikh Hussein Juma, an African, took over Willis's duties. At that time the UTP's membership stood at 11,000, of which 76 per cent were Africans.[1] In March, Ivor Bayldon bluntly accused the government of a "lack of will" in carrying out its declared multi-racial policy. He urged the members of the immigrant races to work for multiracialism by bringing to the front the hidden support of "a vast number of African Tanganyikans" for this form of political development.[2] Bayldon's appeal was to no avail. As the year progressed, the UTP found itself becoming less of a political force and more of an organ of opinion. In a letter to *The Economist,* Amir Jamal set out the reasons for the Party's lack of success:

In the political field, the United Tanganyika Party has failed because it was a party based on expediency, with so many strange and incompatible bedfellows. Its professed multi-racialism was bound to appear an attempt to entrench separate racial streams. And too many educated Africans had already deeply felt the humiliations of European racial arrogance in everyday life. Besides, there never has been any common platform where the masses and the privileged groups could ever stand together.

The Tanganyika African National Union of course met the psychological need, and Mr. Nyerere, apart from being charming, is a person of impeccable integrity and burning with deeply felt patriotism.[3]

In June, supporters of the UTP and TANU were startled by an announcement that their leaders had held talks to determine whether a joint conference should be convened to consider a merger of the two parties. The announcement came from TANU headquarters; the UTP subsequently issued a statement regretting the "premature publicity" given to the matter, since it had intended the talks "to continue in private a little longer."[4] This was the end of the two parties' efforts to effect a merger.

In early July, Nyerere assured his supporters, some of whom had been shocked by the fact that a merger was being even remotely considered, that TANU would not unite with "a dead thing."[5] With reference to the talks, the *Standard* commented on the spirit of moderation that was attending the territory's political development:

Except for the unrealistic and irrational statements of policy which accompanied the birth of nationalist politics in this country, Tanganyika has been particularly fortunate, not only in the moderation of its nationalist party but in the cooperative outlook of its settlers and other members of the immigrant races. So long as moderation continues to mark the approach to party politics, we need have little fear for the economic and political future of the territory.[6]

The fact that Europeans were not alarmed by the prospect of TANU's sweeping the forthcoming elections is borne out by a correspondent's report: he stated that most Europeans in Dar es Salaam remained indifferent both to the possibility of a merger of the parties and to the territory's first elections, hardly two months away.[7]

The polling in Tanga, Western, Northern, Southern Highlands, and Eastern Provinces (this last excluded the Dar es Salaam district) was set to begin on September 8 and would extend over four days in the remote regions. Some 400 polling stations had been established to serve the 28,500 registered voters in the five constituencies. Africans made up more than two-thirds of the electorate. Voting was to be on the basis of a common roll, although each elector had to vote for a candidate of each race in order to make his ballot valid. The government made every effort to enable all registered voters to vote. In one isolated district a polling station team traveled 160 miles on election day so that three voters could cast their ballots.

Nominations of candidates took place in early July. Twelve of the fifteen seats were contested by twelve Africans, eighteen Asians, and six Europeans. One African and two Europeans were unopposed for the other three seats. Six of the fifteen unofficial members of the Legislative Council who held representative seats chose not to seek re-election. In four constituencies TANU members ran against other African candidates, who stood either as independents or as UTP candidates. In Tanga Province both the TANU and the UTP African candidates were confronted by Zuberi Mtemvu, the president of the extremist African National Congress, which had been the Tanganyika African Congress until denied registration. The three European seats were contested by two UTP candidates and four others standing as independents. Several of the eighteen Asian candidates ran under the UTP banner, but most stood as independents.

Although TANU was utterly opposed to the tripartite system of voting, it decided to make the best of the situation. In August it announced its intention to indicate which of the European and Asian candidates it regarded as being the most favorable to African interests. TANU realized that by throwing African support to these candidates it could probably elect a coalition of members who either had been TANU candidates or had enjoyed TANU support. If this move proved successful, the Party would then be in a better position to bargain with the government and to press for rapid advance toward self-government.

One of the most dramatic events of the campaign occurred at Moshi, in the heart of settler country, when a mass meeting of about 5,000 was addressed by Nyerere, by the European and Asian candidates supported by TANU, and by the local TANU candidate. The press reported:

It was an historic event as this was the first time a non-African has been invited to address a mass meeting of Tanu supporters, numbering more than 5,000. For the first time, an African, an Asian, and a European stood on a political platform and talked about Tanganyika to a large and enthusiastic approving crowd.[8]

TANU support was pledged for Derek Bryceson, an organizer of the Tanganyika National Society and until recently Assistant Minister for Labor, who was contesting the European seat for Northern Province. Bryceson and Nyerere both spoke on the theme that there were such people as Tanganyikans, people who cut across the barriers of tribe, race, and religion. Mrs. Sophia Mustafa, contesting the Asian seat, and Solomon Eliufoo, who was the assistant education secretary of the Lutheran Mission, also emphasized the interdependence of the races.[9]

The president of the UTP, Ivor Bayldon, was his party's candidate for the European seat in Southern Highlands Province. During his campaign, Bayldon attacked what he felt was a lack of leadership at the top levels in the government. Because of this, he said, there was a widespread lack of respect for law and order.[10] The Party chairman, Sheikh Hussein Juma, stated that the UTP's "moderate, non-racial policy" was the "only means by which self-government can be speedily achieved."[11] Bayldon was opposed by Lady Chesham, who stood as an independent. Lady Chesham formerly belonged to the UTP, but was receiving TANU's support. Nyerere chose to contest the African seat in Eastern Province. He opposed G. P. Kunambi, who until recently had been an unofficial member of the Legislative Council. The only candidate of the African National Congress was its president, Mtemvu, who contested the African seat in Tanga Province. His main appeal to the electorate was for internal self-government by no later than 1962.

The balloting began on September 8. "Voters dressed themselves in their best clothes and behaved with the utmost decorum. No disorder of any kind occurred."[12] At the various polling stations, voters of all three races queued up together while waiting to cast their ballots. According to one observer, Tanganyika's first elections were so uneventful that "a stranger visiting Tabora would probably not realize there was an election going on."[13]

The result of the election was a clear-cut victory for TANU. In the twelve contested seats, every TANU candidate, or TANU-supported candidate, won the vote. TANU obtained some 67 per cent of the 22,769 ballots cast.[14] In Eastern Province, Nyerere collected more than three times as many votes as his opponent. Lady Chesham outdistanced Ivor Bayldon by the same margin in Southern Highlands Province. In Tanga Province, John Keto of TANU polled 3,455 votes; P. C. Mntambo, the UTP candidate, 1,854; and Zuberi Mtemvu, 53, thus forfeiting his £25 deposit. In other words, the voters showed a clear preferenec for TANU over the UTP and rejected the ANC outright. In Northern Province, Derek Bryceson, Solomon Eliufoo, and Mrs. Sophia Mustafa all outdistanced their opponents.[15] Mrs. Mustafa told the press, "I am very proud to be the first Asian woman to be elected to the Legislative Council. I will do my best for the Northern Province and for Tanganyika, as a true Tanganyikan."[16]

Other Asians receiving TANU's support also won by large majorities. One of these was the president of the Asian Association, Mahumud N. Rattansey, who was a successful candidate in Western Province. Another was Amir H. Jamal in Eastern Province, who maintained that the only way for Asians to live in Tanganyika was to identify themselves with the indigenous majority.[17] Except for G. T. Lewis and J. H. Baker, who were unopposed, all Legislative Council members running for re-election were defeated.

Many people had foreseen a victory for TANU, but not such a complete victory, and some people were disturbed by this. The tripartite vote, in particular, was criticized, as the following letter to the *Kenya Weekly News* shows: "Under the present system the European community cannot prevent one of their number being elected by the TANU vote, although they themselves do not necessarily consider him the most suitable."[18] F. S. Joelson, the editor of a weekly magazine dealing with East Africa, held Sir Edward Twining responsible for TANU's sweeping victory: "Weak administration during the past two or three years undermined the foundations and prepared the way for this landslide, which would certainly not have occurred if intimidation on a very wide scale had not been practised almost with impunity."[19] *The Economist* viewed the elections as confirmation that Tanganyika was "bound to become, ultimately, an African state."[20]

The result of the elections damaged the United Tanganyika Party beyond repair, although this was not admitted by some of the Party's leaders right away. According to Ivor Bayldon, the elections had proved that the UTP was "very much alive"; it took courage from the fact that it had received considerable support.[21] Most others saw that the Party had no political future. Less than a month after the elections Sir Edward Twining (now Lord Twining) told the Royal African Society that the UTP was "a failure, because of apathy and because of lack of leadership"; the capacity for leadership was present, but people had "not got the time to devote to public affairs."[22]

At the end of December, Sheikh Hussein Juma resigned from his position as chairman of the UTP. In a letter to the president he expressed the view that Tanganyika would have self-government within a "comparatively short number of years," and that it could be delayed only by irresponsibility. He felt that the UTP had been successful in moderating extremist opinion.

The scene today is transformed, and the views for which the U.T.P. has always stood are now widely accepted by those who were our political opponents. . . . It has been proved that those who thought that Tanganyika wanted European or Asian leadership were wrong, and my own experience has been that the immigrant populations of Tanganyika are content to see our constitutional development take place under African leadership.[23]

By the end of 1958 the UTP had, according to the administration, "ceased to function as an effective political organisation."[24]

The elections, as one observer noted, introduced "a new era of even stronger T.A.N.U. influence," an era in which Nyerere's personal position would not be an easy one. He had the power either to make life very difficult for the government, or to offer the administration TANU's support in a united drive toward self-government. If he chose the latter course, "the path of moderation and reasonableness," there was the question whether he would "be able to maintain his personal prestige among his followers." Although the opposition to him in the form of the African National Congress was insignificant, it could grow if the TANU rank-and-file became dissatisfied with the rate of progress toward self-government.[25]

Sir Richard Turnbull saw that Tanganyika was at a turning point in its political development. The next few years could be either a period of violence and unrest, or a period in which Africans, Asians, and Europeans worked together for independence. He therefore considered it supremely important at this point in Tanganyika's history for Governor and political leaders to work together, a judgment that showed "both courage and imagination."[26] At the opening of the new session of the Legislative Council on October 14, 1958, Turnbull set out the government's future policy:

A belief appears to exist amongst some people that a "multi-racial"—or, as I would prefer to call it, and intend to call it, a "non-racial"—policy will in some way or other prevent the Africans of Tanganyika from reaching their full political stature and from playing their proper part in the government of this country. This is not so. . . .

In terms of population the Africans always will be an overwhelming majority in Tanganyika, and, as the country progresses, it is right and proper, as indeed it is natural and inevitable, that African participation both in the legislature and in the executive should steadily increase. It is not intended, and never has been intended, that parity should be a permanent feature of the Tanganyika scene.

It is intended, and always has been intended, that the fact that when self-government is eventually attained both the legislature and the Government are likely to be predominantly African should in no way affect the security of the rights and interests of those minority communities who have made their homes in Tanganyika. I am glad to note that the responsible leaders of major political parties in the Territory are in complete agreement on this important matter; and that there is therefore a good prospect that in due course there will exist in Tanganyika a Government to which H.M. Government will be able to devolve their trust as being a Government under which responsible people of all races would feel secure.[27]

One after another, European, African, and Asian elected members rose to commend the Governor's statement. Nyerere, the newly elected chairman of the Elected Members Organization, said that Africans had long awaited such a statement and that Sir Richard was the Governor the country needed to guide it to independence. In the short period that Sir Richard had been in Tanganyika, Nyerere continued, he had earned the respect of all the people. Nyerere pledged that the Africans would take the attitude that was expected of them. He also mentioned that he was glad Sir Richard had cleared up certain misunderstandings about the government's multiracial policy, since Africans had felt "there was something sinister about this multiracial policy."[28] Similarly, one observer reported that Turnbull's speech establishing nonracialism as official policy pleased the African population very much, since it viewed "words like 'multi-racial' or 'partnership' as excuses for giving most privileges and the political power to the minority whites."[29] The speech, however, caused some uneasiness among the immigrant communities, who felt that the progress toward self-government might be too rapid.

In a booklet entitled *Barriers to Democracy,* which was published at this time, Nyerere stated that a "fear complex" haunted the Europeans and Asians and acted as a barrier to the establishment of democratic government. He urged the immigrant communities to forget their color and identify their interests with those of their fellow Tanganyikans.[30] Shortly afterward, in a letter to the *Tanganyika Standard,* he wrote: "It is said that Tanganyika has 120 tribes. I suggest that the way to democracy is to say we have 123 tribes in Tanganyika, the youngest and relatively the most educated being the European and Asian tribes. Let us then have tribal but not racial problems, if we must have problems at all."[31]

There were problems to be faced, however. For several months there had been considerable unrest in different parts of the territory, particularly around Mwanza in Lake Province. TANU's membership in these areas had been built up by soliciting the support of a group of Africans who viewed the government's agricultural policy as a threat to their way of life.[32] As a result of TANU's victory at the polls, some misguided TANU supporters in Lake Province were led into thinking that self-government was imminent and increased their opposition to all Native Authority rules regarding natural resources—not realizing that these measures were for their own benefit. Natural resources centers and cattle dips were forced to close.

The situation was so serious that at the end of November Nyerere flew to Mwanza to make a special appeal to his followers. Speaking to a crowd of some 10,000 people, he emphasized that law and order must be maintained. "TANU intends its members to obey the laws of the country," he said. "All other countries have laws, irrespective of the party in power." He remarked on the recent tendency for large crowds to make their way into Mwanza when any Msukuma was arrested; this was not TANU policy, he declared. Those who thought that a TANU membership card excused them from the ordinary processes of the law were quite wrong. He added without further explanation that the "TANU of today" was quite different from the "TANU of yesterday."[33]

Nyerere was commended in all quarters for his speech at Mwanza. Speaking at Morogoro in December, Turnbull said he was glad to note that "the leader of the major political party of the Territory has himself condemned those who defy the laws of the country." Such actions, the Governor continued, were doing the territory a lot of harm, since the timing of the next steps toward self-government depended on the people themselves. Those who defied the rule of law "through ignorance, ill-will or personal ambition are in fact hindering this development and putting a brake on the constitutional progress of the country."[34] Although the disturbances did not stop right away, by the end of the year the situation was somewhat improved.

A total of 30,791 voters registered for the second phase of the territorial elections in February. Although fifteen seats were at stake in five constituencies, only a few candidates came forward on nomination day, January 5, 1959. The result was that only three seats were contested in the February elections. Since the UTP had disappeared from the scene, TANU was left with little opposition. All five of the African candidates, TANU nominees, were unopposed. The European seat in Dar es Salaam was contested by D. F. Heath, a TANU-supported candidate, and Tom Tyrrell, the incumbent, who had resigned from the UTP after the September elections. K. L. Jhaveri, a lawyer backed by TANU, was opposed by G. M. Daya for the Asian seat in Dar es Salaam. Jhaveri was the candidate of the Asian Association. The only other contest was for the Asian seat in Southern Province. Although there was some question about the outcome of the two races in Dar es Salaam, owing to the preponderance of Asian voters, the TANU-supported candidates were victorious in all three contests. Heath toppled Tyrrell by 4,869 votes to 1,434. Other candidates who were returned unopposed were Rashidi M. Kawawa, the head of the Tanganyika Federation of Labor; Paul Bomani, the African incumbent in South-East Lake constituency; Miss B. C. Johanasson, a Swedish missionary-teacher; and H. W. Hannah of the Church Missionary Society at Mvumi in Central Province.

The *Kenya Weekly News* commented that Tanganyika's first territorial elections were a "significant victory" for TANU under the "shrewd leadership" of Nyerere. It pointed out that Nyerere could now press for constitutional changes "with the backing of votes of all races in Tanganyika." The *News* continued:

He has achieved this with obvious official and unofficial approval, and he has achieved it in spite of having to take a possibly unpopular line in Lake Province, where he berated the extremists. Nyerere has quietly and effectively gained Government's confidence, and that of many non-African voters, in his plan for orderly progress towards self-government.[35]

In early February, John Fletcher-Cooke reported on Tanganyika's recent constitutional progress to the Trusteeship Council. He said the government's nonracial policy was a recognition that Tanganyika was predominantly an African country, but still one in which the immigrant communities would play some role. Although the level of political consciousness was not even throughout the territory, he felt that there was a growing national awareness, and pointed out that tribal loyalties had played no part in the recent elections. The recent unrest in certain sections proved that there was a gulf between the political leaders at the center and their supporters in the provinces, but, nevertheless, he considered that Tanganyika's constitutional progress could be described as "rapid and orderly."[36] The growth in national consciousness was to be attributed in part to the growth of the African middle class: teachers, clerks, medical and agricultural assistants, and the occasional university graduate were now part of the scene in the towns and cities. Often these urbanized

Africans were not of the local tribe and therefore lived in a world apart from the old order. More than anything else they were Tanganyikans.[37]

In its review of developments in Tanganyika the Trusteeship Council expressed its pleasure at the "harmony of purpose and interest among all persons" and hoped that the territory would rapidly make further substantial advances toward self-government. The Council also hoped that the Administering Authority would give early consideration to adopting measures for progressively decreasing official and nominated representation in the Legislative Council and transforming it into a completely elected body. Recalling its previous resolutions on the subject of a timetable for independence, the Council recommended that the Administering Authority, in consultation with the elected representatives of the population, adopt plans for the development of the territory in all fields, "with indications where appropriate of intermediate target dates to create as soon as possible the pre-conditions for the attainment by the Territory of self-government or independence."[38]

According to John Stonehouse, a member of Parliament who visited Tanganyika shortly after the February 1959 elections, Tanganyika was the "nearest to solving its political and racial problems" of any territory in East and Central Africa. He had the opportunity of meeting the TANU executive committee and reported that with the exception of one or two extremists, "who wanted no truck with the other races," the rest of the committee supported Nyerere's program for future policy. Stonehouse reported that the willingness of Tanganyika's Asian population to identify themselves with the African masses contributed to the absence of racial feeling. He also noted that "the rank and file Indians supported the idea of equality with Africans as keenly as their leaders did."[39]

FINAL STEPS TO RESPONSIBLE GOVERNMENT

The fifteen newly elected members took their seats beside their fifteen colleagues elected the previous September at the opening of the new session of the Legislative Council on March 17, 1959. Presiding for the first time was the new speaker, A. Y. A. Karimjee, a member of a distinguished family that has lived in East Africa for five generations. Chief H. M. Lugusha succeeded Karimjee as deputy speaker.

Sir Richard Turnbull opened the session with an important announcement. Since Tanganyika would now move rapidly toward responsible government with elected members holding the majority of the seats in the Council, he considered it desirable to give administrative responsibility to several members of the elected opposition ahead of the grant of responsible government. He therefore porposed to set up, on July 1, a Council of Ministers in which unofficials—three Africans, one Asian and one European—would for the first time be appointed to ministerial office. The Council would assume the functions of the Executive Council in advising the Governor on constitutional and legislative matters. The Executive Council would continue in existence, however, with modified powers. With the appointment of unofficials as ministers, the posts of assistant ministers would disappear. Turnbull said that he hoped it would be possible to find all five unofficial ministers from among the elected members of the Legislative Council.[40]

During the following week the Elected Members Organization deliberated whether they should accept this proposal. Since it would be possible for Turnbull to fill the posts with other unofficials, Nyerere later said, "it was not really important whether we accepted the five ministries or rejected them. What was important is that we accepted them as a team or rejected them as a team."[41] The elected members subsequently decided to accept appointment. The five chosen to head departments were: Derek Bryceson, Minister for Mines and Commerce; S. N. Eliufoo, Minister for Health; Chief Abdullah Fundikira, Minister for Lands and Surveys; Amir Jamal, Minister for Urban and Local Government and Works; and C. G. Kahama, Minister for Social and Cooperative Development. There was general agreement that the Governor had chosen five outstanding members for the posts. Nyerere declined a ministerial appointment; as the leader of the opposition, he thought it best not to accept a position of responsibility until the elected members were granted a majority in the Council of Ministers. On July 1, at the swearing in of the new Council, Turnbull said that the ceremony marked the introduction of

as fundamental a change as any that has been brought about in the fast-moving constitutional progress of the Territory; for it signifies the termination of a long period of wholly official executive government, and the setting up of a different kind of Government—the kind of Government in which Elected Members of the Legislature will share in the formation of Government policies.[42]

After the five elected members had moved over to the Government benches as ministers, the opposition was left with only 25 elected members. When the Legislative Council reconvened in October, the government side consisted of 7 ex officio members, the 5 elected members who had been appointed ministers, and 16 nominated members. Since the three opposition seats reserved for such interests as the Governor saw fit had been left vacant, the other 25 elected members made up the opposition. Thus, although the government had a majority of three, in effect there was an over-all majority of elected members.

In his address to the Legislative Council in March, Turnbull also announced that he was setting up a postelections committee to recommend further African representation in the Legislative Council, changes in the franchise and the system of tripartite voting, and the creation of a Territorial Council. He said that by the time the Committee's report was made public he hoped to be able to make an announcement that would "include a forecast as to when . . . we may expect nonofficial majorities to be introduced into the Council of Ministers and the Legislative Council." Such an announcement, however, would depend on two factors: "First, our ability to operate in a workmanlike manner the substantial executive changes which I have today placed before this House, and, secondly, the maintenance of law and order."[43]

Although TANU had originally asked the Governor for an immediate unofficial majority and a target date for independence, Nyerere accepted the present proposals, but made it clear that he had done so only after the administration had clarified its future intentions. Derek Bryceson, the deputy leader of the elected members, expressed his complete confidence in Nyerere's policy and in Nyerere's keeping faith with Tanganyikans of all races when there came to be an African majority on the Council of Ministers and the Legislative Council.[44] Following Bryceson's speech, a number of letters in the *Tanganyika Standard* called on TANU to open its membership to people of other races. Regarding this, Nyerere told the Arusha Chamber of Commerce: "It is our intention as soon as we feel that it is the right time to do that and throw it open. I feel that there is a right time to do this. I have tried it twice and every time have convinced myself that it was not the right time."[45]

That Bryceson was not alone in placing faith in Nyerere was pointed out by the *Kenya Weekly News*: "Many Europeans and Asians, inside Legislative Council and outside, have committed themselves unreservedly to Mr. Nyerere's care and leadership. They trust him."[46] Even Tanganyika's "old guard" found it possible to say a good word about the territory's political development. Speaking at Tanga, Alec Le Maitre remarked: "All that I have worked for in this country is invested here in Tanganyika. That is my reply to those who ask me what I think of the future . . . politically, I have no fear."[47] According to an American observer who visited Tanganyika in 1959, racialism had practically vanished from the political scene: "The subject is seldom mentioned by the various racial leaders, as if it were some nightmare now passed and best forgotten. Mr. Nyerere gives a reason for this change: 'It is very simple. We are all Tanganyikans now, and no one expects that special privileges will be reserved for racial groups.' "[48]

In May the membership of the postelections committee was announced. Sir Richard Ramage was named as chairman; eight of the fourteen members were elected members of the Legislative Council. TANU representatives on the committee were Rashidi Kawawa, Paul Bomani, and John Keto. In June, TANU submitted a memorandum to the Ramage Committee, outlining four major proposals: (1) that the Legislative Council should have a majority of elected members; (2) that the Council of Ministers should have a majority of elected members; (3) that elections should be by universal adult suffrage and on a common roll; and (4) that the racial parity system of representation should be abolished.

The most important of these was the second proposal; upon its acceptance hinged the realization of responsible government. TANU proposed that nine out of the twelve ministers should be elected members of the Legislative Council. Only the portfolios of Defense, External Affairs, and Legal Affairs would be filled by officials. The Governor would retain his veto. The first proposal envisaged a Legislative Council of 82 members, 79 of them elected. Of the 79 elected seats, 21 would be temporarily reserved for minorities (13 for the Asians and 8 for the Europeans); the remaining 58 seats would be open to candidates of any race. Nyerere insisted on the provision for reserved seats in order to avoid giving the impression to the outside world that the Africans intended to disregard the wishes of the minorities.[49] TANU's memorandum stated:

The proposals we are submitting are not designed to provide representation for Africans, Asians, and Europeans as such. They are designed to pave the way for a truly democratic form of representation. We are not therefore suggesting representation for the African as such. We are suggesting that a majority of seats be free seats which can be contested by any Tanganyikan.[50]

There was little reaction to TANU's proposals in the capital. The Asian Association differed on one point: true to its policy declaration, it asked that there should be no minority privileges for Asians. European opinion outside of Dar es Salaam was more conservative. Several settler groups, feeling that their views were not represented in the Legislative Council by the present elected members, asked for the introduction of a communal roll for the European community. Speaking in London in July, Nyerere said he wished to emphasize that the leaders of the three racial communities were "absolutely determined" to establish a genuine democracy in Tanganyika. "My friends within the Legislative Council are just as united in their demand for what we have put forward—the demand for responsible government this year—as any African in the country." Nyerere reported that an official from the Colonial Office recently in Tanganyika "was taken aback when the demand for responsible government . . .

was put in strong terms, not by the Africans, but by the non-African elected members and by British Europeans in particular."[51]

The Ramage Committee was also responsible for making recommendations on the establishment of a Territorial Council, to be composed of representatives of the chiefs and others and to act in an advisory capacity to the government. TANU's memorandum stated that such a body was unnecessary, since the present Convention of Chiefs already fulfilled this function. Although TANU had expressed no official opinion on what the future position of the chiefs should be, it was becoming obvious that the nationalists saw no place for them in the central government. On one occasion during this period Nyerere stated:

We tell the Chiefs quite frankly that their authority is traditional only in the tribes, which were the traditional units. Tanganyika is not a traditional unit at all, and if the Chiefs want to have a place in this thing we call Tanganyika, they have got to adapt themselves to this new situation. There is nothing traditional in the Central Government of Tanganyika today.[52]

Since the chiefs had not completely identified themselves with the nationalist movement, there existed "a subtle sub-surface conflict between [them] and the nationalist leaders."[53] Afraid that they might be removed from their Native Authority positions after independence, the chiefs were beginning to develop an interest in territorial politics in order to protect their position locally.

July 7, 1959, marked the fifth anniversary of TANU. Nyerere's TANU Day message, which was read in all the branches, noted that the Union was at "the end of five years of relentless struggle for the freedom of Tanganyika."[54] Beginning almost from nothing in 1954, Nyerere had forged a movement of tremendous political power, whose appeal went far beyond the bounds of its membership. TANU headquarters estimated that they now had over three million supporters and about half a million dues-paying members.[55] Those who were not technically members nevertheless felt they were a part of the movement. TANU members were wholeheartedly devoted to their leaders; opposition to the leaders was "incomprehensible and rejected out of hand."[56]

During July and part of August, Nyerere was in London in order to press TANU's demand for responsible government at the Colonial Office. He was disturbed lest Tanganyika's constitutional progress might be held back owing to the strong pressures being applied by parties in Kenya and Central Africa who were afraid of the effect that responsible government in Tanganyika might have on their own internal politics.[57] According to Nyerere, however, Tanganyika could be an example to these other areas by showing that it was possible to have a democratic government in a multiracial society. "We in Tanganyika are determined to do it," he said, "so that our friends . . . can say: 'If it can be done in Tanganyika, it can also be done in Kenya and in Central Africa.' "[58] He expressed the opinion that Tanganyika should get responsible government right away, and independence in five years. He told a press conference: "We are impatient for responsible government. We are not impatient about independence. We want to handle the education of our people, economic development, improvement of communications, and so on. When we are doing the job independence can take care of itself."[59] On his return to Dar es Salaam, Nyerere reported that he was "satisfied" with the British attitude toward Tanganyika.[60]

Ever since the elections Nyerere had been careful to point out in his speeches that responsible government, which TANU was seeking, was not the same as independence. He urged moderation and patience, since it was impossible for Tanganyika to have independence right away. At meetings held after his return from London, he told Africans throughout the territory that freedom had been practically achieved, and that now the really hard work must begin. He spoke of the need for economic development, but pointed out that all of the needed capital could not be obtained outside Tanganyika. In order to retain the capital already invested in the territory, he emphasized that it should be understood that the immigrant races were in Tanganyika to stay. More important, Africans would be called on for hard work in the years ahead.[61] In order to stress the difficulties that lay ahead, TANU changed its slogan from "Uhuru" (Freedom) to "Uhuru na Kazi" (Freedom and Work).[62]

Although he postponed making any announcement on the

Ramage Committee's report, Turnbull informed the Legislative Council on October 20, 1959, that Tanganyika's next general election would be brought forward from 1962 to September 1960. He also said that the tripartite system of voting would be dispensed with. Nyerere expressed his approval of the Governor's statement in these words: "We would like to light a candle, and put it on top of Mount Kilimanjaro, which will shine beyond our borders, giving hope where there was despair, love where there was hate, and dignity where there was humiliation."[63] In November, Turnbull flew to London to discuss the recommendations, not yet made public, of the Ramage Committee with the new Colonial Secretary, Ian Macleod, and what should be the government's reply to them in the announcement now promised for December.

On December 12, 1959, simultaneously with the publication of the report, the Governor announced to the Legislative Council and to a large crowd waiting outside Karimjee Hall that he had been authorized by the Colonial Secretary to say that, provided there were no untoward developments, Tanganyika would be granted responsible government following the coming general election. With only slight modifications the Ramage Committee's report had been accepted in full. The new Legislative Council would have 71 elected members; 50 of these seats would be open to members of any race, 11 would be reserved for Asians, and 10 for Europeans. There would still be a small number of nominated members. As a general rule, districts rather than provinces would be used as the basic constituency. The proposal that the minority representatives should be elected on the basis of a communal roll was rejected by the Committee as being politically impracticable.

The Committee's recommendations on the franchise were modified somewhat by a decision of the Colonial Secretary. In a dispatch published with the report, Macleod stated that he shared the Committee's desire for a substantial widening of the franchise, but that to link the right to vote with the payment of personal tax, as had been proposed, would differentiate against women. He did not think it would be wise to establish separate qualifications for women, and therefore proposed, instead, three alternative qualifications, which would apply to both men and women. These required that the voter be able to read and write in English or Swahili; possess an annual income of at least £75; or be the present or past holder of a prescribed office. The Committee's recommendation that the idea of a Territorial Council be dropped and that, instead, statutory recognition be given to the Convention of Chiefs by means of local legislation was accepted.

Reform of the executive government was not included in the Committee's terms of reference. However, the Governor told the Council:

Her Majesty's Government agreed that . . . the Executive Government will be re-formed after the general election on the basis of an unofficial majority; that is to say, the Council of Ministers will be reconstituted in such a way that the number of Ministers selected from amongst the people of the Territory will be greater than the number of Ministers who are public officers.

Turnbull went on to say that the precise structure of the executive government in its new form had not yet been determined; the details would be worked out at a discussion in London in the spring of 1960.[64]

The new constitutional changes represented a considerable triumph for TANU, since they went a long way to meet the Party's original proposals to the Ramage Committee. The announcement of responsible government in 1960 showed great confidence in Nyerere's leadership. Only five years before, Great Britain had protested in the Trusteeship Council that Tanganyika could not be ready for self-government within even twenty years; now it seemed that self-government and independence were just around the corner. When Nyerere left Karimjee Hall after the Governor's address, he was cheered, garlanded, and hoisted shoulder-high by the laughing and shouting crowd. As the largest procession ever staged in Dar es Salaam wound its way through the city's streets, Africans, Asians, and Europeans enthusiastically greeted each other in "spontaneous instances of inter-racial amity all along the route."[65] In London,

Lord Perth, Minister of State for Colonial Affairs, commented: "Sooner or later we have to take the plunge with all our territories in Africa. . . . We believe this will set a pattern for others."[66]

The government relinquished its majority on the Council of Ministers in early February, when Sir Ernest Vasey, until recently Minister of Finance in Kenya, was sworn into office as Tanganyika's new Minister of Finance. Vasey was not an official, but an appointed unofficial, minister. Although his appointment came from the Governor, Vasey had been personally invited to take the post by Nyerere, who felt that Vasey's experience would win the people's confidence. "People with money to invest sometimes want proof of our intentions," Nyerere had recently remarked.[67] Referring to the appointment, one observer commented that Nyerere "means business and intends to run Tanganyika in a responsible and determined manner."[68]

Before leaving on a month's tour of the United States at the invitation of the U.S. Department of State, Nyerere addressed TANU's annual conference in Dar es Salaam. He used the occasion to criticize some current attitudes among TANU's leaders.

I have seen some Tanu officers getting drunk with power, and scheming to undermine one another. Some officers are too interested in finding ways of dominating others and in seeking to eliminate their friends from their posts. . . . There is a great danger that many of our leaders are working for responsible government to provide themselves with high positions.

It would be a disgrace, he declared, to get rid of colonial rule only to find that one's own government did not please the people as much as the former one.[69]

Stopping off in London on his way back from the United States, Nyerere, together with Vasey and Turnbull, discussed the future structure of the Council of Ministers with the Colonial Secretary. On his return to Dar es Salaam, Nyerere said the talks had gone well but were not concluded.[70] The final announcement was not made until April 26, when Fletcher-Cooke, the Chief Secretary, informed the Legislative Council that the constitution of the Council of Ministers had been settled, with effect from October 1. The post of Chief Minister would be created, the occupant of which would combine the functions of principal adviser to the Governor and leader of government business in the Legislative Council. The Chief Secretary would consequently become head of the civil service. The Council of Ministers would consist of the Governor, the Deputy Governor, the Chief Minister, nine other unofficial ministers, and two civil service or unofficial ministers, these two being the Attorney General and the Minister for Information Service. Responsibility for the use and operational control of the police force would remain vested in the Governor. Lastly, the Executive Council would cease to exist.

Nyerere described these changes as a major step toward full independence. However, he doubted whether the Governor should be on the Council of Ministers, since if the Governor insisted on some particular point, it could lead to a constitutional crisis. He also expressed the hope that the elections could be moved up to early August.[71] The preponderance of unofficial ministers on the new Council was regarded as a sign that Tanganyika would move rapidly on to full independence. The decision "confirms the unchallenged leadership of Mr. Nyerere," remarked one observer. "So peaceful have Tanganyika politics become that these momentous developments have occasioned none of the processions, mass meetings, and green-branch-waving usually associated with constitutional advance. It's all taken quietly for granted."[72]

The fifth United Nations Visiting Mission to Tanganyika, headed by Mason Sears of the United States, spent three weeks touring the territory in April. During this time it received communications from many groups, including a request from TANU "that the proposed September general elections should be mounted as a plebiscite for the independence of the Territory." One of the main reasons given was that the whole country was united and peaceful and was demanding immediate independence. The Mission gained the impression that one of TANU's aims in presenting the memorandum was to make sure that the restricted franchise, to which the organization was opposed, should not be a barrier to the attainment of independence.[73] At the close of the Mission's visit, Sears commented that the outside world was too little informed about the peaceful and important progress that Tanganyika was making.[74]

The Mission's report was presented to the Trusteeship Council in early June. The general conclusion was that "with patience and hard work, great days are ahead for Tanganyika."[75] The Mission felt that Tanganyika was progressing "smoothly and rapidly" toward independence, the problems that remained being largely technical and financial ones. Constitutional advances during the last few years had far exceeded all expectations. "The most noteworthy feature of the political situation . . . is the peaceful and harmonious atmosphere of goodwill. Nowhere did the Mission get the impression that there were any political tensions or any current threat to law and order." At the same time the Mission found what it described as "a steady emotional pressure for *Uhuru,* for complete independence in the near future." It noted that several small groups of Asians and Europeans had expressed apprehension about the rapidity of political progress and feared for their economic rights after independence, but "these cases were somewhat isolated and were accompanied by no suggestions for political action." The Mission said it realized that some feeling of apprehension was inevitable prior to a major change of regime; "such a change is, however, never likely to take place under more favourable circumstances than in Tanganyika."

The Mission also spoke of the "excellent relations existing between persons of various races," adding that "the ease and graciousness of social contacts is very remarkable." As a practical example of racial cooperation in action, it cited the Elected Members Organization. In conclusion, the Mission reported:

In the course of the discussion in London, the Secretary of State for the Colonies stated that he was anxious that Tanganyika should remain a showpiece among territories developing towards independence. Each territory's problems were different and each had to advance at its own pace. He could assure the Mission that Tanganyika would not be held back because of possible repercussions in other territories.[76]

During the Trusteeship Council's review of the Mission's report, Sir Andrew Cohen told the Council that the British government regarded the report as containing "many penetrating and valuable observations and recommendations." Speaking next, Tanganyika's Chief Secretary, John Fletcher-Cooke, said that the Mission's findings had been well received in Tanganyika and that the Mission had left many friends there. He told the Council that the success of the "Grand Design" for Tanganyika would depend on five factors. The first of these was the presence of strong and honest political leadership. "We in Tanganyika believe that we have this in full measure and that in Mr. Nyerere we have an outstanding political leader—indeed a great African statesman." The other factors were wise financial and economic guidance, which Sir Ernest Vasey was furnishing; a spirit of tolerance and good will among all those who had made their homes in Tanganyika; a genuine desire to make the "Grand Design" work; and the presence of an incorruptible, efficient, and contented civil service.[77]

In its conclusions on the situation in Tanganyika the Trusteeship Council welcomed the important constitutional reforms taking place. It was confident that the forthcoming changes in the executive government would only be "a short-lived stage" in Tanganyika's progress toward independence. It expressed satisfaction with the reforms introduced in the electoral system and in the composition of the Legislative Council, but regretted the administration's decision not to introduce universal adult suffrage in the forthcoming elections. It was confident, however, that the new government entering office after the elections would give this matter further attention "and that the introduction of universal adult suffrage will not be long delayed."[78]

Registration for the general election was completed in March and resulted, on final count, in a total of 885,000 registered voters. This apathy—the figure represented only about half the number of persons estimated as potentially eligible to register—was attributed to the absence of substantial competition.[79] Nomination day was July 18. Only 86 candidates presented themselves for the 71 seats. On July 29, 58 of this number were declared elected, since they faced no opposition. Nyerere was one of the 39 Africans elected unopposed. In the remaining constituencies, whose seats would be contested on election day, August 30, eleven TANU African candidates were opposed by two candidates of the African National Congress, TANU's only organized opposition, and nine other independents. In the two other contests, two TANU-supported Europeans were opposed by two independents, one of whom was Ivor Bayldon, the former head of the UTP. *The Times* pointed out that this was "the first time in the Commonwealth that a general election has been won before the voters have gone to the polls."[80] One observer commented that there would have been greater opposition, at least in the non-African communities, if TANU did not have the confidence of all the people.[81]

The campaigning for the thirteen contested seats took place during August, but was overshadowed by news of violence from the Congo. During this time, Nyerere made several speeches which did much to reassure certain sections of the non-African population that the disorders occurring in the Congo would not happen in Tanganyika. Speaking at Moshi, he said: "Changes are going to take place in this country, but there will be no change in Tanu's attitude towards law and order, except to enforce even more respect for law and order. We are pledged to ensure that this is going to continue to be an absolutely peaceful country." He pointed out that TANU was committed to a policy of respect for all human beings irrespective of color or race.[82]

Election day was quiet and passed almost unnoticed. TANU won twelve of the thirteen contested seats. The only unsuccessful TANU candidate lost to a TANU member put forward by the Mbulu branch who had been passed over by the TANU executive committee when nominations were made. The *Kenya Weekly News* commented that TANU's remarkable victory could be "directly attributed to the statesmanlike qualities of its leaders, particularly Mr. Nyerere."[83]

Following the election, Nyerere formed the new government that he was to head as Chief Minister. A decision had previously been made to advance the date for responsible government; the new Council of Ministers, therefore, was sworn into office on September 3. In addition to Nyerere, those taking the oath were as follows: Attorney General, J. S. R. Cole; Minister for Information Services, M. J. Davies; Minister for Finance, Sir Ernest Vasey; Minister for Lands, Surveys, and Water, Chief Abdullah Fundikira; Minister for Health and Labor, Derek Bryceson; Minister for Home Affairs, George Kahama; Minister for Communications, Power, and Works, Amir Jamal; Minister for Agriculture and Cooperative Development, Paul

Bomani; Minister for Education, Oscar Kambona; and Minister for Local Government and Housing, Rashidi Kawawa. Seven of the ministers were holdovers from the previous government. Only two of the posts, Attorney General and Minister for Information Services, were official appointments. After the ministers had taken the oath, the Governor read a message from the Colonial Secretary, Macleod:

The people of the territory have the unique opportunity to show by their example that men and women of all races and all conditions of society can live and work together harmoniously in a spirit of interdependence. I am sure that with wisdom and understanding you will not fail to meet this challenge.[84]

That evening Nyerere made a nation-wide broadcast in English and Swahili. Speaking for the first time as Chief Minister, he told his audience that Tanganyikans had earned the admiration of millions of people outside Tanganyika for the way in which the struggle for freedom had been conducted:

It was the character of our people which made inevitable our achievement of responsible government and which again renders inevitable the achievement of our complete independence. It is that same character which ensures our success in the struggle against ignorance, poverty, disease, and fear—a struggle in which I am proud and privileged to lead you.[85]

AFRICAN MAJORITY GOVERNMENT

The new Legislative Council met for the first time on October 11, 1960, which had been designated "Madaraka Day" by the government, *madaraka* being the Swahili equivalent for "responsible government." Of the 81 members, there were 52 Africans, 16 Europeans, 11 Asians, one Arab, and one Goan. Among these were ten nominated members, who included Sir Ernest Vasey, the Minister for Finance; Miss Lucy Lameck, the organizing secretary of the women's section of TANU; and J. M. Hunter and Alec Le Maitre, both former members. Reaction to the Governor's speech from the throne was "unemotional, almost apathetic," many people being disappointed by his not naming the actual date of independence. Instead it was announced that a constitutional conference would be held in March to discuss the final plans for independence. Sir Richard Turnbull also promised that Britain would do everything in her power to see that any obstacles to independence were speedily overcome. Following Turnbull's address, a public procession through the streets of Dar es Salaam took place before a large, orderly throng.[86]

Soon after Madaraka Day, TANU took the first step toward opening the party's membership to all races. Two Asians and a European, Dossa Aziz, Al Noor Kassum, and Lady Chesham, were named to the new executive committee of the TANU Parliamentary Party. Nyerere became the group's president and Sheikh Amri Abedi, the mayor of Dar es Salaam, its chairman.

By the end of the year it became apparent that there was a growing difference of opinion between the TANU leadership and some of the more fiery nationalists on the back benches. This difference centered upon the Africanization of the civil service. With the granting of independence, many of the British civil servants were expected to leave the country, and plans were therefore being made for their replacement; at the recent election, TANU had promised to carry out a program of Africanization as quickly as possible.

Disagreement about the meaning of Africanization was first voiced by the Tanganyika Federation of Labor. In October the Federation attacked the Minister for Labor, Derek Bryceson, for his statement that TANU believed in localization rather than Africanization. The labor federation claimed that priority must be given to Africanization, the employment of Africans, in preference to "local" people, presumably of other races. Asked his views on the subject, Nyerere supported Bryceson by emphasizing that Africanization meant getting local people into the civil service, which presumably meant local people of any race.[87] Many trade union officials who were members of the Legislative Council supported the position of the Federation in the Council. By the end of the year it was clear that Africanization was going to be one of the most politically explosive problems confronting the new government.

The differences of opinion within TANU went further afield than Africanization. In some ways it began to look more like an all-out attack on the gradualist policies of the TANU leadership. This was particularly evident in the Legislative Council's debate in December at which the government's plans for school integration were discussed. Up to this time a separate school system had existed for African, Asian, and European children. Attacking the integration plan announced by the government, C. K. Tumbo, the head of the railway union, declared, "I am for revolution. If we want integration, we should integrate, and we should not embark on half measures." In reply, Nyerere insisted that evolution, rather than revolution, was the right path. What Tumbo and certain of his colleagues had advocated, he said, would amount not to a revolution, but to an explosion. Nyerere then declared that the government would not undertake what was unnecessary simply to satisfy "the irresponsibles."[88]

Disturbed by the growing rift between TANU and the trade unionists, Nyerere informed the trade unions (through a circular letter sent out early in 1961) that when trade unions formed a political wing of a party, as had happened in TANU, then those workers were a part of the party, and it was absurd for them to talk about independence from the party. He maintained that the Party and the trade unions should cooperate in achieving the goals they both desired.[89]

In January it was announced that the Tanganyika Constitutional Conference planned for March would take place in Dar es Salaam at the Karimjee Hall. The conference began on March 27, following the arrival of the Colonial Secretary, Ian Macleod, and his advisers. Barely two days later it was announced that Tanganyika would receive full internal self-government on May 1 and complete independence on December 28. The measures that would come in force on May 1 were as follows: the Council of Ministers would become a Cabinet; the Governor, the Deputy Governor, and the two official Ministers, J. S. R. Cole and M. J. Davies, would cease to be members; the Legislative Council would become the National Assembly; the post of Deputy Governor would be abolished; and the Governor would continue to be responsible for defense and external affairs until December 28. During the conference the Tanganyika government reaffirmed its intention to apply for membership in the Commonwealth after the attainment of independence. It was also agreed that the British government would introduce a resolution at the United Nations proposing the termination of the Trusteeship Agreement on December 28.

At the closing session of the conference, formal addresses were made by Macleod, Nyerere, and Turnbull. When Macleod announced that the date of independence would be December 28, his words were drowned by cheering, which spread from the public galleries of the hall to the thousands waiting outside. Speaking after Macleod, Nyerere said that the changes in the Council of Ministers were "no more than a matter of form, because my colleagues and I have a relationship, and an understanding, with the Governor, which is so close that we are far from feeling that his chairmanship of the Council of Ministers has ever been any kind of a burden or frustration to us." Nyerere concluded his address with the words: "This is a day of triumph for Tanganyika. . . . I rejoice to say that it is not a day of triumph *over* anybody. It is a happy victory for a good cause in which all are winners. One and all in Tanganyika can rejoice with us in saying '*Uhuru* 1961.' "[90]

When the Governor got up to speak, Nyerere and all his fellow ministers rose to their feet, cheering and applauding with the entire audience. Following this spontaneous expression of good will, Turnbull expressed his confidence that "under the wise guidance and far-seeing direction of our Chief Minister—soon to be our Prime Minister—Tanganyika will, with God's help, fulfill the high expectation we place in her."[91] As they left the conference hall, the three speakers had garlands placed about their necks by the jubilant crowd; Nyerere was lifted shoulder-high by his supporters. A triumphal procession through the capital followed.

On May 1 Tanganyika received internal self-government, and Julius Nyerere took office as the territory's first Prime Minister. The new Cabinet was sworn in by Sir Richard Turnbull at a ceremony in Government House. Before administering the oaths to Nyerere and his colleagues, the Governor recalled the two previous governments in which elected members of the Legislative Council played an increasing role in the formulation of government policy. "Both Governments measured up to their responsibilities in a manner worthy of the highest praise," Turnbull said, "and it is for that reason that we are able today to embark on the final stage of our constitutional march to independence."[92]

The composition of the Cabinet was as follows: Prime Minister, Julius Nyerere; Minister for Finance, Sir Ernest Vasey; Minister for Legal Affairs, Chief Abdullah Fundikira; Minister for Health and Labor, Derek Bryceson; Minister for Home Affairs, George Kahama; Minister for Communications, Power, and Works, Amir Jamal; Minister for Agriculture, Paul Bomani; Minister for Commerce and Industry, Nsilo Swai; Minister for Education, Oscar Kambona; Minister for Lands and Surveys, Tewa Saidi; Minister for Local Government, Job Lusinde; and Minister without Portfolio, Rashidi Kawawa. The portfolio of the Minister for Information Services was taken over by the Prime Minister, thus keeping the number of ministers at twelve. Kawawa's appointment as Minister without Portfolio was virtually that of Deputy Prime Minister, his job being to relieve Nyerere of much of the detailed work.

There were two new ministers in the Cabinet, Tewa and Lusinde. The appointment of Chief Fundikira as Minister for Legal Affairs was well received by the European and Asian communities because of his commendable record as Minister for Lands and Surveys. Roland Brown, a London advocate, succeeded J. S. R. Cole as Attorney General, but was not included in the Cabinet. The rest of the Cabinet remained unchanged from the previous Council of Ministers. Of the twelve ministers, nine were Africans, two were Europeans, and one was an Asian. All were elected members of the National Assembly except Sir Edward Vasey, a nominated member. Collectively the Cabinet must have been one of the youngest in the history of the Commonwealth: the average age of the twelve ministers was 37, with Sir Edward Vasey as the oldest at 59.

At the same time, three parliamentary secretaries were appointed —to assist the Prime Minister, the Minister for Agriculture, and the Minister for Education, respectively. Two of them were Africans and one was an Asian. All three were elected members of the National Assembly, but were not, of course, members of the Cabinet.

After May 1, the Governor was bound by the Constitution to

accept the advice of the Cabinet, or in certain specified circumstances of an individual minister, on all matters relating to the internal government of Tanganyika, but continued to be responsible for defense and external relations. Although this was the constitutional position, the situation in practice was different. After May 1, ministers were increasingly associated with the conduct of Tanganyika's external affairs and its defense arrangements. In fact, a special section of the Prime Minister's Office was established to deal with these matters, with the intention that after independence it would become the new Ministry of External Affairs and Defense. In addition, preparations were made to establish a Tanganyikan Foreign Service and to open certain Tanganyikan missions overseas.

Although in the previous period from September 3, 1960, to May 1, 1961, the Governor was not legally bound to accept the advice of the Council of Ministers, it was later revealed at the United Nations that there was no occasion during this time on which he did not, in fact, accept the advice of his ministers, only two of whom were officials. In practice, therefore, Tanganyika enjoyed internal self-government for eight months before it was formally granted.[93]

The first meeting of the legislature under its new title of National Assembly began on May 16 and lasted until June 6. This, the budget session, was the longest continuous meeting of the legislature's 35-year history. During this session the members of the Assembly subjected Tanganyika to "probably the most exhaustive stocktaking of its history, . . . when everything from vast irrigation projects to Ministers' use or misuse of Government motorcars was put under the legislative microscope."[94] The general tenor of the debate accurately reflected political feeling in the territory. Speeches of a number of backbenchers exhibited growing impatience with certain government policies. To some, the supposed material benefits of independence seemed as far away as ever. In particular, this unofficial opposition called for a more liberal expenditure of government funds and faster Africanization.

Although the government's position was not seriously challenged, it was now quite evident that an opposition group was forming. It was helped along by the dissatisfaction of certain TANU backbenchers who had been demoted in the party hierarchy to make way for younger and better educated men. Some TANU regional officials, unhappy with the size of their representation in the National Assembly, also tended to identify with this group.[95] One observer commented, "It is true that no particular leader of such an opposition group has yet emerged. . . . But once a leader emerges, it is clear that he will have many followers in the Assembly.[96]

The long budget session closed with the Prime Minister's moving that the British government be requested to introduce legislation establishing Tanganyika as an independent sovereign state on December 28, and that other member governments of the Commonwealth be requested to join with the British government in supporting Tanganyika's desire to become a Commonwealth member. Nyerere pointed out that Tanganyika's one qualification to joining the Commonwealth, namely, the expulsion of South Africa from Commonwealth membership, had been removed. Therefore he could see "nothing but good" from Tanganyika's entry into the Commonwealth. Stronger than treaties, less selfish than alliances, less restrictive than any other association, Commonwealth membership seemed to him to offer "the best hope in the world today of lasting peace and friendship among the peoples of the world."[97] After a few muttered objections from the back benches, the motion was approved unanimously amid the loudest applause of the session.[98] Shortly afterward the date for independence was moved forward to December 9 so that Prince Philip could attend the celebrations.

The only organized opposition to TANU continued to be that of the African National Congress led by Zuberi Mtemvu. Although it suffered a complete defeat in the 1960 elections, the ANC managed to keep itself in existence. At the end of 1960 it had nine organized branches as opposed to TANU's 498.[99] Early in 1961 Mtemvu visited Red China and other Communist countries. Following his return, the ANC proceeded to form provincial headquarters and branches in five new areas. Although it still had little support from the general public, the fact that officials and money were found to open new branches indicated that the ANC was by no means dormant.

The Trusteeship Council conducted its last annual review of conditions in Tanganyika in July. Already the General Assembly, by its resolution 1609 (XV) of April 21, 1961, had resolved that the Trusteeship Agreement for the territory should cease to be in force upon Tanganyika's gaining independence. The Administering Authority informed the Trusteeship Council at its July meeting that the date of independence had been advanced from December 28 to December 9. John Fletcher-Cooke outlined recent constitutional developments in the territory, and A. Z. N. Swai, the Minister for Commerce and Industry, described the new government's policies and objectives. On the final day of the Council's consideration of Tanganyika, Nyerere, who was visiting the United States on another matter, presented a short statement to the Council. He said Tanganyika hoped that before the end of the year she would become a full-fledged member of the United Nations; he pointed out that former trust territories, particularly Tanganyika, had a "very soft spot" for the United Nations; and he paid tribute to the Council and to the British for their contributions to Tanganyika's independence.[100]

During August and September the government embarked on an extensive program to explain to the people what *uhuru* would mean. All of the Cabinet devoted as much time as possible to touring and speaking in the provinces. The objectives of the new three-year development plan were explained, and it was pointed out that much of the plan's success would depend on the people themselves. The slogan *"Uhuru na Kazi"* (Freedom and Work) was supplemented by the slogan *"Uhuru na Jasho"* (Freedom and Sweat).

The government's proposals for Tanganyikan citizenship were published in October and debated by the National Assembly later that month. The bill stated that dual nationality would not be permitted after December 9, 1963: all persons becoming Tanganyika citizens who also remained citizens of some other country would have up to two years in which to renounce their other citizenship. Anyone who was a citizen of a Commonwealth country and had lived in Tanganyika for a period of five years would be eligible to obtain citizenship by registration after December 9, 1961.

This latter provision provoked a flood of anti-immigrant and anti-Commonwealth sentiment in the National Assembly. The rift between the TANU leadership and the extremist wing of the party became wider than ever. Supporting the view that non-Africans should not automatically become citizens after independence were Assembly members Tumbo, Msindai, Mtaki, Mwakangale, and Wambura. Mwakangale went so far as to ask the non-African Ministers to resign on Independence Day, since the country had no confidence in them. In a forceful reply, Nyerere accused the extremists of racialism, likening their ideas to those of the Nazis. "This Government has rejected, and rejected completely," he said, "any ideas that citizenship, with the duties and the rights of citizenship of the country, are going to be based on anything except loyalty to this country." Moreover, since the government considered this a serious matter of principle, a free vote would be permitted. He added that he and his government would resign if they did not carry a majority of the elected members with them.[101] In the end the bill was carried overwhelmingly.

This trouble within TANU led Sir Richard Turnbull to comment to a visiting reporter, "Julius, who is an exceptional man of a type too infrequently produced in any society, used to be the fair-haired boy of the extremists; now he runs the risk of becoming their Colonel Blimp."[102] In England the Institute of Race Relations pointed out that "the present situation in Tanganyika is to a considerable extent the result of a few inspired leaders of the different races and that undercurrents of racial and political intolerance still flow."[103]

This growing criticism of Nyerere and his government's policies needs to be viewed in its proper perspective. Hitherto, TANU had been a national movement rather than a political party; but once the goal of independence had been achieved, as was virtually the case now, the vague principles and sentiments used during the struggle for independence had to be transformed into concrete policies. This is what happened in the case of such matters as Africanization and the extension of citizenship to non-Africans. Such policies could hardly be expected to appeal to everyone. For the present the opposition was contained within TANU, but in the future a full-fledged opposition party might well emerge. Although he regarded one-party government as the ideal, Nyerere said he would be the first to defend the rights of a responsible opposition in Tanganyika. He added, however, that his government could not permit an irresponsible opposition that played on racial, religious, and tribal differences and hindered the task of building a unified nation. Nyerere compared this task of a young country with that of a country facing war or some other national emergency.[104] Soon after this, the publicity secretary of the African National Congress, a Kenyan, was expelled from Tanganyika for exploiting "racial differences."[105]

The greatest danger to Tanganyika's racial harmony as an independent nation was the disparity in the relative degrees of wealth between the three racial communities. As Nyerere pointed out to the Dar es Salaam Chamber of Commerce at its annual dinner in July, the economic divisions in Tanganyika were almost identical with the racial divisions. He warned that Tanganyika's harmonious race relations would not long survive if the standard of living of the masses was not quickly raised.[106] Unless they were given immediate personal benefits following independence, the situation could all too easily be used by the unscrupulous to foster racial antagonisms and antigovernment activity. The European farmers would probably be left in peace, partly because there were relatively few of them and also because there was no shortage of land in Tanganyika; but the outlook for the territory's 100,000 Asians was less secure. Envy approaching racial resentment had been aroused by the Asians' success as traders and middlemen. Already the growth of trading cooperatives threatened to squeeze out the Asian businessman.

The matter was not so simple as this, however. All during the pre-independence period, Amir Jamal, the Minister for Communications, Power, and Works, tried to get his people to face up to their responsibilities under the new order. On one occasion he said: "It would be a matter of great pity if all we felt we needed was a piece of paper to make us citizens, something we could wave and display as an identity card. Instead of asking what am I going to get out of it, the question they should be asking is what am I going to put into it." Jamal went on to suggest that the failure of the privileged few to identify themselves completely with Tanganyika's efforts to raise the general standard of living was as great a danger as any irresponsible behavior on the part of the uninitiated masses.[107] As one writer accurately pointed out prior to independence: "The importance of the racial factor is that it will be the barometer of Tanganyika's progress. As long as she moves forward satisfactorily in solving her economic problems, the barometer will be set fair—but should she not do well, then there will be immediate repercussions in race relations."[108]

There was no sign of trouble in Dar es Salaam in November, but there were some disturbing reports from several upcountry districts, notably in Lake Province where Asian shopkeepers had been threatened. Non-Africans in some of the smaller centers were becoming increasingly alarmed by the developing situation. On several occasions during November, the Minister for Home Affairs, George Kahama, urged the people to behave with restraint at the forthcoming independence celebrations, and particularly to treat members of other races with respect.[109] Disturbed by the situation in Mbeya District, the Parliamentary Secretary to the Ministry of Local Government, Austin Shaba, appealed to the people of Mbeya to refrain from reprisals and violence, and to forget about their differences.[110]

The possibility of upcountry unrest was not the only cause of anxiety at this time. As a result of intra-union rivalries and trade disputes, relations between the government and the trade union movement had never been worse, and a head-on clash seemed imminent. Various unions, notably the teachers' and medical workers' unions, were threatening strike action. Nyerere, seeing that the situation demanded a strong stand by the government, declared that the country simply could not afford at this time to meet the wage demands of the people. Furthermore, he threatened to dismiss all government workers who went on strike after their demands had been considered. This statement provoked some of the most concentrated and persistent criticism Nyerere had ever faced. On the eve of Tanganyika's independence a veteran correspondent in Dar es Salaam wrote: "This is the shadow cast over the *Uhuru* celebrations and while this is a time for rejoicing and optimism, it would be foolish to ignore the signs and portents of trouble, which, strangely enough, have gathered more and more force as the great day approaches."[111]

8

LOCAL GOVERNMENT, LAND, AND INTERTERRITORIAL RELATIONS

LOCAL GOVERNMENT

In contrast to the tremendous advances made at the central government level during the years 1955–60, progress at the local government level, especially in rural government, was much less systematic. According to Sir Richard Turnbull, the administration's task was "to devise by consultation and experiment a basic form of local government generally suited to the whole Territory but sufficiently flexible to be adjusted to the special needs of particular areas"[1]—no easy matter, as the administrators themselves were the first to admit.[2]

By the end of 1957 there were some 2,500 rural councils in existence; this figure included councils that acted in an advisory capacity to the Native Authorities established under the Native Authority Ordinance, as well as many others at the chiefdom, subchiefdom, and village levels. In all of these councils there was an elected element. Moreover, non-Africans had been invited by the Native Authorities to sit with them in 30 districts.[3] Attempts, however, to incorporate non-Africans in rural government bodies in more than an advisory capacity were generally unsuccessful. For example, the two local councils established at Mafia and Newala following the enactment of the Local Government Ordinance of 1953 found that Africans were extremely reluctant to admit Europeans into what was felt to be a traditional African function. These two councils had replaced the former Native Authorities. The ordinance also provided for the setting up of multiracial county councils, but only one, the South-East Lake County Council, was ever established. This county council "found itself too unwieldy and too remote from the people" and was eventually dissolved in 1959.[4]

Since it was found that the natural unit of loyalty was the district, the government decided to concentrate upon the development of smaller units of government at the district level. The administration's new policy, embodied in the Local Government (Amendment) Ordinance of 1957, was to set up statutory district councils with a wider range of functions than the former local councils. The district councils were to be established on a nonracial basis so that if the non-African interests in an area were extensive, they could be represented. In districts in which non-African interests were limited, a wholly African district council would not be barred. Although the government attempted to make sure that there was a general desire for a district council before it was established, four of the nine set up during 1958 failed to function properly owing to a lack of popular support. The Geita District Council encountered severe opposition because of its multiracial character and, following a government inquiry, was replaced by a purely African council in 1960. Also during 1958, some Native Authorities were hampered by nationalist elements of the population that had become impatient with all government authority. In October 1959, recognizing that the administration's plans for advancing rural local government had largely been frustrated, Turnbull announced the appointment of a ministerial committee to study the question further.

By 1960, according to the Visiting Mission's report, disturbances provoked by local government measures were "a thing of the past, in part because of the general improvement in political atmosphere and in part because of the abandonment of coercive measures in the natural resources field."[5] In the new government appointed in September 1960, urban as well as rural local governments were joined under the Ministry for Local Government and Housing. Rashidi Kawawa, the minister for this division, announced in the Legislative Council that it would be the government's policy to have a majority of directly elected councilors in all of the 2,800 rural councils. (Previously only the village councils had had representatives directly elected by the people.) It was thought that nonofficial elected members would exceed ex officio members in these councils by at least two to one.[6] Although this policy was immediately put into force, the majority of councils continued to have neither executive nor legislative powers and were purely advisory to the superior councils of the districts.

In May 1961, Kawawa was appointed Minister without Portfolio and Job Lusinde assumed the post of Minister for Local Government. Before election to the Legislative Council, Lusinde had served as Executive Officer of the Gogo Council in the Dodoma district. His first address as Minister stressed the importance of strong local government bodies to the country: "No country of the size of Tanganyika can possibly hope to develop steadily unless the Central Government is firmly and faithfully supported by a system of Local Governments, based on the very firmest foundation. Any cracks there are liable to undermine the whole edifice of the government."[7] He stated that the government's policy toward rural local government was "to establish, as soon as possible, democratic and efficient Local Government Authorities, to which Central Government may safely delegate more of its powers and responsibilities." He announced that the process of democratization, by which he meant the introduction of a majority of elected members on all rural councils, was "virtually complete." Nevertheless, "the more important and more difficult task of making these Authorities efficient still remains." Written constitutions had been approved for most of the 50 Native Authority Councils.[8]

Although no additional district councils had been set up since 1958, Lusinde announced that at least nine Native Authorities were considering the adoption of district council status. Six of the original nine district councils established in 1958 still remained in existence. Explaining the need for additional district councils, Lusinde pointed out that although the Native Authorities had played an important part in the era of indirect rule, "the limitations imposed on their jurisdiction and the lack of clear definition of their powers and functions, hardly make them suitable to our present day needs."[9] At the end of the year, two more district councils came into being with the formation of Lindi and Kilwa district councils. The Lindi Council consisted of 32 members and the Kilwa Council of 22 members; each member represented a ward of the district. Provision was made for up to six co-opted members on each council. No ex officio members were appointed, since there were no traditional chiefs in the two districts. The establishment of these two councils brought the number of district councils in Southern Province to six.

As independence approached, the question arose of TANU's future role at the provincial and district levels. Previously, provincial and district administration had been carried out as a function of central government rather than of local government. It was clear that such an arrangement was no longer satisfactory. In October the Prime Minister announced that a political head would be appointed in each province to assume responsibility for all the political functions formerly carried out by the Provincial Commissioner, leaving the latter with administrative responsibilities only. According to Nyerere, the relationship between the Provincial Commissioner and the political head would be similar to that of a permanent secretary to his minister. One observer pointed out, however, that the job of a permanent secretary is chiefly to advise his minister in the making of policy, yet nothing had been said to indicate that the political appointee would be responsible for policy-making, and even if he were, the Provincial Commissioner was not necessarily the best person to advise him.[10] Nyerere's aim, no doubt, was to incorporate into provincial administration, and perhaps later into district administration, some of the capable young men of the TANU party organization and at the same time to use the party machinery in the development of the country. The ultimate role of the former provincial and district administrators was by no means clear. However, there was little question that TANU would from then on play the dominant role.

The problem of the position of the chiefs in the new local government structure was not solved before independence. Nyerere made a statement in July 1960 that no major changes would be immediately forthcoming, but that as the people continued to have more say in their own affairs, the status of the chiefs must change. He added, however: "If an instrument of Government is doing its work properly, there is no need to do away with it or to replace it with another instrument. I believe that if the Native Authorities of Tanganyika need polishing up they will be polished up so that they can perform their work properly." He described the "fever of uprooting the chiefs" as stupid and futile.[11]

In June 1961 the Minister for Local Government announced that *liwalis* and other nontraditional chiefs would not be appointed by councils as executive officers. Similar conditions were to apply to subchiefs and village headmen "as opportunity arises"; in other words, there was to be no automatic dismissal of existing subchiefs and headmen. The position of traditional chiefs was left for later clarification. However, Lusinde did indicate that the administrative functions of chiefs would be separated from their judiciary functions, suitable chiefs becoming executive officers or magistrates.[12] This statement, coupled with the appointment two months earlier of eleven African district commissioners designate, none of whom were chiefs, indicates that the traditional chiefs were being eased out of their administrative and political responsibilities. In October 1961, representatives of the chiefs met with the government to consider the future position of chiefs as a whole. The only decision reached was for the establishment of a committee to pursue the question further and to offer recommendations on what the government's policy should be.

The councils created at the urban level of local government have been much more successful than their rural counterparts. By the end of 1959, ten town councils in addition to the Dar es Salaam Municipal Council had been established. An eleventh was set up at Bukoba in July 1960. These eleven town councils and the Dar es Salaam Municipal Council are self-financing authorities. The other category of urban local authorities is the non-self-financing kind such as exists in the townships and minor settlements. The new government's policy toward these non-self-financing authorities was that they must be able to command sufficient financial resources to enable them to provide the services for which they would be responsible before they could be upgraded to the status of town councils. "Financial viability is an essential preliminary to Town Council status," Lusinde told the National Assembly in June 1961. Furthermore, there was no longer any justification, he said, for establishing an artificial barrier between a rural authority and an urban authority, particularly in districts in which district council status either had been granted or was being considered. Since district councils were designed as nonracial, all-purpose local government authorities, Lusinde continued, their juris-diction would extend over all areas within the district. The only ex-ception would be a town administered by a town council, since under the Local Government Ordinance town councils and district councils had equal status.[13] Previously the township authorities had been removed from the jurisdiction of the Native Authorities, which had jurisdiction only over Africans in their areas under the Native Author-ity Ordinance; the townships themselves were chiefly non-African in composition.

The Local Government Election (Urban Areas) Ordinance, en-acted in 1956, provided for elections to town councils to be held in areas in which there was a public demand for them. The first elec-tion under this ordinance took place at Arusha in January 1958. By the middle of 1960, similar elections had been held for seven other town councils. Voters qualified on a combination of age, residence, and property; in some places there was an additional business quali-fication. One of the first announcements Rashidi Kawawa made as Minister for Local Government and Housing was that the property qualification in urban areas would be eliminated.[14] Accordingly, early in 1961, the local government franchise in urban areas was ex-tended to all adults who either had resided in the town for two out of the last three years, or owned or occupied premises in the town. Additional elections were held under this extended franchise, and by October 1961 all of the town councils contained a majority of elected members. TANU candidates usually won these elections, and in many cases an African was elected as mayor or chairman. The normal composition of a town council is therefore as follows: a large ma-jority of elected members, three ex officio members, the district commissioner, a medical officer, an engineer of the Public Works Division, and up to three members nominated by the Ministry for Local Government.

The first elections for the Dar es Salaam Municipal Council took place in January 1960 and resulted in an entirely elected council of 24 members. The new council elected Dar as Salaam's first African mayor, Sheikh Amri Abedi, at its initial meeting. During the 1961 independence celebrations, Dar es Salaam was raised from the status of a municipality to that of a city, and the royal charter granted by the Queen was conferred by the Duke of Edinburgh.

LAND POLICY

During the years 1955–60, land alienation ceased to be the explosive issue noted by the 1954 Visiting Mission, a policy of caution with regard to future alienations having been instituted by the government in this period. Beginning in 1957, the net increase in alienated land was less each year, and in 1959 it was the lowest since 1948. As of December 31, 1959, the total amount of land alienated to individuals and companies was 3,173,078 acres, or about 1.6 per cent of the total land area. Of the total amount, 487,651 acres were covered by freehold right granted during the period of German administration, 2,544,864 acres were held under long-term leases, and 130,563 acres were covered by mining leases.[15] In 1960, more land held under long-term rights of occupancy was surrendered than was alienated. The 1960 annual report pointed out that "a considerable portion of the land originally alienated to non-Africans is now being used by Africans.[16]

The 1957 Visiting Mission reported that it had received a number of communications concerning land alienation. It observed that although the economic benefits of alienation were undeniable, the government's policy of permitting limited alienation still "raised fears and a feeling of insecurity in the minds of the Africans regarding their heritage which it will be difficult to eradicate."[17] By 1960, government policy was to grant long-term rights of occupancy to non-Tanganyikans only in special circumstances, or when it was considered necessary to obtain a particular development that could not be undertaken out of the territory's own resources. Accordingly, the 1960 Mission heard few complaints concerning land alienation. There was continuing dissatisfaction among the Meru arising from the alienation of the farms at Engare Nanyuki in 1951, but this was an isolated case. Although 3,290 acres of land had been turned over to the tribe in 1956, their resentment of the government's earlier action persisted. Moreover, the Mission stated, this residual sense of grievance would continue so long as the problem remained unsettled. On the other hand, there had been a "remarkable change" in the spirit of the tribe over the last few years: "The sense of frustration that followed the events of 1951 has now completely disappeared and the Meru are now one of the most progressive tribes in the Territory."[18]

With this single exception, the 1960 Mission reported that as a result of the substantial reduction in the rate of alienation and also of the improved political conditions, "which have brought about a relaxation of inter-racial tensions and a broader realization of the Territory's development needs, local resentment against land alienation seems to have greatly diminished." It was now the settlers who expressed anxiety about their future security of tenure in view of the territorys' rapid advance toward independence.[19]

Chief Fundikira, the Minister for Lands and Surveys, attempted to allay these fears. The new government, he said, would respect the rights of tenure of non-African farmers, and in no circumstance would it confiscate freehold land. He promised that as the rights of tenure of non-African farmers "granted long ago by the German Government had been respected by the British Government, so the new Tanganyika Government would in turn respect the existing rights of tenure in exactly the same way."[20] Similarly, in July 1961, Chief Fundikira's successor as Minister for Lands and Surveys, Paul Bomani, said that the government after independence had every intention of respecting the land titles of those already in the country.[21]

INTERTERRITORIAL RELATIONS

During these years Tanganyika's relations with the East African High Commission remained unchanged. Although the High Commission met with increased confidence in Tanganyika over the years, local suspicion of Kenyan domination was never completely removed. It was still felt that Tanganyika did not benefit sufficiently from the operation of the common services and that Kenya, where most of the services were based, was the main beneficiary. Although several of the elected members had expressed these views with some heat, the Tanganyikan Legislative Council unanimously passed a motion at the end of 1959 extending the life of the East African Central Legislative Assembly (the legislative arm of the High Commission) for a period of two years, during which time a review of the operation of the existing services could be carried out. A later motion extended the period to three years.

With Tanganyika's further advance toward independence, a question was raised concerning the future of the High Commission. If the administrative union between the three East African territories was to continue after Tanganyika gained its independence, some of the basic statutes would have to be redrawn. The Raisman Commission was therefore appointed to consider the subject. At the Tanganyika Constitutional Conference in March 1961, it was agreed that all matters relating to the country's continued association with the High Commission should be discussed at a special conference to be attended by delegates from all the East African territories.

This conference was subsequently held in London in late June, with Ian Macleod, the Colonial Secretary, presiding. The talks were attended by delegates from Tanganyika, Kenya, Uganda, Great Britain, and the East Africa High Commission, as well as by an observer from Zanzibar. Since Tanganyika had already expressed the desire to continue participating in the common services, the work of the conference was to consider the ways this could be done in a manner consistent with Tanganyika's sovereignty. The delegates agreed that it would be in the interests of all the territories for the common services to continue to be provided on an East African basis, and that a new organization, to be called the East African Common Services Organization, should take over these functions from the High Commission following Tanganyika's independence. Tanganyika, Kenya, and Uganda would participate as equal partners in the control of this new organization.

Control would be exercised through an authority to be known as the East African Common Services Authority, which would be composed of three principal elected ministers from the three territories. The Authority would be supported by four policy-formulating groups, each composed of three ministers, one from each territory. Each group would deal with one of the four specified fields of responsibility: communication, finance, commercial and industrial coordination, and social and research services. There would also be a Central Legislative Assembly composed of thirteen members from each territory and the Secretary-General and Legal Secretary of the Organization. The matters over which the Assembly would have the power to legislate were agreed to.[22]

In a statement to the press, Macleod said:

I am delighted with the results of the conference. They have an importance and significance going far beyond the actual agreements reached. The spirit which has prevailed throughout the conference has made manifest the wishes of the Governments and peoples of East Africa that their association in a common organization should continue, and, indeed, that in due course the institutions of the organization could well become the basis of an even wider and more general form of association.[23]

The "even wider and more general form of association" referred to by the Colonial Secretary was the possibility of an eventual East African federation, a matter that once again was being discussed. Two factors were behind the renewed discussions: a growing East African consciousness and a growing sense of African unity. Africans in all three territories were becoming more conscious not only of their own problems, but of each others' problems as well, and they began to see their situation as one held in common.[24] This feeling of African solidarity was strongest among the continent's nationalist leaders and led to the first All African People's Conference, held in Accra in December 1958. The Accra Conference was actually preceded by a meeting of nationalists from Kenya, Uganda, Tanganyika, Zanzibar, and Nyasaland, which was held at Lake Tanganyika in September 1958. Under the leadership of Nyerere, the convener of the meeting, the Pan-African Freedom Movement for East and Central Africa was formed to coordinate the nationalist movements of the five territories. A series of resolutions condemned the continued existence of colonial rule. Nyerere was elected the organization's first chairman.

Within less than a year of this meeting, the possibility of an East African federation was being mentioned in public. Outlining the policies that an eventual African government would follow in Tanganyika, Nyerere said in August 1959: "Our relations with our East African neighbours will be friendly and the chances are that the territories will eventually federate—after the question of domination from the Kenya Highlands has dropped out."[25] The crux of the matter lay in this final proviso, as is shown by the fact that Tanganyika was much more favorably disposed toward the idea of federation once the Kenya constitutional conference of early 1960 had virtually assured African control of the next Kenya government. Speaking in the Legislative Council in May 1960, Nyerere pointed out that the High Commission could do a great deal to help bring about the unity of the East African territories.[26] Sir Ernest Vasey's emphasis on the need to preserve East Africa's economic unity also helped to modify opposition to the High Commission.

Talk of a possible federation took an entirely new turn in June, when Nyerere, speaking at the Conference of Independent African States at Addis Ababa, suggested that Tanganyika might be willing to postpone independence, if such a measure would improve the prospect of federation.[27] Following his return to Dar es Salaam, he spoke of Tanganyika's responsibility to help bring about independence in Kenya, Uganda, Nyasaland, and Zanzibar by encouraging federation. Nyerere's strong support for federation surprised many people, especially since it came at the beginning of an important election campaign. Some of his lieutenants in the trade unions failed to back him in this matter. C. K. Tumbo, the head of the railway union and the chief critic of the High Commission in the Legislative Council, said it was "unthinkable" that the High Commission should continue to function in Tanganyika after independence.[28]

Nyerere kept the subject alive, however. "A federation would enable all of the states involved to move to independence as a political unit," he stated in an interview. He expressed the opinion that a federation should be formed after Kenya, Uganda, Tanganyika, and Zanzibar became self-governing and before they gained full independence. "If we waited to federate after each gained its independence separately, there would be obstacles to unity that would be difficult to overcome." Finally, he stressed that the type of federation he had in mind would be limited and that only such matters as external affairs, defense, international trade, common research projects, currency, and regional communications would come under its jurisdiction.[29]

In September 1960 the leaders of the Pan-African Freedom Movement for East and Central Africa held discussions on federation. The result of the session was a shift in policy. The suggestion to delay Tanganyika's independence until a federation could be established was no longer entertained. What was needed, Nyerere said, was to bring Kenya and Uganda up to Tanganyika's level of constitutional advancement so that the Chief Ministers of the three territories could discuss whether they wished to go their separate ways or move toward federation.[30] He added that Tanganyika had to know before March what was going to happen in the other East African territories, since that was the date of the Tanganyika Constitutional Conference.[31]

Opposition to a continuation of the East African common services following Tanganyika's independence persisted, particularly in the trade unions. It was felt that a continued association would mean a delay in the Africanization of Tanganyika's share of the common services. Existing difficulties in wage negotiations would also not be alleviated. After talks with Nyerere in December, Tumbo said that his "struggle" against the High Commission would continue until "regionalisation" was achieved. However, there seemed to be a growing feeling among the delegates to that month's session of the Central Legislative Assembly that after certain changes had been made in its structure, the High Commission should form the basis of any federation.[32]

By the time of the Tanganyika Constitutional Conference in March, all hopes for immediate steps toward federation had been dashed by the political deadlock in Kenya. Nyerere decided that Tanganyika must move on to independence, but at the same time maintain as many of the interterritorial links provided by the High Commission as possible. This would facilitate federation immediately African governments assumed power in Kenya and Uganda. The plan for an East African Common Services Organization was the result of this decision.

During the months prior to Tanganyika's independence, discussions on federation continued, and Kenneth Kaunda, who was visiting Dar es Salaam in August, proposed that the area to be covered by an eventual federation should be expanded to include Nyasaland and Northern Rhodesia.[33] In October, leaders of the Pan-African Freedom Movement for East and Central Africa met in Dar es Salaam for further talks on federation and other problems. At this meeting representatives were present from all the East African territories except Uganda.

The final meeting of the Central Legislative Assembly took place in November. In its last communication to that body, the High Commission stressed the importance of fostering "the concept of an East African community of interests" through the Common Services Organization that was to come into being sometime after Tanganyika's independence.[34] Speaking to the journalists during the period of the independence celebrations, Prime Minister Nyerere said that it would be inappropriate to hold formal talks on an East African federation until Kenya and Uganda had governments with a clear mandate from their people. Attempts to settle the question of East Africa's future interterritorial relations, therefore, must await further constitutional development in these two territories. Nevertheless, as one writer has pointed out, "the groundwork has been laid for a truly Federal Parliament and framework—though, for the moment, its powers will be restricted to certain economic matters—within which Tanganyika fully intends to work."[35]

9

INDEPENDENCE ACHIEVED

On the night of December 8, 1961, over 75,000 people were gathered in Dar es Salaam's huge, new national stadium to celebrate the coming of independence. Among them were Tanganyika's first Governor-General, Sir Richard Turnbull, her first Prime Minister, Julius Nyerere, and members of the Cabinet and the National Assembly. Two days earlier, Prince Philip had flown in to represent the Queen. Leading the British government's delegation was the Secretary of State for Commonwealth Relations, Duncan Sandys. Also present were the leaders of the nationalist movements in the rest of East and Central Africa, Jomo Kenyatta, Ronald Ngala, Joshua Nkomo, Kenneth Kaunda, and Hastings Banda, as well as representatives of nearly every independent African country.

Band music and a military tattoo opened the evening's ceremony. These were followed by the handing over of the colors of the Tanganyika Regiment of the King's African Rifles to the newly formed Tanganyika African Rifles. Shortly before midnight, Turnbull and Nyerere walked together to the center of the field near the flagstaff. The lights of the stadium dimmed, and the Union Jack was lowered for the last time while the band played "God Save the Queen." Then a spotlight reached out to illuminate the new green, black, and gold flag of Independent Tanganyika. By now the wildly cheering crowd was on its feet; the band struck up "Mungu Ibariki Afrika," a Swahili version of "God Bless Africa" specially written for the new country, and everybody joined in the singing. Turnbull and Nyerere shook hands and returned to their seats on the platform.

At the same time, 300 miles away from Dar es Salaam, in the middle of a snowstorm on Mount Kilimanjaro, Lieutenant Alexander Nyirenda, the country's first African commissioned officer, hoisted the new flag on the summit and lit a torch as a symbol of Tanganyika's unity. Rockets were fired, signaling to the tribesmen gathered on the foothills below that independence had been achieved.

Back in Dar es Salaam the Prime Minister was delivering his independence address to the huge throng. This message was read at all centers of celebration throughout the country at one minute after midnight on December 9.

Fellow countrymen, here is a moment we shall all remember, when for the first time we see our flag flying aloft to mark our country's independence. This is the moment for which we have been working these last seven years, and for which we have longed above all others.

How have we come to this great event? The answer is that we are free because we spoke with one voice; you have all stood shoulder to shoulder in unity and in a common determination to run our own affairs. So today we can rejoice in our country's triumph, and we can rejoice too in the way the victory has been won. Your self-discipline and good temper have enabled us to gain our freedom with good will towards all and injury to none.

Today we rejoice but tomorrow we have our freedom to preserve and strengthen. We Tanganyikans will not seek to do this with armies and navies and air forces. We shall do it by work, work that will increase our riches, so that we do not have to depend on our friends to provide us with our daily bread; and so that we ourselves can lift from our own shoulders the burdens of poverty, ignorance, and disease. We shall convince all people by the visible efforts that we make day by day that we are indeed working for our country.

But this, my friends, is not a time for many words, it is a time for joy. *Uhuru na furaha! Uhuru na Tanganyika! Uhuru na Afrika!*[1]

The following morning Prince Philip, on behalf of the Queen, formally presented Nyerere with the instruments of sovereignty. Having been sworn in as Governor-General, Sir Richard Turnbull administered the oath of allegiance to the Prime Minister and the Cabinet. The constitution of the Cabinet remained the same as before. A message from Queen Elizabeth was delivered by Prince Philip:

I am confident that your country, standing firmly by the ideals of unity and co-operation and the principle of tolerance in human relations, all of which are so evident in your national life today, will make a worthy and significant contribution to the future of the great continent of which you form part.[2]

The Independence Monument in Dar es Salaam was also unveiled. It took the form of an obelisk 30 feet high, at the top of which was a bronze torch that would be illuminated at night.

The following day, Sunday, December 10, Dar es Salaam was raised to the status of a city, when Prince Philip presented the charter and letters patent. He was made the first freeman. On Monday the National Assembly was redesignated the Tanganyika Parliament; it was to consist of Her Majesty the Queen, as head of state, and the National Assembly.

In all the messages, both printed and spoken, that Nyerere delivered during the independence celebrations, he emphasized the economic realities of independence, rather than purely the joys of celebration. The great changes and improvements the people wanted, he explained, would not come unless they themselves were willing to work hard. He also announced that 85 per cent of the British civil servants had decided to stay on in the country following independence. Consequently the country was not faced with an immediate administrative crisis. The number who had elected to stay far exceeded earlier expectations.[3]

The independence celebrations ended on Monday, December 11. Significantly, there was not a single serious racial or political incident reported anywhere in the country during these days.[4] The people of Tanganyika, the police, and the TANU Youth League, which gave valuable assistance during the celebrations, all contributed to this excellent record.

Immediately after the close of the celebrations, Nyerere, accompanied by Rashidi Kawawa, the Minister without Portfolio, flew to New York to attend the debate on Tanganyika's application for membership in the United Nations. On Thursday morning, December 14, the Security Council unanimously approved the application, and that afternoon the General Assembly adopted by acclamation a resolution approving Tanganyika's membership. After many tributes from member states, Nyerere was called upon to speak. He made a moving statement of his country's aims:

The basis of our actions, internal and external, will be an attempt, an honest attempt, to honour the dignity of man. We believe that all mankind is one, that the physiological differences between us are unimportant in comparison with our common humanity. We believe that black skin or white, straight or curly hair, differences in the shape of our bodies, do not alter or even affect the fact that each one of us is part of the human species and has a part to play in the development of mankind.[5]

As the first truly multiracial state in Africa to achieve independence in recent years, Tanganyika has set an admirable example, which others would do well to follow. Despite several minor racial incidents just before and after the independence celebrations, racial harmony has never been seriously endangered. The Africans have long envied the Asian community for its economic advantages; at times this envy has approached racial resentment. But the new government, by giving full support to the older, African-dominated agricultural cooperative societies and by helping to finance a new system of consumer cooperatives, is trying to redress the economic balance. Thus Tanganyika gained its independence with few manifestations of the harsh racial feelings that have characterized other plural societies in Africa. There are a number of factors that have contributed to this.

In the first place, Tanganyika was especially fortunate in having a nationalist leader of the stature of Julius Nyerere. Throughout TANU's seven-year campaign for independence, Nyerere remained a person of great reasonableness and modesty. Although his aim was always complete independence for Tanganyika, he used only moderate and peaceable methods in his approach to this goal. Demagoguery was never one of his political tactics. His ability, wit, and reasonableness won him friends and admirers not only among his own people but among members of the immigrant communities as well. In all of East and Central Africa, Nyerere is the only African politician to have won the confidence of more than a minority, usually a very small minority, of the non-Africans. The importance of his ability to inspire the trust of the Asian and European communities cannot be overstressed. On this point, one observer has written: "If a one-word explanation had to be given for the trust placed in him [Nyerere] by the non-African communities, the best answer would probably be 'sincerity'; and sincerity dilutes fear and predisposes to faith even when elements of anxiety remain."[6]

The people of Tanganyika have also to thank their first Governor-General, Sir Richard Turnbull, for the country's smooth advance to independence. He realized that any attempt to hold back the nationalist movement might discredit its moderate leadership and cause more extreme elements to come to the front, an event that could have severely damaged the country's good racial relations. Instead of resisting TANU, Turnbull persuaded the British government and the former Colonial Secretary, Ian Macleod, to allow Tanganyika to move rapidly through the intermediate stages of responsible government and internal self-government to full independence. Because of this Nyerere was able to show his followers the success of his moderate, nonracial policy.

Racial harmony did not come about overnight, however. Mention must be made of the men who laid the foundations for racial cooperation in Tanganyika. Notable among these is Lord Twining, formerly Sir Edward Twining, who was Governor from 1949 to 1958. People who dismiss Twining as a man who deliberately tried to hold back Tanganyika's march to independence overlook his great contribution in this respect. Not only was Twining a constant critic of those Europeans who thought that the government should remain almost wholly in European hands, but he also encouraged Africans to seek greater responsibility. Perhaps more important, the practice of looking at Tanganyika in racial compartments was done away with during his administration. "We are trying to build up a community where merit is the criterion, not color," he is quoted as saying.[7]

But the factors that have contributed to Tanganyika's racial harmony go further back than this. Much of Tanganyika's recent history has simply been a continuation of what was begun during the period that the territory was under British Mandate. Many years ago Sir Donald Cameron saw that Tanganyika would be primarily an African country. Consequently he started to prepare the African population for the time, which must have seemed very far off in his day, when Africans would take over the operation of the central government. His scheme of indirect administration was a first step toward giving Africans greater political responsibility, and Tanganyika's long tradition of unofficial participation at the central government level began in 1926, when he inaugurated the first Legislative Council.

In addition, Cameron did everything possible to defeat the hopes of those who wished to see a great white dominion of East Africa established. Realizing that a white settler-controlled federation would permanently relegate Tanganyika's African population to a secondary place in the governing of their own country, he withstood the combined pressure of the Colonial Secretary, the Governors of Kenya and Uganda, and the East African settler community, all of whom wanted him to bring Tanganyika into the proposed federation. And if the advocates of closer union had carried the day, the course of political development in Tanganyika would certainly have been very different. It is entirely appropriate that TANU had as its first national headquarters a house given many years before by Cameron to the Tanganyika African Association.

Under the Mandate Agreement, Great Britain had undertaken to prepare Tanganyika and its African inhabitants for eventual self-government, and it is clear that one of Cameron's chief reasons for opposing closer union was that such an arrangement would not be in keeping with the intentions of the Mandate System. The Mandate Agreement also banned discriminatory legislation. For these reasons I cannot accept Lord Hailey's contention that Tanganyika's constitutional development was not significantly affected by the fact that it was a mandated territory of the League of Nations during this period.[8] It is true that no specific developments can be directly attributed to the Mandate Agreement, but it certainly served as the background for constitutional development.

Much depended as well upon the fact that Great Britain was the Administering Authority for Tanganyika, a point that Margaret Bates brings out very clearly in her study of the country:

It is apparent that the mandate and trust agreements have had a major effect on developments, but it is also obvious that British policy and influence have played an equally important role, perhaps in day-to-day administration an even more important one. The stamp of Britain is today as evident in Tanganyika as anywhere else in Africa.

This is not, I think, to beg the question. It has been for Tanganyika a happy fact that national and international policy have frequently coincided. If Britain had been an unusually reluctant or unwilling trustee, the history of the territory would have been far different and less fortunate.[9]

Nyerere made the same point in his address to the General Assembly, when he said, "I would not be honest if I did not admit openly and graciously that the fact that we have been a Trust Territory under British administration has greatly helped us to achieve our independence in the way in which we have achieved it."[10]

If, as has been suggested, a monument should be erected in West Africa in honor of the anopheles mosquito, the same might be done in Tanganyika for the tsetse fly. The fact that so much of the land is infested by the tsetse, combined with the rather general lack of water, made Tanganyika one of the less popular countries with European settlers. Those Europeans who did come settled in widely separated parts of the territory, and poor communications prevented effective political organization. They never had the advantage of occupying a compact block of land such as the Highlands, in which most of the Europeans of Kenya are concentrated. Moreover, Tanganyika's Europeans are a far less homogeneous group than the European community of Kenya, another factor that makes the organization of a united European political unit difficult. Consequently, Tanganyika was comparatively untroubled by settler problems.

Tanganyika's nationalist movement was also fortunate with respect to the country's African population. For one thing, it did not have to combat strong tribal feelings of the kind that exist in Kenya. Instead of being divided into a few large tribes, Tanganyika Africans are dispersed among some 120 tribes, and the existence of so many units discouraged any tendency for political parties to form along tribal lines. Furthermore, some of Tanganyika's leading chiefs, notably Chief Fundikira, supported TANU. For another thing, TANU benefited from the fact that tribal organization in Tanganyika is not for the most part very strong, whereas in some African countries, particularly in Ghana, the nationalist movements have had to contend with strong attachments to traditional rulers. And, finally, political organization was made easier for TANU by the existence of a common language in Swahili. This lingua franca enabled TANU to communicate effectively with all elements of the population. The Swahili press also helped to spread the nationalists' message to the masses.

According to some claims, the fact that many Europeans and Asians abandoned their own privileged political position to support TANU played a major part in reducing racial tension. It certainly encouraged the British government to hasten Tanganyika's independence. According to the *Kenya Weekly News,* however, this factor in the country's racial harmony "is probably overrated by Europeans and Asians. . . . What *has* been a big contribution to progress is Mr. Nyerere's acceptance of his European and Asian allies. He could well have . . . gone it alone without them."[11]

George Shepherd, an American political scientist with wide experience in East Africa, attributes Nyerere's attitude in this respect to the fact that he is a devout Christian. "His program combining firm nationalist demands with racial reconciliation arises out of strong Christian convictions," Shepherd wrote nearly two years before the achievement of independence.[12] Although the intervening period saw the re-emergence of racial feeling on a small scale, Nyerere never departed from his original stand. And because of his strong influence, people continued to remain loyal to the principles he had so eloquently set forth in his speech to the General Assembly in December 1961. The Tanganyikan achievement of political progress by means of racial cooperation is one of the most encouraging events in the recent history of Africa.

On January 22, 1962, people all over the world were shocked to hear that after only 44 days in office, Nyerere had resigned as Prime Minister in order to give full time to being President of the Tanganyika African National Union. After some initial speculation about whether he had been forced out of office by the more radical wing of TANU, it became clear that he had resigned on his own and that the reasons for the change were in fact those given in his announcement of resignation:

I have taken this action and have won the support of my colleagues after a long debate that has gone on for days, because of our firm belief that this is the way of achieving our new objective—the creation of a country in which the people take a full and active part in the fight against poverty, ignorance and disease.

To achieve this purpose it is necessary to have an able, elected Government which has the full support and co-operation of the people. This we have had and will have. It is also necessary to have a strong political organisation active in every village, which acts like a two-way, all-weather road along which the purposes, plans and problems of Government can travel to the people at the same time as the ideas, desires and misunderstandings of the people can travel direct to Government. This is the job of the new TANU.

I believe that these two needs of Tanganyika can now best be served by the Government being carried on by a very able set of Ministers, in whom I have full confidence, while I myself devote full time to the work of TANU. . . .

We know that it is unusual for a Prime Minister to step down from his position as a leader of the Government to undertake leadership in the country of the party which supports the new Government. But we do not believe that it is necessary for us to copy the institutions of other countries. We believe that we must work out our own pattern of democracy and that the step we have announced today is the best way to proceed at the present.[13]

Nyerere then announced that he had selected Rashidi Kawawa, formerly Minister without Portfolio and in effect Deputy Prime Minister, to succeed him as Prime Minister. He also announced that Sir Ernest Vasey had resigned as Minister for Finance, but would continue to take part in the government as Adviser on Finance and Economic Affairs. Although he had the fullest confidence in Vasey's loyalty and devotion to Tanganyika, Nyerere said it was inappropriate for a noncitizen to be a member of the Cabinet.[14] Having come to Tanganyika only three years before, Vasey could not meet the requirements for citizenship.

A better understanding of these changes can be obtained from looking at the events that preceded them. Nyerere has stated that the idea of resigning in order to reorganize TANU first came to him in October 1961.[15] It was during that month that the storm over the citizenship bill broke out in the National Assembly, and Nyerere was undoubtedly shocked and dismayed by the intense racial feeling displayed by some of the members on that occasion.

Soon after independence an open rupture with the Tanganyika Federation of Labor occurred. Several trade unions began to press new wage demands in spite of calls for *Uhuru na kazi* and restraint in wage demands on the part of the country's leaders. Then, in January, the Federation of Labor announced that it was opposing the re-election of Sheikh Amri Abedi, TANU's nominee, as mayor of Dar es Salaam, an announcement that was strongly attacked by TANU's Dar es Salaam District Committee.

Apart from these problems, the nation as a whole was suffering from disappointment. In spite of the attempt made by the country's leaders to impress upon the population the need for even greater efforts following independence, many people were disappointed that there were so few personal benefits deriving from independence. This letdown after independence came at the end of a hard year from an economic viewpoint. For the first time in recent years there was no increase in the national income, and a decrease in exports and in imports of consumer goods caused government revenue to fall. Farmers were suffering from heavy rains and depressed world prices for their goods. This combination of circumstances made it seem likely that the people's disappointment would find an outlet in a burst of racialism. The government had hoped that the three-year development plan would lessen popular resentment of the economic-racial divisions of society; but the goals of the plan seemed far off to the workers and villagers.

As the unrest began to build up, Nyerere at first bowed to it, signing expulsion orders against one Swiss and four British subjects accused of racial discrimination. Even if he could not show his followers the economic fruits of independence, at least he could show them that they no longer had to suffer the indignity of being discriminated against because of the color of their skin. Meanwhile, the division of thought within his own party was once again brought home to him, when a party newspaper, *Uhuru,* stated in a leading article that Africans who caused annoyance to the British were doing the right thing.

Disturbed by all of these danger signs, Nyerere decided to call a meeting of the 120-member national executive of TANU on January 16 for an airing of grievances and a session of policy-making. It was not until this meeting, the first since the achievement of self-government the preceding May, that Nyerere realized how widespread the grievances were. The trade union representatives again pressed their demands for increased wages and faster Africanization. Nyerere, however, sought to avoid a direct clash with his more militant critics in the TANU executive, a clash that would doubtless have caused a complete split between TANU and the Tanganyika Federation of Labor. A firm believer in one-party government for underdeveloped countries, he was convinced that Tanganyika's progress would not be served by the creation of a strong opposition party at this time. Instead of consuming its energy in dealing with a political opposition, the government's "supreme task" was to build up the country's economy so as to raise the living standards of the people.[16] Prior to independence Nyerere had written: "A second party will not need to grow provided that a broad two-way channel of ideas and education is maintained through T.A.N.U. between the people and the Government. It is the establishment and maintainance of this channel of communication which is the real problem of democracy in Tanganyika." He wrote in the same article that the growth of a second political party would in one sense represent a failure by TANU.[17]

Clearly, then, in Nyerere's view the Party was failing in its function. It was not providing the two-way channel of communication between the people and the government that he saw as its proper role. As a result, the people were becoming discouraged because they lacked information about their place in the new Tanganyika. Nyerere knew that the Party organization had suffered since the removal of all its leaders into government positions two years before. Though there were a number of dedicated men in the Party structure, there were a number of political hacks as well. The Party simply could not go on untended without endangering the collapse of the government's whole program, especially the development program. The people needed a new spirit—negative racial envy needed to be replaced by positive aspiration. Always a shrewd tactician, Nyerere decided to turn over the premiership to a trusted lieutenant in order to devote his full energies to the organization of "the new TANU."

After Nyerere had announced this decision to the TANU executive, it took three days of prolonged persuasion before they finally agreed to it. He then personally appointed his successor, Rashidi Kawawa, and the new Cabinet. At the press conference of January 22 at which the changes in the government were announced, Nyerere was still seen very much as the national leader. In the words of the new Prime Minister: "He is the commander-in-chief and we are his troops. He is the Father of the Nation to whom we will continue to go for advice."[18] Tanganyikans received the news of Nyerere's sudden resignation with far greater composure than the rest of the world. A common reaction among many of them was pleasure that the former Prime Minister had now "come closer to his people."[19]

Nyerere's action was described by Sir Ernest Vasey as "a touch of political genius." This view was supported by *The Spectator*:

The process Arnold Toynbee called "withdrawal and return" ought to be standard practice for the leaders of national movements, when liberation is achieved. It is not simply that to lead a movement requires different qualities before independence is achieved, and after. The leader also—as Nyerere seems to have understood—needs to restore closer contact with his people.[20]

Rashidi Kawawa was sworn into office as Tanganyika's new Prime Minister by the Governor-General, Sir Richard Turnbull, on January 22. In the Cabinet reshuffle, Paul Bomani relinquished the Agricultural portfolio to become Minister for Finance, succeeding Sir Ernest Vasey. Both Derek Bryceson and Amir Jamal were retained in the new Cabinet, Bryceson as Minister for Agriculture and Jamal continuing as Minister for Communications, Power, and Works. Three new members were appointed to the Cabinet, Jerry Kasambala as Minister for Cooperative and Community Development, Solomon Eliufoo as Minister for Education and Information Services, and Saidi Maswanya as Minister without Portfolio.

As one observer has put it, Kawawa is "not a new and disruptive force in Tanganyikan politics, but an experienced administrator and tactician who has been quietly groomed behind the scenes over a period of time."[21] As a government civil servant, he helped to found the Tanganyikan Federation of Labor in 1955 and was elected its first secretary-general. Under his guidance the trade unions emerged as a major force in the country's economy. On leaving government employment in 1956, he joined TANU and became a member of the Party's central committee the following year; in 1960 he became its vice-president. First appointed as a nominated member of the Legislative Council in 1957, he was elected to the Council in February 1959, and re-elected in 1960. He resigned his post with the Tanganyika Federation of Labor after being appointed Minister of Local Government and Housing in September 1960, and he became Minister without Portfolio in May 1961. With his background of trade unionism, it was hoped that his appointment as Prime Minister might help to heal the breach between TANU and the labor movement.

At his first press conference, Prime Minister Kawawa confirmed that the government had been requested by the national executive of TANU to initiate steps toward making Tanganyika a republic as soon as possible, but he denied rumors that the country might leave the Commonwealth. "We became members of the Commonwealth because we thought it was the right thing to do," he said, "and we believe it is in our interest to continue."[22] He stressed that there would be no change in government policy and that racial tolerance would continue to be a guiding principle.

The partnership of Kawawa as Prime Minister and Nyerere as President of TANU is merely the continuation of an association that was begun five years ago. In 1957, when Nyerere resigned his seat on the Legislative Council in protest against the slow rate of progress being made toward self-government, Kawawa remained within the Council to exert pressure from the inside while Nyerere agitated for faster political advancement on the outside.[23] This partnership continued and became more important in 1961, when Nyerere appointed Kawawa to the post of Minister without Portfolio so that he might share some of the duties of the premiership.

The partnership could take on yet another form after Tanganyika becomes a republic. Provided he has finished reorganizing TANU by then, Nyerere is almost sure to be the country's first President. And should an eventual East African federation emerge, Nyerere and Kawawa will no doubt play a prominent part in its development. In the meantime, both men can be expected to provide sound and balanced leadership to the new Tanganyika.

NOTES

Complete authors' names, titles, and publication data are given in the Bibliography, pp. 244–49. The following abbreviations are used in the Notes:

AD   *African Digest* (London)
KWN   *Kenya Weekly News* (Nakuru)
Month *The Month in Tanganyika* (Dar es Salaam)
TS   *Tanganyika Standard* (Dar es Salaam)
VMR   United Nations, Trusteeship Council, *Visiting Mission's Report* (1948, 1951, 1954, 1957, 1960)

CHAPTER ONE

1. Leakey, pp. 37–38, 41–42.
2. Davidson, pp. 7–9.
3. *Ibid.*, pp. 7–8.
4. Clarke, pp. 7–8.
5. Marsh, p. 2.
6. Colonial Office, *Report 1958*, p. 9.
7. Moffett, p. 27.
8. Oliver, p. 50.
9. Hill and Moffett, p. 27.
10. Reusch, pp. 216–19.
11. Davidson, pp. 224–27, 231–34.
12. Coupland, p. 319.
13. *Ibid.*, pp. 382–92.
14. Moffett, p. 50.
15. *Ibid.*, p. 52.
16. Coupland, p. 459.
17. *Ibid.*, pp. 474–75.
18. *Ibid.*, pp. 484–85.
19. Marsh and Kingsnorth, p. 221.
20. Moffett, pp. 69–71.
21. *Ibid.*, p. 57.
22. *Ibid.*, p. 71.
23. Sayers, p. 72.
24. Skeffington, p. 8.
25. Datta, p. 6.
26. Marsh and Kingsnorth, pp. 226–27.
27. Moffett, p. 78.
28. *Ibid.*, pp. 80–81.
29. Marsh, p. 196.
30. Marsh and Kingsnorth, pp. 229–30.
31. Buell, pp. 432–33.

CHAPTER TWO

1. Hill and Moffett, p. 34.
2. Sayers, pp. 32–33.

3. Colonial Office, *Report on the Administration of Tanganyika for 1938,* pp. 165–67; Maisel, p. 295.

4. See "Tanganyika and the Mandates System," p. 240.

5. Commisson on Closer Union, *Report 1929,* p. 93.

6. Colonial Office, *Report on the Administration of Tanganyika for 1938,* p. 167.

7. "Tanganyika and the Mandates System," p. 240.

8. Hill and Moffett, p. 29.	15. Colonial Office, *Report 1958,* p. 7.
9. Moffett, p. 301.	16. Tanganyika, *Tanganyika,* p. 8.
10. Hill and Moffett, pp. 29–30.	17. Buell, pp. 438–39.
11. Moffett, p. 149.	18. Datta, p. 17.
12. *Ibid.,* p. 285.	19. *Ibid.,* pp. 18–19.
13. *Ibid.,* p. 287.	20. Joelson, p. 21.
14. Hill and Moffett, p. 33.	21. Datta, p. 15.

22. *Ibid.,* p. 25.

23. Tanganyika, *Detribalisation,* p. 14. The figure given for the total African population is that recorded by the 1948 census.

CHAPTER THREE

1. Datta, pp. 26–27.

2. Sayers, p. 114.

3. Datta, p. 33.

4. Cameron, *Tanganyika Service,* pp. 28–29.

5. Buell, p. 429.

6. Cameron, *Tanganyika Service,* pp. 30–31.

7. Datta, pp. 28–29.

8. *Ibid.,* p. 37.

9. Sayers, pp. 114–15.

10. Hailey, *African Survey 1938,* p. 164.

11. British Information Services, *Towards Self-Government,* p. 45.

12. *Tanganyika Service,* p. 29.	14. Buell, p. 433.
13. Datta, pp. 30–31.	15. Sayers, pp. 94–104.

16. Marsh and Kingsnorth, pp. 230–31.

17. Sayers, pp. 124–25.	20. *Ibid.,* pp. 31–34.
18. *Ibid.,* p. 125.	21. *Ibid.,* pp. 89–90.
19. *Tanganyika Service,* pp. 22–23.	22. *Ibid.,* p. 20.

23. Buell, pp. 451–52.

24. Cameron, "Native Administration," p. 8.

25. *Tanganyika Service,* pp. 84–86.

26. Colonial Office, *Papers,* pp. 112–13. Italics are Cameron's own.

27. Hailey, *Native Administration,* p. 219.

28. Hailey, *African Survey 1938,* pp. 439–40.

29. Macmillan, pp. 203–4.	31. Buell, pp. 461–62.
30. Datta, p. 60.	32. Sayers, pp. 128–29.

33. Hailey, *African Survey 1938,* p. 438.

34. Hailey, *Native Administration,* p. 218.

35. *Tanganyika Service,* p. 95.
36. *Ibid.,* p. 97.
37. Buell, p. 454.
38. Colonial Office, *Papers,* p. 113.
39. Cameron, "Native Administration," p. 8.
40. *African Survey 1938,* p. 443.
41. Culwick, pp. 190–92.
42. Upthegrove, pp. 106–7.
43. Leys, pp. 103–4.
44. Hailey, *Britain,* p. 45.
45. *Tanganyika Service,* p. 116.
46. *Ibid.,* pp. 115–16.
47. Dundas, pp. 135–36.
48. *Tanganyika Service,* pp. 24–25.
49. Hailey, *African Survey 1956,* p. 689.
50. *Ibid.,* p. 686.
51. Buell, pp. 486–87.
52. Sayers, p. 100.
53. Tanganyika, *Arusha-Moshi Report,* pp. 17–20.
54. Buell, p. 488.
55. Upthegrove, p. 104.
56. Buell, p. 491.
57. Richter, p. 6.
58. Buell, p. 491.
59. Leubuscher, p. 29.
60. *Tanganyika Service,* pp. 37–40.
61. *Ibid.,* p. 125.
62. *Ibid.,* pp. 125–26.
63. Buell, p. 495.
64. Leubuscher, p. 30.
65. Hailey, *African Survey 1938,* pp. 767–68.
66. Colonial Office, *Memorandum,* pp. 8–11.
67. Mair, p. 143.
68. Leubuscher, p. 33.
69. Colonial Office, *Report on the Administration of the Tanganyika Territory for 1938,* p. 143.
70. Leubuscher, pp. 33–35.
71. Colonial Office, *Report on the Administration of the Tanganyika Territory for 1938,* pp. 165, 167.
72. Rothchild, p. 16.
73. Buell, p. 523.
74. Rothchild, p. 18.
75. Buell, p. 523.
76. Huxley, p. 200.
77. *Ibid.,* p. 206.
78. *Ibid.,* pp. 221–23.
79. Rothchild, p. 52.
80. *Ibid.,* p. 18.
81. Legislative Council, *Proceedings,* Part I, pp. 127–31.
82. *Ibid.,* pp. 133–36.
83. East Africa Commission, *Report,* p. 7.
84. *Tanganyika Service,* pp. 225–26.
85. Commission on Closer Union, *Report 1929,* pp. 144, 236–37.
86. Colonial Office, *Report of Sir Samuel Wilson,* Sect. IV.
87. Great Britain, *Statement,* p. 14.
88. Colonial Office, *Memorandum,* pp. 4–5.
89. Rothchild, p. 31.
90. *Tanganyika Service,* pp. 230–31.
91. Colonial Office, *Papers,* pp. 111–14.
92. Rothchild, pp. 33–34, 44–45, 53–54.
93. *Ibid.,* p. 43.

94. *Ibid.*, pp. 34–35.

95. Cameron, *Tanganyika Service*, p. 282.

96. Twining, "Last Nine Years," pp. 15–24.

97. Buell, p. 432.

98. Africanus, "Shall We Betray Our Trust?," *National Review* (London), CVII (November 1936), 595–97.

99. Colonial Office, *Report on the Administration of Tanganyika for 1938,* p. 188.

100. Buell, pp. 539–40.

101. Upthegrove, p. 124.

102. Mitchell, p. 67.

103. Bates, p. 37.

104. East Africa Royal Commission, *Report,* p. 22.

CHAPTER FOUR

1. "Tanganyika and Trusteeship," *African Transcripts* (May 1946), p. 74.

2. *Ibid.*

3. Toussaint, pp. 46–47.

4. Colonial Office, *The Colonial Empire*, pp. 111–12.

5. British Information Services, *Britain and Trusteeship*, p. 13.

6. U.N. General Assembly, *Trusteeship Agreement*.

7. House of Commons, *Parliamentary Debates*, DII, col. 2240.

8. *KWN*, June 7, 1957, p. 20.

9. Moffett, pp. 121–24, 129.

10. Hailey, *African Survey 1956*, p. 302.

11. "British M.P.'s Visit Tanganyika," *Crown Colonist*, XV (January 1945), 66.

12. Hailey, *African Survey 1956*, p. 195.

13. U.N. Trusteeship Council, *Official Records*, 4th sess., Suppl. No. 3 (Lake Success, 1950), p. 12.

14. *Ibid.*, p. 10.

15. "Situation in Tanganyika," p. 299.

16. Colonial Office, *British Territories*, pp. 11–12.

17. Colonial Office, *Report 1948*, p. 212.

18. *VMR 1948*, pp. 3–4.

19. *Ibid.*, pp. 11–12.

20. *Ibid.*, pp. 201–22.

21. *Ibid.*, pp. 34–35. Italics in the original.

22. Bates, p. 42.

23. Mortimer, p. 19.

24. *VMR 1948*, pp. 237, 246–47.

25. "Tanganyika's 'Go Ahead' for Port Development," *Crown Colonist*, XIX (August 1949), 511.

26. "Tanganyika Governor Opens Ground-nut Rail Link," *Crown Colonist*, XIX (December 1949), 780–81.

27. Tanganyika, *Constitutional Development Report 1951*, p. i.

28. "Tanganyika Benefits from O.F.C. Activities," p. 54.

29. "Tanganyika Not Ready for Constitutional Change?," *New Commonwealth*, XXII (July 1951), 59.

30. "Tanganyika's Political Future Under Discussion," *Crown Colonist*, XX (May 1950), 321.

31. Colonial Office, *Report 1950*, p. 23.

32. Tanganyika, *Constitutional Development Report 1951*, p. ii.

33. *Ibid.*, p. 5.

34. *Ibid.*, pp. 18–21.

35. *Ibid.*, p. 36.

36. "Rains Do Their Worst to Tanganyika Roads," *New Commonwealth*, XXI (June 1951), 702.

37. *VMR 1951*, p. 6.   39. Bartlett, p. 206.

38. *Ibid.*, pp. 6–7.   40. *VMR 1951*, p. 6.

41. U.N. Trusteeship Council, "Petition from the Chagga Cultural Association," p. 2.

42. *VMR 1951*, p. 6.

43. U.N. Trusteeship Council, "Petition from the Tanganyika African Association," pp. 9–10.

44. *VMR 1951*, p. 6.   46. Buell, p. 441.

45. *Ibid.*, p. 7.   47. Bates, p. 42.

48. *VMR 1951*, p. 51.

49. U.N. Trusteeship Council, *Official Records*, 11th sess., 425th meet. (T/PV.425), 1952, pp. 2–3.

50. *Ibid.*, p. 13.

51. House of Commons, *Parliamentary Debates*, DII, col. 2239.

52. Tanganyika Constitutional Development Commission, *Report of the Special Commissioner*.

53. Datta, pp. 36–37.

54. Colonial Office, *Colonial Territories 1953–54*, Cmd. 9169, p. 17.

55. Colonial Office, *Colonial Territories 1954–55*, Cmd. 9489, pp. 13–14.

56. House of Commons, *Parliamentary Debates*, DII, col. 2240.

CHAPTER FIVE

1. Meeker, p. 284.

2. *VMR 1954*, p. 68.

3. Colonial Office, *Report 1954*, p. 20.

4. *VMR 1954*, pp. 45, 74.

5. *Ibid.*, p. 64.

6. Colonial Office, *Report 1954*, p. 20.

7. *VMR 1951*, p. 6.

8. Colonial Office, *Report 1952*, p. 39.

9. "Tanganyika," *AD*, II (September-October 1954), 20.

10. H. W. Flannery, "Julius Nyerere, Great Leader," *Catholic Association for International Peace,* XXI (February 1960), 9–10.

11. Hatch, "Bright Star," p. 300.   13. *Ibid.,* pp. 62–63.

12. *VMR 1954,* p. 62.   14. Moffett, p. 131.

15. Colonial Office, *Report 1952,* p. 28.

16. Hailey, *Native Administration,* pp. 225–32.

17. *Ibid.,* p. 278.   20. *Ibid.,* p. 26.

18. *VMR 1948,* p. 32.   21. *Ibid.,* pp. 244–45.

19. *Ibid.,* p. 244.   22. *Ibid.,* p. 33.

23. *Ibid.,* p. 245.

24. "Tanganyika Benefits from O.F.C. Activities," p. 54.

25. Colonial Office, *British Territories,* p. 20.

26. F. A. Montague and F. H. Page-Jones, "Some Difficulties in the Democratisation of Native Authorities in Tanganyika," *Journal of African Administration,* III (January 1951), 22.

27. Colonial Office, *Development of African Local Government,* p. 21.

28. Twining, "Situation in Tanganyika," p. 299.

29. Tanganyika, *Constitutional Development Report 1951,* p. 13.

30. Tanganyika Constitutional Development Commission, *Report of the Special Commissioner,* p. 3.

31. Mackenzie, p. 129.

32. *VMR 1954,* p. 9.

33. Colonial Office, *Report 1954,* p. 15.

34. Colonial Office, *Development of African Local Government,* pp. 31–33.

35. Tanganyika, *Constitutional Development Report 1951,* pp. 14–17.

36. P. H. Johnston, "Chagga Constitutional Development," *Journal of African Administration,* V (July 1953), 134–40.

37. Colonial Office, *Report 1952,* p. 34.

38. Colonial Office, *Report 1954,* p. 16.

39. Colonial Office, *Annual Report on the East Africa High Commission,* 1952, p. 2.

40. *Ibid.*

41. Hailey, *African Survey 1956,* p. 196.

42. "Tanganyika Council's Eventful Session," *Crown Colonist,* XVI (February 1946), 135.

43. Rothchild, pp. 63–64.

44. F. J. Khamisi, "The African Viewpoint," *African Affairs,* XLV (July 1946), 141.

45. "Tanganyika's Views on East African Affairs," *Crown Colonist,* XVI (January 1946), 63.

46. Rothchild, p. 70.

47. Legislative Council, *Proceedings, April 15 & 16, 1947,* Extraordinary Meeting (Dar es Salaam: Government Printer, 1947).

48. *VMR 1948,* p. 64.

49. House of Commons, *Parliamentary Debates,* CDLXXXII, col. 1167.

50. Rothchild, p. 78.

51. *VMR 1954*, p. 11.
52. *Ibid.*, p. 64.
53. Colonial Office, *British Territories*, p. 33.
54. Rothchild, pp. 82–83.					59. *VMR 1954*, pp. 78–80.
55. *VMR 1948*, p. 60.					60. *Ibid.*, p. 88.
56. *Ibid.*, pp. 253–60.					61. *Ibid.*, p. 87.
57. Rothchild, pp. 83–84.					62. *VMR 1948*, pp. 77–78.
58. *VMR 1951*, p. 17.					63. *VMR 1954*, p. 88.
64. Colonial Office, *Report 1952*, pp. 79–88.
65. Tanganyika, *Arusha-Moshi Report*, p. 5.
66. *Ibid.*, pp. 44–45.					68. *Ibid.*, p. 96.
67. *VMR 1948*, p. 268.					69. *Ibid.*, p. 270.
70. *VMR 1951*, p. 24.
71. Colonial Office, *Report 1951*, p. 56.
72. *VMR 1948*, p. 76.
73. *Ibid.*, pp. 261–62.
74. Colonial Office, *Report 1951*, p. 62.
75. Colonial Office, *Report 1952*, p. 294.
76. Colonial Office, *Report 1953*, p. 148.
77. Colonial Office, *Report 1954*, pp. 175–76.
78. *VMR 1954*, p. 128.
79. Colonial Office, *Report 1954*, p. 175.
80. *VMR 1954*, pp. 88–90.					90. *Ibid.*, p. 4.
81. *Ibid.*, p. 12.					91. *Ibid.*, p. 73.
82. *Ibid.*, pp. 47–48.					92. Bates, pp. 43–45.
83. *Ibid.*, pp. 52–54.					93. *VMR 1954*, p. 61.
84. *Ibid.*, pp. 54–55.					94. Asbeck, p. 29.
85. *Ibid.*, p. 88.					95. Datta, p. 140.
86. *Ibid.*, pp. 96–97.					96. Bates, p. 43.
87. *Ibid.*, p. 92.					97. *VMR 1954*, p. 74.
88. *Ibid.*, pp. 92–95.					98. *Ibid.*, p. 59.
89. *Ibid.*, p. 66.

CHAPTER SIX

1. *VMR 1954*, pp. 66–75.					4. Jan. 26, 1955, p. 4.
2. Sears, p. 14.					5. Jan. 26, 1955, p. 9.
3. *TS*, Jan. 26, 1955, p. 1.					6. *TS*, Feb. 11, 1955, p. 1.
7. *AD*, II (March-April 1955), 20–21.
8. *TS*, Feb. 17, 1955, p. 1.
9. *Ibid.*, p. 4.
10. *VMR 1954*, pp. 108–9.
11. U.N. Trusteeship Council, *Verbatim Records* (T/PV.584), pp. 72–73.
12. *Ibid.*, p. 86.

13. U.N. Trusteeship Council, *Official Records*, 15th sess., 585th–587th meets., 1955, pp. 170–91.

14. *Ibid.*, 590th–591st meets., pp. 209–14.

15. *Ibid.*, 592d meet., pp. 219–23.

16. U.N. Trusteeship Council, *Report*, 1954–55 (A/2933), p. 35.

17. *AD*, III (May-June 1955), p. 18.

18. *KWN*, Apr. 1, 1955, p. 20.

19. *New York Times*, Apr. 20, 1955, p. 33.

20. Legislative Council, *Council Debates*, 30th sess., pp. 8–11.

21. Sept. 5, 1955, p. 7.

22. Colonial Office, *Report 1955*, p. 31.

23. "Congratulations, T.A.N.U.!," *Venture*, VII (December 1955), 2.

24. Hatch, *New From Africa*, pp. 53–54.

25. "Parties and Politics in Tanganyika," *Venture*, VIII (May 1956), 8.

26. *Ibid.*, pp. 8–9.

27. Apr. 20, 1956, p. 15.

28. U.N. Trusteeship Council, *Official Records*, 17th sess., 670th–672d meets., 1956, pp. 137–52.

29. *Ibid.*, 697th meet., pp. 337–41.

30. *KWN*, Apr. 20, 1956, p. 15.

31. Legislative Council, *Council Debates*, 31st sess., pp. 6–10.

32. *TS*, Apr. 5, 1956, p. 5.

33. *Ibid.*, Apr. 27, 1956, p. 1.

34. *Ibid.*, May 28, 1956, p. 2.

35. *TS*, July 2, 1956, p. 3.

36. *Ibid.*, July 3, 1956, pp. 1, 6.

37. *Ibid.*, p. 2.

38. *AD*, IV (September-October 1956), 45.

39. Apr. 4, 1956, p. 2.

40. Apr. 20, 1956, p. 15.

41. *TS*, Apr. 27, 1956, pp. 1, 6.

42. *Ibid.*, July 2, 1956, p. 2.

43. *Ibid.*, June 25, 1956, p. 5.

44. *Ibid.*, Sept. 21, 1956, p. 2.

45. *Ibid.*, Sept. 25, 1956, p. 5.

46. *Ibid.*, p. 4.

47. *Ibid.*, June 20, 1956, p. 4.

48. *KWN*, Apr. 27, 1956, p. 21.

49. *TS*, Sept. 19, 1956, p. 3.

50. *KWN*, Oct. 5, 1956, p. 20.

51. *TS*, Sept. 22, 1956, p. 3.

52. *KWN*, Oct. 5, 1956, p. 3.

53. *AD*, IV (November–December 1956), 98.

54. U.N. General Assembly, *Official Records*, 11th sess., 4th comm., 579th and 582d meets., pp. 149–51, 163–65.

55. *Ibid.*, Resolutions, res. 1065.

56. Dec. 22, 1956, p. 4.

57. Dec. 31, 1956, p. 2.

58. *KWN*, Mar. 1, 1957, p. 20.

59. Tanganyika, *Some Comments*.

60. Feb. 20, 1957, p. 2.

61. *KWN*, Nov. 2, 1956, p. 20.

62. *Ibid.*, Jan. 4, 1957, p. 20.

63. *TS*, June 20, 1957, p. 5.

64. *The Times* (London), Feb. 15, 1957, p. 7.

65. *TS*, Feb. 25, 1957, p. 1.

66. *Ibid.*, Jan. 29, 1957, p. 3.

67. *Ibid.*, p. 2.

68. *KWN*, July 26, 1957, p. 20.

69. *Ibid.*, May 3, 1957, p. 20.

70. *Ibid.*, July 26, 1957, p. 20.

71. *The Times* (London), May 30, 1957, p. 9.

72. *AD*, IV (May-June 1957), 187–88.

73. U.N. Trusteeship Council, *Official Records,* 20th sess., 817th–820th meets., pp. 143–58.

74. U.N. Trusteeship Council, *Report of the Trusteeship Council Covering the Period from 15 August 1956 to 12 July 1957,* Doc. A/3595 (New York, 1957), pp. 30–32.

75. *TS,* June 21, 1957, p. 2.

76. *Ibid.,* June 19, 1957, p. 4.

77. *Ibid.,* June 20, 1957, p. 5.

78. *Ibid.,* Aug. 5, 1957, p. 1.

79. Aug. 16, 1957, p. 20.

80. *TS,* July 27, 1957, p. 1.

81. Colonial Office, *Report 1957,* p. 11.

82. Legislative Council, *Council Debates,* 33d sess., pp. 15–16.

83. *TS,* Oct. 29, 1957, pp. 1–3.

84. *KWN,* Aug. 16, 1957, p. 20.

85. "United Tanganyika," pp. 142–43.

86. "Colour Disharmony," pp. 1131–32.

87. "Multi-Coloured Programmes," *Economist,* CLXXXV (Oct. 26, 1957), 300.

88. *KWN,* Dec. 13, 1957, p. 28.

89. Legislative Council, *Council Debates,* 30th sess., p. 6.

90. *Ibid.,* 32d sess., p. 6.

91. *KWN,* May 31, 1957, p. 20.

92. "United Tanganyika," p. 143.

93. Legislative Council, *Council Debates,* 33d sess., pp. 330–48.

94. *TS,* Oct. 4, 1957, p. 5.

95. *Ibid.,* Dec. 19, 1957, p. 1.

96. *VMR 1957,* pp. 4–12.

97. *Ibid.,* p. 55.

98. Jan. 9, 1958, p. 2.

99. *VMR 1957,* pp. 89–89.

100. U.N. Trusteeship Council, *Official Records,* 21st sess., 872d–875th meets., 1958, pp. 169–96.

101. U.N. Trusteeship Council, *Report of the Trusteeship Council Covering the Work of Its Twenty-First and Twenty-Second Sessions,* II (A/3822) (New York, 1958), 4, 6.

102. U.N. Trusteeship Council, *Document T/PET.2/L.10/Add.1* (New York, 1958).

103. *TS,* Jan. 27, 1958, p. 1.

104. *Ibid.,* Feb. 18, 1958, pp. 1, 5.

105. *Ibid.,* p. 4.

106. *KWN,* Feb. 28, 1958, p. 24.

107. *TS,* Jan. 20, 1958, p. 2.

108. *KWN,* Apr. 25, 1958, p. 22.

109. *TS,* Jan. 9, 1958, p. 2.

110. "Progress in Tanganyika Under British Administration," *East Africa and Rhodesia,* XXXIV (May 15, 1958), 1157.

111. "Colour Disharmony," p. 1132.

112. Twining, "Tanganyika's Middle Course," pp. 216–18.

113. Hatch, "Bright Star," p. 300.

114. Central Office of Information, *Tanganyika,* p. 9.

115. *KWN,* Sept. 5, 1958, p. 24.

116. *Ibid.*

117. *TS,* July 10, 1958, p. 1.

118. *Ibid.,* July 12, 1958, pp. 1, 3.

119. *Ibid.,* Aug. 12, 1958, pp. 1, 3.

120. Hatch, "Bright Star," p. 300.

CHAPTER SEVEN

1. *TS*, Feb. 24, 1958, p. 2.
2. *AD*, V (March–April 1958), 178.
3. "Tanganyika," *Economist*, CLXXXVII (May 3, 1958), 396.
4. *TS*, June 26, 1958, p. 1.   8. *TS*, Aug. 12, 1958, p. 3.
5. *Ibid.*, July 8, 1958, p. 1.   9. *Ibid.*
6. *Ibid.*, June 24, 1958, p. 2.   10. *TS*, Aug. 25, 1958, p. 3.
7. *KWN*, July 8, 1958, p. 22.   11. *Ibid.*, July 10, 1958, p. 5.
12. Colonial Office, *Report 1958*, p. 34.
13. *TS*, Sept. 9, 1958, p. 1.
14. Colonial Office, *Report 1958*, p. 35.
15. *KWN*, Sept. 19, 1958, p. 22.
16. *TS*, Sept. 13, 1958, p. 3.
17. "Tanganyika's New M.L.Cs.," *East Africa and Rhodesia*, XXXV (Sept. 25, 1958), 113.
18. *KWN*, Oct. 24, 1958, p. 17.
19. "Matters of Moment," *East Africa and Rhodesia*, XXXV (Sept. 25, 1958), 97.
20. "Voting the TANU Ticket," *Economist*, CLXXXVIII (Sept. 20, 1958), 921.
21. *TS*, Sept. 13, 1958, p. 1.
22. Twining, "Last Nine Years," p. 22.
23. *TS*, Dec. 27, 1958, p. 1.
24. Colonial Office, *Report 1958*, pp. 35–36.
25. *KWN*, Sept. 19, 1958, p. 23.
26. Skeffington, p. 6.
27. "Tanganyika Must Concentrate on Quality," p. 191.
28. *KWN*, Oct. 24, 1958, p. 24.   31. *Ibid.*, Sept. 17, 1958, p. 4.
29. Stonehouse, p. 135.   32. Young and Fosbrooke, p. 151.
30. *TS*, Sept. 11, 1958, p. 4.   33. *TS*, Nov. 25, 1958, p. 1.
34. "Discreditable Defiance of the Rule of Law in Tanganyika," *East Africa and Rhodesia*, XXXV (Jan. 8, 1959), 561.
35. Feb. 20, 1959, p. 22.
36. U.N. Trusteeship Council, *Official Records*, 23d sess., 942d–945th meets., 1959, pp. 5–10, 14–15, 17–29.
37. Macmillan, p. 243.
38. U.N. Trusteeship Council, *Report 1958–59* (A/4100), pp. 23–26, 41.
39. Stonehouse, pp. 134–41.
40. *TS*, Mar. 18, 1959, p. 1.
41. *KWN*, May 1, 1959, p. 23.
42. Tanganyika Public Relations Department, *Tanganyika Progresses Towards Self-Government* (Dar es Salaam: Government Printer, 1959), p. 4.
43. "Disrespect for Law and Contempt for Authority in Tanganyika," *East Africa and Rhodesia*, XXXV (Mar. 26, 1959), 875.
44. *TS*, Mar. 20, 1959, p. 1.   45. *KWN*, May 3, 1959, p. 23.

46. *Ibid.,* Apr. 24, 1959, p. 22.			47. *Ibid.,* May 8, 1959, p. 22.

48. George W. Shepherd, Jr., "Tanganyika Today," *Africa Today,* VI (November 1959), 13.

49. Stonehouse, p. 137.

50. Skeffington, p. 32.

51. Nyerere, "Tanganyika Today," p. 46.

52. *Ibid.,* pp. 3–4.			55. Shepherd, p. 12.

53. Young and Fosbrooke, p. 179.			56. Young and Fosbrooke, p. 177.

54. *KWN,* July 17, 1959, p. 20.			57. Shepherd, p. 14.

58. Nyerere, "Tanganyika Today," p. 47.

59. "Self-Government Now," p. 1404.

60. *KWN,* Aug. 21, 1959, p. 20.

61. *Ibid.,* Sept. 25, 1959, p. 20.

62. Nyerere, "We Cannot Afford to Fail," p. 10.

63. *KWN,* Oct. 30, 1959, p. 20.

64. *TS,* Dec. 16, 1960, pp. 1, 3.

65. Hill, p. 127.

66. "Bumps in Freedom Road," *Time,* LXXIV (Dec. 28, 1959), 20.

67. "Self-Government Now," p. 1404.

68. "Tanganyika to Have Responsible Government," *Central African Examiner,* III (Dec. 19, 1959), 9.

69. *KWN,* Jan. 22, 1960, p. 20.			73. *Ibid.,* p. 5.

70. *Ibid.,* Apr. 1, 1960, p. 20.			74. *Month,* April 1960, p. 2.

71. *VMR 1960,* p. 7.			75. "Tanganyika's Progress," p. 51.

72. *KWN,* May 6, 1960, p. 22.			76. *VMR 1960,* pp. 4–6, 36–37.

77. *Ibid.,* pp. 42–54.

78. U.N. Trusteeship Council, *Report, 1959–60* (A/4404), pp. 31–35.

79. *VMR 1960,* p. 10.			84. *Month,* September 1960, p. 2.

80. July 25, 1960, p. 7.			85. *Ibid.,* p. 3.

81. *KWN,* Sept. 9, 1960, p. 21.			86. *KWN,* Oct. 21, 1960, p. 20.

82. *Month,* August 1960, p. 3.			87. *Ibid.,* Oct. 14, 1960, p. 22.

83. *KWN,* Sept. 9, 1960, p. 21.			88. *Ibid.,* Dec. 16, 1960, p. 20.

89. *Ibid.,* Jan. 6, 1961, p. 18.

90. Tanganyika Information Services, *Day of Triumph,* pp. 3–4. Italics in the original.

91. *Ibid.,* p. 5.

92. Tanganyika Information Services, *Tanganyika's Parliament,* p. 11.

93. U.N. Trusteeship Council, *Verbatim Records,* 27th sess., 1169th meet. (T/PV.1169), pp. 4–6.

94. Osborn, p. 423.

95. Martin Lowenkopf, "Outlook for Tanganyika," *Africa Report,* VI (December 1961), 6.

96. *KWN,* June 2, 1961, p. 18.

97. *Ibid.,* June 16, 1961, p. 18.

98. Osborn, p. 422.

99. Colonial Office, *Report 1960,* Part I, p. 32.

100. U.N. Trusteeship Council, *Report 1960–61* (A/4818), pp. 20–21.

101. National Assembly, *Debates,* 36th sess., 4th meet., cols. 335–36.

102. Smith Hempstone, "Tanganyika; Bright Spot in a Dark Continent," *Saturday Evening Post,* CCXXXIV (Dec. 2, 1961), 18.

103. "Preparations for Uhuru," *Institute of Race Relations Newsletter* (October 1961), p. 22.

104. Nyerere, "One Party Government," pp. 7–9.

105. Ginwala, p. 5.

106. *KWN,* Aug. 4, 1961, p. 18.

107. "Tanganyika's Torch," *Economist,* CCI (Dec. 9, 1961), 1041.

108. Ginwala, p. 6.　　　　　　110. *Ibid.,* Dec. 8, 1961, p. 18.

109. *KWN,* Nov. 10, 1961, p. 18.　　111. *Ibid.,* Dec. 1, 1961, p. 19.

CHAPTER EIGHT

1. "Tanganyika Must Concentrate on Quality," p. 192.

2. See Liebenow, p. 136.

3. *VMR 1957,* p. 20.

4. Legislative Council, *Council Debates,* 33d sess., p. 17.

5. *VMR 1960,* p. 11.

6. Colonial Office, *Report 1960,* Part I, p. 20.

7. National Assembly, *Debates,* 36th sess., 4th meet., p. 945.

8. *Ibid.,* pp. 951–52.

9. *Ibid.,* p. 951.

10. John Smythe, "Political Prefects," *Spearhead,* I (November 1961), 6.

11. *Month,* July 1960, p. 5.

12. National Assembly, *Debates,* 36th sess., 4th meet., p. 953.

13. *Ibid.,* p. 947.

14. *Month,* November 1960, p. 4.

15. U.N. Trusteeship Council, *Report 1959–60* (A/4404), p. 43.

16. Colonial Office, *Report 1960,* Part I, p. 62.

17. *VMR 1957,* p. 30.　　　　19. *VMR 1960,* p. 17.

18. *VMR 1960,* p. 19.　　　　20. *Month,* August 1960, p. 6.

21. *Tanganyika News Review,* July 1961, p. 7.

22. Colonial Office, *The Future of the East African High Commission Services.*

23. "Future of E. Africa High Commission," *East Africa and Rhodesia,* XXXVII (July 6, 1961), 1173.

24. Rothchild, p. 85.　　　　　26. *Month,* May 1960, p. 6.

25. "Self-Government Now," p. 104.　27. *KWN,* June 24, 1960, p. 20.

28. *Ibid.,* July 15, 1960, p. 20.

29. *New York Times,* Aug. 28, 1960, p. 6.

30. *Month,* November 1960, p. 2.　33. *Ibid.,* Aug. 18, 1961, p. 18.

31. *KWN,* Dec. 2, 1960, p. 20.　　34. *Ibid.,* Nov. 10, 1961, p. 18.

32. *Ibid.,* Dec. 9, 1960, p. 20.　　35. Ginwala, p. 6.

CHAPTER NINE

1. "How Independence Was Celebrated," p. 372. *Furaha* is the Swahili word for "joy."
2. *Ibid.*
3. *KWN,* Dec. 15, 1961, p. 20.
4. *Ibid.,* Dec. 22, 1961, p. 19.
5. U.N. General Assembly, *Provisional Verbatim Record,* p. 61.
6. "Matters of Moment," *East Africa and Rhodesia,* XXXVIII (Dec. 7, 1961), 335.
7. Gunther, p. 406.
8. Hailey, *African Survey 1956,* p. 301.
9. Bates, p. 50.
10. U.N. General Assembly, *Provisional Verbatim Record,* p. 57.
11. *KWN,* Apr. 15, 1960, p. 22. Italics in the original.
12. George W. Shepherd, Jr., "Tanganyika's New Force," *Christian Century,* LXXVII (Feb. 17, 1960), 190.
13. *KWN,* Jan. 26, 1962, p. 6.
14. *Tanganyika News Review,* Jan. 15–31, 1962, p. 2.
15. Kitchen, p. 7.
16. Nyerere, "One Party Government," p. 8.
17. Nyerere, "Challenge of Independence," pp. 339–40.
18. *African Daily News* (Salisbury), Feb. 2, 1962, p. 10.
19. "Mr. Nyerere's Decision," *Economist,* CCII (Jan. 27, 1962), 329.
20. "Withdrawal and Return," *Spectator,* No. 6970 (Jan. 26, 1962), p. 91.
21. Friedland, p. 8.
22. Kitchen, p. 7.
23. Friedland, p. 7.

BIBLIOGRAPHY

Asbeck, Frederick Mari van. Leaps and Approaches Towards Self-Government in British Africa. The Hague: van Hoeve, 1954.

Bartlett, Vernon. Struggle for Africa. London: Muller, 1953.

Bates, Margaret L. "Tanganyika: The Development of a Trust Territory," International Organization, IX (February 1955), 32–51.

Buell, Raymond Leslie. The Native Problem in Africa. Vol. I. New York: Macmillan, 1928.

Cameron, Donald C. My Tanganyika Service and Some Nigeria. London: Allen and Unwin, 1939.

——. "Native Administration in Nigeria and Tanganyika." Supplement to the Journal of the Royal Africa Society, XXXVI (November 30, 1937).

Clarke, P. H. C. A Short History of Tanganyika. London: Longmans, 1960.

"Colour Disharmony," The Economist, CLXXXIII (June 29, 1957), 1131–32.

Coupland, Reginald. The Exploitation of East Africa. London: Faber, 1939.

Culwick, A. T. and G. M. "What the Wabena Think of Indirect Rule," Journal of the Royal African Society, XXXVI (April 1937), 176–93.

Datta, Ansu Kumar. Tanganyika: A Government in a Plural Society. Leiden, 1955.

Davidson, Basil. The Lost Cities of Africa. Boston: Little, Brown, 1958.

Dundas, Charles. African Crossroads. London: Macmillan, 1955.

East Africa High Commission. East African Statistical Department. Tanganyika Population Census, 1957. [Nairobi?], 1958.

Friedland, William H. "Tanganyika's Rashidi Kawawa," Africa Report, VII (February 1962), 7–8.

Ginwala, Frene. "Tanganyika's Challenge," Central African Examiner, V (December 1961), 5–6.

Great Britain. Statement of the Conclusions of His Majesty's Government in the United Kingdom as Regards Closer Union in East Africa. Cmd. 3574. London: H.M. Stationery Office, 1930.

——. British Information Services. Britain and Trusteeship. New York, 1947.

———. ———. Towards Self-Government in the British Colonies. New York, 1947.

———. Central Office of Information. Reference Division. Tanganyika. London: Swindon Press, 1959.

———. Colonial Office. Annual Report on the East Africa High Commission, 1952. London: H.M. Stationery Office, 1953.

———. ———. The British Territories in East and Central Africa, 1945–1950. Cmd. 7987. London: H.M. Stationery Office, 1950.

———. ———. The Colonial Empire, 1939–1947. Cmd. 7167. London: H.M. Stationery Office, 1947.

———. ———. The Colonial Territories, 1953–54, 1954–55. Cmd. 9169, 9489. London: H.M. Stationery Office, 1954, 1955.

———. ———. Development of African Local Government in Tanganyika. Colonial No. 277. London: H.M. Stationery Office, 1951.

———. ———. The Future of the East African High Commission Services. London: H.M. Stationery Office, 1961.

———. ———. Future Policy in Regard to Eastern Africa. Cmd. 2904. London: H.M. Stationery Office, 1927.

———. ———. Memorandum on Native Policy in East Africa. Cmd. 3573. London: H.M. Stationery Office, 1930.

———. ———. Papers Relating to the Question of the Closer Union of Kenya, Uganda, and the Tanganyike Territory. Colonial No. 57. London: H.M. Stationery Office, 1931.

———. ———. Report by Her Majesty's Government in the United Kingdom of Great Britain and Northern Ireland to the General Assembly of the United Nations on the Administration of Tanganyika for the Years 1947, 1948, 1949, 1950, 1951, 1952, 1953, 1954, 1955, 1956, 1957, 1958, 1959, 1960. London: H.M. Stationery Office.

———. ———. Report by His Majesty's Government in the United Kingdom of Great Britain and Northern Ireland to the Council of the League of Nations on the Administration of the Tanganyika Territory for the Year 1938. London: H.M. Stationery Office, 1939.

———. ———. Report of Sir Samuel Wilson on His Visit to East Africa, 1929. Cmd. 3378. London: H.M. Stationery Office, 1929.

———. ———. Report on Tanganyika Territory for the Year 1921. Cmd. 1732. London: H.M. Stationery Office, 1922.

———. Commission on Closer Union of the Dependencies in Eastern and Central Africa. Report. Cmd. 3234. London: H.M. Stationery Office, 1929.

———. East Africa Commission. Report. Cmd. 2387. London: H.M. Stationery Office, 1925.

———. East Africa Royal Commission. Report. Cmd. 9475. London: H.M. Stationery Office, 1955.

———. House of Commons. Parliamentary Debates, CDLXXXII, DII. London: H.M. Stationery Office, 1951, 1952.

Gunther, John. Inside Africa. New York: Harper, 1955.

Hailey, William Malcolm Hailey. An African Survey. London: Oxford University Press, 1938.

———. An African Survey, Revised 1956. London: Oxford University Press, 1957.

———. Britain and Her Dependencies. London: Longmans, 1943.

———. Native Administration in the British African Territories: Part I, East Africa. London: H.M. Stationery Office, 1950.

Hatch, John. "Bright Star of Africa," *New Statesman,* LVIII (September 12, 1959), 300, 302.

———. Everyman's Africa. London: Dobson, 1959.

———. New From Africa. London: Dobson, 1956.

Hill, J. F. R. "Green Branches in Tanganyika," *Corona,* XII (April 1960), 126–28.

Hill, J. F. R., and J. P. Moffett. *See under* Tanganyika, A Review.

"How Independence Was Celebrated in Tanganyika," *East Africa and Rhodesia,* XXXVIII (December 14, 1961), 372.

Huxley, Elspeth. White Man's Country: Lord Delamere and the Making of Kenya. Vol. II. London: Chatto and Windus, 1956.

Ingham, Kenneth. A History of East Africa. London: Longmans, 1962.

Joelson, Ferdinand Stephen. Eastern Africa Today. London: East Africa, 1928.

Kitchen, Helen. "Why Did Julius Nyerere Resign?," *Africa Report,* VII (February 1962), 7.

Leakey, L. S. B. The Progress and Evolution of Man in Africa. London: Oxford University Press, 1961.

Leubuscher, Charlotte. Tanganyika Territory: A Study of Economic Policy Under Mandate. London: Oxford University Press, 1944.

Leys, Norman M. The Colour Bar in East Africa. London: Hogarth Press, 1941.

Liebenow, D. Gus. "Some Problems in Introducing Local Government Reform in Tanganyika," *Journal of African Administration,* VIII (July 1956), 132–39.

Mackenzie, W. J. M. "Changes in Local Government in Tanganyika," *Journal of African Administration,* VI (July 1954), 123–29.

Macmillan, William Miller. Road to Self-Rule: A Study in Colonial Evolution. London: Faber, 1959.

Mair, Lucy Philip. Native Policies in Africa. London: Routledge, 1936.

Maisel, Albert Q. Africa, Facts and Forecasts. New York: Duell, Sloan, and Pearce, 1943.

Marsh, Zoe (ed.). East Africa Through Contemporary Records. London: Cambridge University Press, 1961.

Marsh, Zoe, and G. W. Kingsnorth. An Introduction to the History of East Africa. Cambridge, Eng.: Cambridge University Press, 1957.

Meeker, Oden. Report on Africa. New York: Scribner's, 1954.

Mitchell, Philip Euen. African Afterthoughts. London: Hutchinson, 1954.

Moffett, J. P. (ed.). Handbook of Tanganyika. Dar es Salaam: Government Printer, 1958.

Mortimer, Molly. Trusteeship in Practice: A Report to the Fabian Colonial Bureau. London: Fabian Publications and Gollancz, 1951.

Nyerere, Julius. "The Challenge of Independence," *East Africa and Rhodesia*, XXXVIII (December 7, 1961), 339–40.

———. "One Party Government," *Spearhead*, I (November 1961), 7–9.

———. "Tanganyika Today: The Nationalist View," *International Affairs*, XXXVI (January 1960), 43–47.

———. "We Cannot Afford to Fail," *Africa Special Report*, IV (December 1959), 8–10.

Oliver, Roland. The Dawn of African History. London: Oxford University Press, 1961.

Osborn, Joyce. "Emergent Tanganyika," *Corona*, XIII (November 1961), 422–23.

Reusch, Richard. History of East Africa. Stuttgart: Evang. Missionverlag, 1954.

Richter, D. Julius. Tanganyika and Its Future. London: World Dominion Press, 1934.

Rothchild, Donald S. Toward Unity in Africa: A Study of Federalism in British Africa. Washington: Public Affairs Press, 1960.

Sayers, Gerald F. (ed.). The Handbook of Tanganyika. London: Macmillan, 1930.

Sears, Mason. "The Congo, Africa, and the U.N.," *Africa Today*, VII (September 1960), 14–15.

"Self-Government Now and Independence in Five Years," *East Africa and Rhodesia*, XXXV (August 13, 1959), 1404.

Skeffington, Arthur. Tanganyika in Transition. London: Fabian Commonwealth Bureau, 1960.

Stonehouse, John. Prohibited Immigrant. London: Bodley Head, 1960.

Tanganyika. Arusha-Moshi Lands Commission. Report. Dar es Salaam: Government Printer, 1947.

———. Committee on Constitutional Development. Report, 1951. Dar es Salaam: Government Printer, 1952.

————. Constitutional Development Commission. Report of the Special Commissioner. Dar es Salaam: Government Printer, 1953.

————. Detribalisation. Dar es Salaam: Government Printer, 1957.

————. Legislative Council. Council Debates. 30th–33d Sessions. Dar es Salaam: Government Printer, 1955–58.

————. ————. Proceedings. 2d Session. Dar es Salaam: Government Printer, 1928.

————. National Assembly. Debates. 36th Session. 4th and 5th Meetings. Dar es Salaam: Government Printer, 1961–62.

————. Some Comments on Mr. Nyerere's Speech at the Fourth Committee of the United Nations. Dar es Salaam: Government Printer, 1957.

————. Tanganyika. Dar es Salaam: Government Printer, 1957.

————. Tanganyika, A Review of Its Resources and Their Development. Compiled by J. F. R. Hill. Edited by J. P. Moffett. Dar es Salaam, 1955.

————. Tanganyika Information Services. Day of Triumph for Tanganyika. Dar es Salaam: Government Printer, 1961.

————. ————. Tanganyika's Parliament. Dar es Salaam: Government Printer, 1961.

"Tanganyika and the Working of the Mandates System," *Crown Colonist,* XV (April 1945), 240.

"Tanganyika Benefits from O.F.C. Activities," *Crown Colonist,* XX (January 1950), 54.

"Tanganyika Must Concentrate on Quality and Economy," *East Africa and Rhodesia,* XXXV (October 16, 1958), 191–92.

"Tanganyika's Progress Toward Independence Harmonious and Rapid," *United Nations Review,* VII (July 1960), 13, 51–53.

"Too Many Official Visits to Tanganyika," *Crown Colonist,* XVIII (June 1948), 333.

Toussaint, Charmian Edwards. The Trusteeship System of the United Nations. New York: Praeger, 1956.

Twining, Edward. "The Last Nine Years in Tanganyika," *African Affairs,* LVIII (January 1959), 15–24.

————. "The Situation in Tanganyika," *African Affairs,* L (October 1951), 297–310.

————. "Tanganyika's Middle Course in Racial Relations," *Optima,* VIII (December 1958), 211–18.

United Nations. General Assembly. Official Records. 7th and 11th Sessions. 4th Committee. New York, 1953, 1957.

————. ————. Provisional Verbatim Record. 1078th Meeting. Document A/PV.1078. New York, 1961.

————. ————. Trusteeship Agreement for the Territory of Tanganyika, as Approved by the General Assembly on 13 December 1946. Document T/A/2. Lake Success, 1947.

————. Secretariat. "British Mandate for East Africa (Tanganyika Territory)." Terms of League of Nations Mandates. Document A/70. Lake Success, 1946.

————. Trusteeship Council. Official Records. 11th, 15th, 17th, 21st, 23d Sessions. New York, 1952, 1955, 1956, 1958, 1959.

————. ————. "Petition from the Chagga Cultural Association, Moshi, Concerning Tanganyika." Document T/PET.2/134. New York, 1951.

————. ————. "Petition from the Tanganyika African Association, Headquarters, Dar es Salaam, concerning Tanganyika." Document T/PET.2/120. New York, 1959.

————. ————. "Petition from Tanganyika National Congress Concerning Tanganyika." Document T/PET.2/L.10/Add.1. New York, 1958.

————. ————. Report, 1954–55, 1955–56, 1956–57, 1957–58, 1958–59, 1959–60, 1960–61. New York.

————. ————. Verbatim Records. Documents T/PV.584, T/PV.1169. New York, 1955, 1961.

————. ————. Visiting Mission to Trust Territories in East Africa. Report on Tanganyika, 1948. Lake Success, 1950.

————. ————. Visiting Mission to Trust Territories in East Africa. Report on Tanganyika, 1951, 1954, 1957, 1960. Documents T/1032, T/1169, T/1401, T/1550. New York, 1952, 1955, 1958, 1960.

"United Tanganyika Party's Statement of Policy," *East Africa and Rhodesia,* XXXIV (October 3, 1957), 142–43.

Upthegrove, Campbell L. Empire by Mandate. New York: Bookman Associates, 1954.

Young, Roland, and Henry Fosbrooke. Smoke in the Hills: Political Tension in the Morogoro District of Tanganyika. Evanston: Northwestern University Press, 1960.

INDEX